TEACHER'S MANUAL

SOCIOLOGY

The Study of Human Relationships

Fifth Edition

SOCIOLOGY
The Study of Human Relationships
Fifth Edition

W. LaVerne Thomas

HOLT, RINEHART AND WINSTON
Harcourt Brace & Company
Austin • New York • Orlando • Chicago • Atlanta
San Francisco • Boston • Dallas • Toronto • London

A *Teacher's Manual* is not automatically included with each shipment of a classroom set of textbooks. However, a *Teacher's Manual* will be forwarded when requested by a teacher, an administrator, or a representative of Holt, Rinehart and Winston, Inc.

SOCIOLOGY: The Study of Human Relationships, Fifth Edition, is complemented by the *Teacher's Manual* and the *Teacher's Resource Binder.* When used with the pupil's textbook, they provide a comprehensive sociology program.

Printed in the United States of America

7 8 9   082   01 00 99

ISBN 0-03-098216-2

CONTENTS

TO THE TEACHER

The Fifth Edition of *SOCIOLOGY: The Study of Human Relationships* continues the long tradition of excellence established by earlier editions of the textbook. The introductory pages of this *Teacher's Manual* are designed to provide the sociology teacher with a comprehensive overview of the program.

OBJECTIVES OF THE TEXTBOOK

SOCIOLOGY: The Study of Human Relationships, Fifth Edition, provides teachers and students with a comprehensive examination of the basic concepts, principles, and methods central to the scientific study of sociology. The textbook is designed to meet three major goals. The first goal is to teach students to think like sociologists. The second goal is to help students develop a sociological imagination, which will enable them to view their own lives within a larger social and historical context. The third goal is to help students understand and thus appreciate the rich diversity that is possible in social life by exposing them to data from a wide variety of cross-cultural and historical sources.

Teaching Students to Think Like Sociologists

SOCIOLOGY: The Study of Human Relationships achieves the goal of teaching students to think like sociologists by approaching sociology as a science. The concepts, principles, theories, and methods used by sociologists in the examination of social life are presented in a clear and concise manner. The tools of sociological inquiry then are applied to the study of contemporary social issues and events so that sociology becomes personally meaningful for the students.

The clear narrative style of the textbook makes sociological concepts and methods easily understandable to students and teachers alike. Headings and subheadings in every chapter provide students with a workable outline and overview. Each paragraph centers on one clearly defined idea and paragraphs build upon one another to produce a logical flow of ideas. The clear and logical presentation of information promotes and facilitates learning.

Developing Sociological Imagination

An effective sociology textbook should provide students with skills that are applicable outside the classroom situation. *SOCIOLOGY: The Study of Human Relationships* accomplishes this goal by helping students to develop a sociological imagination. A sociological imagination is the ability to perceive how people's lives are shaped by the social environment and how the social environment is in turn shaped by people. Such an imagination is the mark of every good sociologist and student of society.

SOCIOLOGY: The Study of Human Relationships helps students to develop a sociological imagination by consistently applying concepts and methods to the analysis of real-world situations. By relating concepts to contemporary and historical events, students come to appreciate the relevance of sociology to their own daily lives and social relationships. In addition, review, enrichment, and assessment activities assist students in developing a sociological imagination by requiring them to analyze the connections between individual actions and the larger social world.

Appreciating Social Diversity

Unlike other animals, human beings are not locked into a set of predetermined behaviors. Thus people can adapt to and change their physical and social environments in a wide variety of ways. The author of *SOCIOLOGY: The Study of Human Relationships* believes strongly that students should be introduced to the rich diversity that is possible in social life. Developing an appreciation for social diversity is one of the keys to understanding our complex social world.

By providing students with a broad range of contemporary and historical cross-cultural examples, *SOCIOLOGY: The Study of Human Relationships* is able to meet its goal of helping students to understand and appreciate social diversity. Understanding and appreciating social diversity, in turn, helps students to become more open to new ideas, lifestyles, and philosophies—an ability that is of vital importance in our rapidly changing and increasingly interdependent world.

FLEXIBILITY OF THE TEXTBOOK

SOCIOLOGY: The Study of Human Relationships is designed so that it can be used to meet a variety of curriculum and personal needs. By varying the amount of time spent on each chapter or by choosing to concentrate on specific areas, teachers can use the textbook successfully in a full-year course, a semester course, a quarter-year course, or in a number of special-topic courses. You will find the textbook readily adaptable to your own particular course of study.

Full-Year Course

When *SOCIOLOGY: The Study of Human Relationships* is used in a 36-week course, it is possible for you to spend two weeks on each of the 18 chapters in the textbook. During a full-year course, you will be able to cover all of the textbook information, as well as utilize all of the teaching, skills, enrichment, and review materials included in the *Teacher's Manual.*

If you wish to emphasize research methods throughout the course, you might wish to spend the first week of the course covering Chapter 1 and the second week covering the Appendix, which begins on textbook page 485. The *Teacher's Manual* contains teaching strategies, enrichment activities, and assignments that will assist you in instructing your students in basic research methods.

Semester Course

Motivated students can cover all of the chapters in the textbook in an 18-week period, allowing one week per chapter. If you wish to include the Appendix in the course schedule, it may be advisable to devote slightly less time to Chapter 1 and combine the discussion of Chapters 2 and 3. The teaching strategies, enrichment activities, and assignments in the *Teacher's Manual* are keyed according to level of difficulty. All level I strategies, activities, and assignments are applicable to a semester course.

If you wish to devote more time to specific areas of interest, the organization of *SOCIOLOGY: The Study of Human Relationships* is ideally suited to selective assignments. The core concepts, theories, and principles are presented in the first five chapters of the textbook. Once this core material is covered, it is possible to vary the level of attention paid to other chapters without detracting from the overall effectiveness of the course.

Quarter-Year Course

When using *SOCIOLOGY: The Study of Human Relationships* in a quarter-year course, it is best to emphasize some chapters more heavily than others and to limit assigned activities. The following course organization will allow you to highlight all of the major topics and concepts central to the study of sociology:

Week 1

Chapter 1. The Sociological Point of View
Chapter 2. Cultural Diversity
Present a brief overview of sociology's subject matter, early history, and current theoretical approaches; outline the components of culture; and discuss cultural diversity, including subcultures and countercultures.

Week 2

Chapter 3. Cultural Conformity and Adaptation
Chapter 4. Social Structure
Discuss internalization of norms, sanctions, components of social structure, types of groups and societies, and bureaucracies.

Week 3

Chapter 5. Socializing the Individual
Chapter 6. The Adolescent in Society
Chapter 7. The Adult in Society
Examine the theories of Locke, Cooley, and Mead; and discuss agents of socialization, characteristics and problems of adolescence, and the world of work.

Week 4

Chapter 8. Deviance and Social Control
Cover the entire chapter.

Week 5

Chapter 9. Social Stratification
Chapter 10. Racial and Ethnic Relations
Chapter 11. Gender, Age, and Health
Discuss types of stratification systems, social classes in the United States, social mobility, race and ethnicity, discrimination and prejudice, and the social inequality faced by some of the groups mentioned in Chapters 10 and 11.

Week 6

Chapter 12. The Family
Chapter 13. The Economy and Politics

Chapter 14. Education and Religion
Chapter 15. Science and Sport

After a brief discussion of the nature of social institutions, focus on one or more of the specific social institutions presented in the unit.

Week 7

Chapter 16. Collective Behavior and Social Movements
Chapter 17. Population and Urbanization
Chapter 18. Social Change and Modernization

Discuss types of collectivities and social movements, measures of population change, the evolution of the city, theories of city life, and the effects of modernization.

Special-Topic Courses

Chapters 8, 9, 10, 11, 16, and 17, as well as Section 3 of Chapter 6, Section 2 of Chapter 7, Section 2 of Chapter 12, and Section 2 of Chapter 18, can be used as the basis of a course focusing on social problems. The chapters cover such topics as adolescent sexual behavior, drug use, and suicide; unemployment; deviance and crime; social stratification; poverty; discrimination and prejudice; racial and ethnic relations; social inequality based on gender, age, and health; divorce and family violence; collective behavior and social movements (including revolution and terrorism); population pressures; urbanization; alienation; and the environmental and social effects of modernization.

INSTRUCTIONAL DESIGN OF THE TEXTBOOK

SOCIOLOGY: The Study of Human Relationships is designed to make the exploration of sociology an enjoyable and exciting experience for teachers and students alike. The clear and lively writing style, logical organization, colorful visuals, and countless cross-cultural and historical examples make the subject matter readily accessible to students of every ability level. In addition, high-interest primary source readings representing a wide variety of viewpoints and theoretical perspectives, a balanced examination of issues at the center of public debate, and an emphasis on social studies and research skills provide students with valuable tools for understanding the changing social environment.

The coverage and organization of *SOCIOLOGY: The Study of Human Relationships* mirrors the theoretical and research emphases currently found in the discipline. Thus students who wish to pursue the study of sociology on a college level will have a firm foundation on which to build. These students already will be familiar with the basic concepts, theories, methods, and areas of specialization recognized by sociologists in academia, government, and the private sector.

Textbook Organization

SOCIOLOGY: The Study of Human Relationships has been carefully organized to assist students of all ability levels in gaining an understanding of the discipline of sociology. Information is presented in manageable segments, with each segment building on previous material. Paragraphs build on topic sentences, subsections build on paragraphs, sections build on subsections, chapters build on sections, and new chapters build on previous chapters. Chapters then are grouped into five units that address the major areas of emphasis in sociology. At every step of the way, students are assisted in determining major points and are given opportunities to self-test their understanding of the material.

Units

SOCIOLOGY: The Study of Human Relationships is organized into five units. Each unit begins with a two-page opener that includes a dramatic page-and-a-half visual, a relevant quotation, and a list of chapter titles (see textbook pages 290–291, for example). The opener gives students a quick preview of the major topics covered in the unit. Each unit closes with a one-page feature—Across Space and Time—that examines a sociological topic from a cross-cultural or historical perspective (see textbook page 288 or page 400, for example) and a one-page unit review.

Chapters

There are 18 chapters in *SOCIOLOGY: The Study of Human Relationships.* Each chapter begins with a two-page opener. The left-hand page of the opener contains a full-page photograph chosen to motivate student interest. On the right-hand page is a chapter outline, chapter focus questions, and a list of key terms. This material is designed to alert students to important topics and areas of emphasis (see textbook pages 45, 231, and 319, for example). An introduction also is included to spark student interest and set the tone for the chapter.

Each chapter closes with a summary, a two-page skills presentation entitled Developing Sociological

Imagination, and a two-page Chapter Review. The left-hand page of the review consists of fact-recall questions, critical-thinking questions, and projects. The right-hand page contains a primary source reading with accompanying review questions (see textbook pages 198–199 and 398–399, for example). Each chapter also includes a Case Study feature and an Applying Sociology feature.

Sections

SOCIOLOGY: The Study of Human Relationships is organized into 45 sections. The title of each section indicates the section's major theme. Each section closes with a Section Review, which includes fact-recall and critical-thinking questions. Sections are designed to be suitable for a daily lesson in most sociology classes. The organization of the textbook into 45 sections ensures that teachers will have adequate time for enrichment activities and tests.

Appendix: Sociological Research Methods

The Appendix provides students with an overview of the research process and basic research methods. Placing the discussion of research methods in the Appendix rather than including it as a chapter in Unit 1 allows teachers maximum flexibility. Teachers who wish to emphasize research methods can teach the Appendix as the second chapter in the course and or can refer to the Appendix throughout the course.

The Appendix includes a discussion of research interests, causation and correlation, the steps in the research process, and ethics in social research. The information presented in the Appendix is supplemented by the Applying Sociology feature that appears in each chapter and by the Developing Research Skills Worksheets that are contained in the *Teacher's Resource Binder* component. In addition, many of the Developing Sociological Imagination features teach research-related skills.

Careers in Sociology

Careers in Sociology offers college admissions guidelines to students wishing to major in sociology and discusses the applicability of a sociology major to a range of entry-level positions. In addition, the section discusses the steps needed to become a professional sociologist and presents an overview of areas of specialization in sociology.

The Sociologist's Bookshelf

SOCIOLOGY: The Study of Human Relationships is grounded in an impressive body of sociological research and theory. The sources used in the preparation of the textbook, as well as additional sources of interest to students of sociology, are included in The Sociologist's Bookshelf. For ease of use, the listing is organized by chapter.

Glossary

Every boldfaced term that appears in *SOCIOLOGY: The Study of Human Relationships* also is included in the Glossary. Each boldfaced glossary entry is followed by a definition and a textbook page reference. The page reference refers to the place in the textbook where the term is first introduced. Guide words at the top of each column in the Glossary assist students in quickly locating glossary entries.

Index

The comprehensive Index to *SOCIOLOGY: The Study of Human Relationships* assists students in quickly locating information in the textbook. Guide words at the top of each column, cross-references, and italicized page references to charts, graphs, and photographs make the Index particularly easy to use.

The Sociologist's Code of Ethics

Ethical considerations are an important element of the research process in sociology. In fact, ethics are of such importance to sociologists that the American Sociological Association (ASA) has published a code of ethics to which all sociologists are expected to adhere. The author of *SOCIOLOGY: The Study of Human Relationships* believes that students of sociology also must be aware of and follow ethical guidelines in their research, and so has excerpted a portion of the ASA *Code of Ethics* for inclusion in the textbook.

Student Learning Program

In addition to a clear writing style, logical organization, and extensive illustration program, *SOCIOLOGY: The Study of Human Relationships* has many built-in features to assist students of all ability levels in learning the material presented in the textbook. These features include unit and chapter openers; chapter introductions; boldfaced terms; chapter summaries; and section, chapter, and unit reviews.

Unit and Chapter Openers

Each unit begins with a two-page opener that includes a dramatic page-and-a-half montage visual, a relevant quotation, and a list of chapter titles. The unit opener provides students with a quick preview of the major topics covered in the unit. Each chapter also begins with a two-page opener. On the left-hand page is a high-interest four-color photograph. The right-hand page includes a chapter outline, consisting of section and major subsection headings, a Chapter Focus, consisting of key study questions to guide student reading, and a list of key terms. This material is designed to alert students to important topics and areas of emphasis.

Chapter Introductions

The running text of each chapter begins with a boxed introduction. The introduction is designed to generate student interest and set the tone for the chapter. In addition, the information contained in the introduction often can be used as the basis of a class discussion.

Boldfaced Terms

Important sociological concepts and principles are indicated in the text in boldface type. The meaning of the boldfaced term can be determined from the sentences surrounding it. Each boldfaced term also appears in the Glossary that begins on textbook page 507.

Section Reviews

Each of the 45 sections in *SOCIOLOGY: The Study of Human Relationships* concludes with a Section Review. Section Reviews can have up to three parts. The first part, DEFINE, asks students to review bold-faced terms that were discussed in the section. The second part, IDENTIFY, asks students to identify people, societies or cultures, objects, legislation, or organizations discussed in the section. The third part consists of numbered questions designed to reinforce knowledge of key facts and main ideas. Each question is labeled with the critical-thinking skill students need to apply in order to answer the question.

The Section Reviews serve three general pedagogical purposes. First, the review questions serve as a detailed guide to reading if students are directed to familiarize themselves with the questions before reading the material in the section. Second, the questions serve as a review of the material in the section. Section Reviews may be assigned as homework or may be used as the basis of an oral review in class. Finally, taken as a whole, Section Reviews help students to organize the details presented in the section.

Chapter Summaries

The running text of each chapter in *SOCIOLOGY: The Study of Human Relationships* ends with a summary. The summary encapsulates and reinforces the main points of the chapter.

Chapter Reviews

Each of the 18 chapters in *SOCIOLOGY: The Study of Human Relationships* concludes with a two-page Chapter Review. The left-hand page of the review consists of fact-recall questions, critical-thinking questions, and projects. Each question is labeled with the critical-thinking skill needed to answer the question. The right-hand page contains a primary source reading with accompanying review questions. Following is a description of the specific elements:

Reviewing Sociological Terms. This section of the Chapter Review measures students' understanding of the sociological terms introduced in the chapter.

Thinking Critically about Sociology. This section consists of questions or activities that require students to recall and interpret or apply information presented in the chapter. Each item carries a label that clearly identifies the critical-thinking skill that students must apply in order to answer the question or complete the activity.

Exercising Sociological Skills. This section reinforces the skills and enrichment features presented in each chapter. The first question or activity reinforces the Applying Sociology feature. The second question or activity reinforces the Case Study, while the third question or activity reinforces the Developing Sociological Imagination feature. Once again, each item is labeled with the critical-thinking skill that students must apply in order to answer the question or complete the activity.

Extending Sociological Imagination. This section provides enrichment activities for students who are willing and able to work independently. Most activities require students to utilize supplemental material or engage in activities or research outside of the classroom.

Interpreting Primary Sources. This feature of the Chapter Review provides students with a primary source reading relevant to the subject content of the chapter. Students are asked to read the selection and answer the accompanying review questions.

Unit Reviews

Each of the five units in *SOCIOLOGY: The Study of Human Relationships* concludes with a one-page Unit Review. The Unit Review has three parts, which consist of the following elements:

Reviewing Sociological Ideas. This section of the review asks students to recall factual information from the various chapters in the unit. The questions often assist students in integrating material from more than one chapter.

Synthesizing Sociological Ideas. This section requires students to synthesize information from the various chapters in the unit. Each item is labeled with the critical-thinking skill that students must apply in order to answer the question or complete the activity.

Applying Sociological Imagination. This section provides enrichment activities for students who are willing and able to work independently. Most activities require students to utilize supplemental material or engage in activities or research outside of the classroom.

Skills Program

Believing that successful skills instruction depends on a systematic presentation, the author of *SOCIOLOGY: The Study of Human Relationships* has integrated comprehensive skills instruction into the textbook. The skills program contains two chapter features: Developing Sociological Imagination and Applying Sociology.

Developing Sociological Imagination

Each two-page Developing Sociological Imagination feature presents students with the steps needed to master an activity that falls into one of four general skill strands: reading about sociology, writing about sociology, interpreting the visual record, or thinking about sociology. Most of the skills are general skills applicable to all of the social sciences. The subject matter of each skill, however, is closely tied to the topics discussed in the chapter.

Each skill presentation utilizes a three-part approach, consisting of an introduction that includes step-by-step instructions, a directed application, and a practice application. Most Developing Sociological Imagination features use primary source readings or graphics to assist students in mastering the skills. For examples of the skills program, see textbook pages 116–117, 170–171, and 226–227.

The skills presented in the Developing Sociological Imagination feature are reinforced in the Exercising Sociological Skills section of the Chapter Review. In addition, the *Teacher's Manual* contains suggested teaching strategies, enrichment activities, or assignments for each skill feature.

Applying Sociology

Each two-page Applying Sociology feature introduces students to skills central to the study of sociology or reinforces skills presented elsewhere in the textbook. Each Applying Sociology feature focuses on one of six research methods: the historical method, content analysis, the survey method, observation, the case study, or statistical analysis. Through the use of primary sources, charts and graphs, and small research projects, students are afforded the opportunity to apply the concepts and methods presented in the textbook.

Enrichment Program

SOCIOLOGY: The Study of Human Relationships has three types of enrichment features. Each feature is designed to enliven the study of sociology and help students appreciate the rich diversity of social life and sociological thought.

Case Study

Each chapter in *SOCIOLOGY: The Study of Human Relationships* contains one Case Study. Each one-page feature examines a single issue related to the chapter material. Topics include Native American assimilation, American youth gangs, the rural poor, women in the military, alcoholism and the family, terrorism, and tropical deforestation.

Interpreting Primary Sources

In addition to the many primary sources that are included in the running text and in the Applying Sociology and Developing Sociological Imagination features, each chapter of *SOCIOLOGY: The Study of Human Relationships* contains a one-page Interpreting Primary Sources feature. The feature, which forms the second page of each Chapter Review, enriches the students' study of sociology by exposing them to a wide range of viewpoints.

Each feature begins with a brief introduction that details the background of the source and alerts students to points to consider while reading. The feature ends with one or more review questions. These questions provide students with a test of comprehension and an additional opportunity to apply critical-thinking skills to source material.

Across Space and Time

Each unit contains one Across Space and Time feature. The one-page feature always precedes the Unit Review. Each feature examines a specific sociological issue from a cross-cultural or historical perspective. Among the topics discussed in the features are family-planning policies in China, Japanese American internment during World War II and the women's movement of the 1800s.

INSTRUCTIONAL DESIGN OF THE *TEACHER'S MANUAL*

The *Teacher's Manual* that accompanies *SOCIOLOGY: The Study of Human Relationships* is designed to help teachers achieve the three major goals of sociology education. Teachers will find that the wide variety of overviews, support material, teaching strategies, enrichment strategies, and assignments are ample for the needs of all classrooms. For ease of use, the material presented in the *Teacher's Manual* is organized by unit, chapter, and section.

Beginning the Unit

The *Teacher's Manual* contains an introduction for each unit of the textbook. The introduction includes the following elements:

Unit Title. Lists the title of the unit and the page numbers covered by the unit in the textbook.

Unit Outline. Lists all of the chapters in the unit.

Unit Overview. Describes the principal themes found in the unit.

Unit Goals. Provides learning objectives to be used in evaluating student knowledge of the unit material.

Unit Skills. Lists the Developing Sociological Imagination skill features contained in the unit.

Introducing the Unit. Suggests an activity to be used in introducing the unit.

References for Teachers. Lists books that might prove useful for teachers.

Readings for Student Enrichment. Suggests fiction and nonfiction works of sociological interest to students.

Multimedia Materials. Lists audiovisual materials that complement the topics discussed in the unit. The list of addresses for the multimedia sources mentioned in the unit introductions begins on page xviii of this *Teacher's Manual*.

Beginning the Chapter

The *Teacher's Manual* contains an introduction for each chapter of the textbook. The introduction includes the following elements:

Chapter Title. Lists the title of the chapter and the pages covered by the chapter in the textbook.

Chapter Outline. Lists all of the sections in the chapter.

Chapter Overview. Describes the principal themes and ideas found in the chapter.

Chapter Objectives. Provides learning objectives to be used in evaluating student knowledge of the chapter material.

Introducing the Chapter. Suggests an activity to be used in introducing the chapter.

Suggested Lesson Plans. Provides a detailed chart of the daily materials and procedures that may be used to teach the chapter.

Using the Sections

The *Teacher's Manual* contains an introduction for each section of the textbook. The introduction includes the following elements:

Section Title. Lists the title of the section and the page numbers covered by the section in the textbook.

Section Overview. Describes the principal themes and ideas found in the section.

Previewing Key Terms. Lists all important vocabulary terms that are presented in boldface type in the section and suggests an activity for introducing students to these terms before they read the section material.

Introducing the Section. Suggests an activity to be used in introducing the section.

Suggested Teaching Strategies. Presents three or more possible approaches to teaching the section material. The activities help students master content and skills. Where appropriate, teaching strategies reinforce the Developing Sociological Imagination skill strand found in the section. These suggestions are identified with a ★. Each teaching strategy is geared to a particular ability level. For an explanation of the criteria used in determining each level, see the chart on this page.

Suggested Enrichment Activities. Presents one or more activities that may be used to expand textbook content. Students are required to use a variety of materials, including library materials, community resource people, and supplementary readings. In addition, many activities require students to employ research methods.

Suggested Assignments. Presents two or more assignments that teachers may give to assess student comprehension of the material presented in the section, and to expand on this material. One assignment in each section is a homework assignment that is designed to be completed in an evening.

Closing the Section. Suggests an activity to be used as a wrap-up of the section.

Assessment

At the close of each section in the *Teacher's Manual,* "Assessing the Section" directs the teacher to assign the Section Review. At the close of each chapter, "Assessing the Chapter" directs the teacher to assign the Chapter Review and other assessment materials. At the close of each unit, "Assessing the Unit" directs the teacher to assign the Unit Review and other assessment materials.

Answers Keys

The *Teacher's Manual* provides answers for each Section Review, Chapter Review, and Unit Review in the textbook. In addition, answers are provided for each skill feature and special feature in the textbook. Answers to the Section Reviews and the special features are found at the end of the section materials. Answers to the skill features are found following the last section of the chapter. Answers to the Chapter Reviews are located at the close of each chapter, and answers to the Unit Reviews are found at the close of each unit in the *Teacher's Manual.*

TEACHER'S RESOURCE BINDER

The *Teacher's Resource Binder* that accompanies *SOCIOLOGY: The Study of Human Relationships* contains the following components:

Unit Sections

There are five tabbed unit sections, one for each unit in the textbook, organized by chapter. These blackline masters provide a comprehensive program of reinforcement, enrichment, review, and assessment. The *Teacher's Manual* offers suggestions when to assign these materials. Each unit section contains the following elements:

Graphic Organizer Worksheets. One Graphic Organizer Worksheet is provided for each chapter in the unit. These worksheets serve to reinforce chapter content by organizing information in a visually graphic form.

Ability Guidelines	
Level I (Basic)	Strategy or activity requires full class participation, is basic to content comprehension, and should be within the range of all students. Only the textbook is required for successful completion of the task.
Level II (Average/Group)	Strategy or activity requires group participation, selective assignments, and teacher direction. It is expected that the majority of students will be able to handle their assigned tasks successfully. The activity may require the use of supplementary sources and the application of a variety of study and thinking skills.
Level III (Challenging)	These are challenging activities especially applicable to those students willing and able to work independently. Successful completion of these tasks will require the use of several sources other than the textbook and the integration of creativity and higher-level critical-thinking skills.

Understanding Sociological Ideas Worksheets.
One Understanding Sociological Ideas Worksheet
is provided for each chapter in the unit. These
worksheets serve to reinforce student understanding of key sociological concepts.

Critical Skills Mastery Worksheets. One Critical
Skills Mastery Worksheet is provided for each chapter in the unit. These worksheets serve to reinforce
student understanding of basic sociological skills.

Developing Research Skills Worksheets. One
Developing Research Skills Worksheet is provided
for each chapter in the unit. These worksheets contain enrichment activities that assist students in
developing basic research skills.

Cross-Cultural Perspectives Worksheets. One
Cross-Cultural Perspectives Worksheet is provided
for each chapter in the unit. These worksheets introduce students to issues of sociological interest in
societies other than the United States.

Review Worksheets. Review Worksheets are provided for each chapter and unit in *SOCIOLOGY: The
Study of Human Relationships*. Mid-Book and End-
of-Book Review Worksheets are included as well.
These Review Worksheets are designed to prepare
students for chapter, unit, mid-book, and end-of-
book tests.

Tests. Form A and Form B Tests are provided for
each chapter and unit of *SOCIOLOGY: The Study of
Human Relationships*. In addition, Mid-Book and
End-of-Book tests allow cumulative assessment.
The format of the tests is logical and easy to grade.
Critical-thinking questions are an integral part of
every test.

Reteaching Worksheets. Reteaching Worksheets
are provided for each chapter and unit of *SOCIOL-
OGY: The Study of Human Relationships*. Mid-book
and End-of-Book Reteaching Worksheets are provided as well. These Reteaching Worksheets follow
the format of the Form A and Form B Tests, thus
allowing them to be used as additional reviews and
practice tests.

Answer Keys. Answer Keys are provided for all
chapter worksheets and tests in the *Teacher's
Resource Binder* and are located at the end of each
chapter. Answer keys also are provided for all unit,
mid-book, and end-of-book materials.

Alternative Assessment Forms

The assessment process in American schools is
undergoing dramatic changes. Many schools
around the nation have adopted alternative systems
of assessment that emphasize projects, performances, and portfolios. The *Teacher's Resource
Binder* that accompanies *SOCIOLOGY: The Study
of Human Relationships* contains a complete package of alternative assessment materials. These materials include blackline masters that can be used to
assess projects, performances, and portfolios.

Student Writer's Guide

The Student Writer's Guide component of the
Teacher's Resource Binder contains a wide variety
of blackline master materials that provide students
with guidelines for effective writing. These materials will serve students well throughout their academic experience.

Transparencies with Teacher's Notes

The *Teacher's Resource Binder* that accompanies
SOCIOLOGY: The Study of Human Relationships
also provides a transparency package that consists
of 18 graphic transparencies with accompanying
teacher's notes. The teacher's notes contain a series
of comprehension and critical-thinking questions
pertaining to each transparency. Suggestions for
using the transparencies and accompanying teacher's notes are given in the *Teacher's Manual*.

HELPING STUDENTS WITH SPECIAL NEEDS

Your classroom may include students who come
from a variety of cultural backgrounds and who
have various learning styles. The materials contained in the *SOCIOLOGY: The Study of Human
Relationships* program can be used to meet the
needs of all types of students.

Strategies for Teaching Students with Limited English Proficiency

As a teacher, you make a variety of instructional
decisions in addressing the needs of students with
various learning abilities. This task becomes more
complex when teaching the student with limited
English proficiency, who often faces stress and anxiety in being unable to understand instructions or

communicate in the classroom. These strategies will help you meet the needs of students with limited English language skills.

Provide Intensive Exposure to English. Use intensive language activities that incorporate a variety of methods and materials. Devote a high percentage of time to direct teacher instruction.

Vary the Context of Language Learning. Use excursions, role playing, and dramatization to help students practice using English for a variety of purposes.

Build Positive Self-Esteem. Reduce stress and anxiety by accepting simple responses such as nodding and *yes/no* answers. Give students opportunities to achieve goals and see their progress.

Make Learning Comprehensible. Use exaggerated body movements and facial expressions, as well as visuals, props, and demonstrations to convey meaning. Stress important points by repeating, labeling, and using voice inflection.

Strategies for Teaching Students with Various Learning Styles

It is likely that you have auditory, visual, tactile, and kinesthetic learners in your classroom. *SOCIOLOGY: The Study of Human Relationships* provides ample opportunities to meet each of these needs.

Auditory Learners. Auditory learners benefit from discussions and any other oral activities. These activities reinforce the use of language and listening skills as well as provide opportunities for students to further investigate information in the text narrative. The *Teacher's Manual* provides for the needs of auditory learners through teaching strategies such as "Making Oral Presentations" and "Evaluating Ideas."

Visual Learners. Visual learners benefit from activities such as studying pictures, analyzing charts, and interpreting visuals. All of the components in the *SOCIOLOGY: The Study of Human Relationships* program contain materials to meet the needs of visual learners. The *Teacher's Manual*, for example, provides teaching strategies such as "Learning from Charts" and "Learning from Photographs."

Tactile Learners. Tactile learners benefit from hands-on activities that require the manipulation and organization of objects. The *Teacher's Manual* provides teaching strategies such as "Creating a Bar Graph" and "Creating a Time Line" that address the needs of tactile learners.

Kinesthetic Learners. Kinesthetic learners benefit from activities that require movement and action. The *Teacher's Manual* provides for the needs of kinesthetic learners through teaching strategies such as "Dramatizing Sociology."

Strategies for Teaching Gifted Students

Teaching gifted students can be a rewarding experience. At the same time, such teaching presents the teacher with a variety of challenges. Gifted students are a diverse group. Keep in mind the individual learning styles of each of these students while motivating them to develop their natural abilities.

Allow Gifted Students to Choose Their Own Topics for Assignments or Activities. Activities that allow gifted students to research topics of special interest tend to keep them motivated and promote independent thinking.

Utilize Group Activities. You may wish to have students take part in panel discussions, information discussions, debates, and interviews, all of which allow gifted students to exchange ideas. Suggestions for many activities such as these are given in the *Teacher's Manual.*

Employ Activities That Address Real Problems Requiring Real Solutions. By asking your gifted students to research issues facing the nation and the world today and to propose possible solutions to these problems, you are helping them to broaden their perspectives and increase their ability to meet challenges. Examples of problems to be researched are: What are some ways to help the homeless? How can science deal with air and water pollution? How can the government reduce the federal budget?

Strategies for Teaching Less Prepared Students

Less prepared students are those who are not able to learn at an average rate from the available written materials. Teachers usually can identify less prepared students by noticeable characteristics such as short attention span, deficiency in basic language skills, and an inability to grasp abstract ideas and concepts. Teaching less prepared students is especially challenging. These instructional strategies will help you to meet their needs.

Plan Lessons Around the Interests and Experiences of Less Prepared Students. Less prepared students need to feel included in the instruction. Lessons involving their interests and experiences raise their interest level and increase their attention span.

Make Frequent Use of Audio and Visual Materials. Usually, less prepared students are auditory or visual learners. By using audio and visual materials, you are adapting the learning situation to accommodate their learning strengths, which in turn can produce a positive learning experience.

Provide Reteaching and Review Activities. Because less prepared students need constant reinforcement, reteaching and review activities at the end of a lesson and before a quiz or test are essential to these students' needs.

Strategies to Ensure Successful Cooperative Learning

Many of the strategies and activities in the *SOCIOLOGY: The Study of Human Relationships* program involve cooperative learning. In cooperative learning, small groups of students of various ability levels work together to solve problems and complete tasks. The purpose of this instructional strategy is to create an environment in which students work together toward a common goal. Simply putting students in groups and asking them to complete cooperative assignments, however, will not guarantee learning. To help ensure that cooperative learning will succeed in your classroom, include the following elements:

Positive Interdependence. Students must feel that they need each other in order to complete the assignment. Establish positive interdependence by requiring the group to turn in one assignment that they have worked on together. Also, tell students that answers must reflect ideas from *every* member of the group.

Individual Accountability. Stress to students that they will be held accountable for learning and for helping their group. Circulate around the room while the groups are working, and quiz individuals to see if they can explain answers that their group has finished so far. If they cannot, ask group members to review until every student understands. Reward groups when all members of the group show that they can explain answers. Also, give each member a specific job to do, such as acting as reader or recorder.

Face-to-Face Interaction. Maximize learning by ensuring that all members in each group exchange ideas, information, and explanations orally.

Cooperative Skill Teaching. To encourage students to take responsibility for interacting with their group, insist on standards of group behavior. Discuss with students the behavior you expect to see, display a list of these standards in a prominent location, remind students of them before commencing group activities, and keep a checklist to document their use. Behavioral standards might include: *Everyone contribute; listen carefully; ask others to explain; praise good ideas;* and *disagree with ideas, not with people.*

Processing Group Effectiveness. Groups will improve only if students take the time to evaluate their group's progress and formulate a plan for improvement. At the end of each cooperative learning assignment, have groups list what they are doing well and how they can improve. Also, have students tell other group members positive things they can do to help the group. Such statements will help all students feel valuable to the group and will help build students' self-esteem.

MULTIMEDIA SOURCES

The following list provides the names and addresses of the multimedia sources listed in the unit introduction sections of this *Teacher's Manual*. The abbreviations in boldface are the abbreviations used to designate the companies in the multimedia lists. It is a good idea to order material well in advance and to preview the material yourself before using it in class.

AM: AIMS Media, 9710 DeSoto Avenue, Chatsworth, CA 91311

BF: Beacon Films, 1560 Sherman Avenue, Suite 100, Evanston, IL 60201

CE: Cambridge Educational, P.O. Box 2153, Dept. DC8, Charleston, SC 25328

CFV: Coronet Film & Video, 108 Wilmot Road, Deerfield, IL 60015

CMFV: Coronet/MTI Film & Video, 108 Wilmot Road, Deerfield, IL 60015

CSS: Cambridge Social Studies, P.O. Box 2153, Dept. SS4, Charleston, SC 25328

EBEC: Encyclopaedia Britannica Educational Corporation, 310 South Michigan Avenue, Chicago, IL 60604

FHS: Films for the Humanities & Sciences, P.O. Box 2053, Princeton, NJ 08543

FIV: Films Incorporated Video, 5547 Ravenswood Avenue, Chicago, IL 60640

FM: Focus Media, Inc., 485 South Broadway, Suite 12, Hicksville, NY 11801

GA: Guidance Associates, P.O. Box 1000, Mount Kisco, NY 10549

NGS: National Geographic Society, Educational Services, Washington, DC 20036

NY: Nystrom, 3333 Elston Avenue, Chicago, IL 60618

PBS: PBS Video, Public Broadcasting Service, 1320 Braddock Place, Alexandria, VA 22314

SSSS: Social Studies School Service, 10200 Jefferson Boulevard, Room AO, P.O. Box 802, Culver City, CA 90232

SVE: Society for Visual Education, Inc., Department BV, 1345 Diversey Parkway, Chicago, IL 60614

ZM: Zenger Media, 10200 Jefferson Boulevard, Room VC, P.O. Box 802, Culver City, CA 90232

TEACHER'S COURSE PLAN

	MON.		TUES.		WED.		THURS.		FRI.
A U G									
S E P									
O C T									
N O V									
D E C									
J A N									

TEACHER'S COURSE PLAN

	MON.		TUES.		WED.		THURS.		FRI.
F E B									
M A R C H									
A P R I L									
M A Y									
J U N E									

UNIT 1 *(pages 1–95)*

CULTURE AND SOCIAL STRUCTURE

CHAPTER 1
THE SOCIOLOGICAL POINT OF VIEW

CHAPTER 2
CULTURAL DIVERSITY

CHAPTER 3
CULTURAL CONFORMITY AND ADAPTATION

CHAPTER 4
SOCIAL STRUCTURE

Unit Overview

Sociology is the science that studies human society and social behavior. Sociologists concentrate their attention on social interaction—the ways in which people relate to one another and influence each other's behavior. Consequently, sociologists tend to focus on the group rather than on the individual.

The study of sociology provides students with the basic tools they need to develop a sociological imagination. The sociological imagination is the ability to see the connection between the larger social world and our personal lives. The development of a sociological imagination enables students to examine how society shapes human behavior and beliefs and how such actions and beliefs in turn shape society. A sociological imagination is the mark of every good sociologist and student of sociology.

Unit 1 provides a comprehensive overview of the nature of sociological inquiry and social life. The unit begins by discussing the benefits of studying sociology and examining sociology's place in the social sciences, its historical development, and its major theoretical perspectives. In the remainder of the unit, the basic concepts that are central to all sociological inquiry are examined in the context of culture and social structure. A rich variety of cross-cultural examples are used to illustrate the ways in which people adapt to and are changed by their physical and social environments.

Unit Goals

At the end of the unit, students should be able to

1. Identify the ways in which sociology is similar to and different from the other social sciences.
2. Trace the development of sociology, and discuss the ideas of five early sociologists.
3. Compare and contrast sociology's three main current theoretical perspectives.
4. Recognize and describe the components of culture.
5. Discuss cultural universals and cultural variations.
6. Describe both the traditional and emerging values contained in the American value system.
7. Explain how culture is both maintained and changed.
8. Describe the components of social structure; the structure of groups, societies, and formal organizations; and the nature of social interaction.

Unit Skills

Four skills are developed in Unit 1.

★ READING ABOUT SOCIOLOGY: *Using Textbook Features* (Chapter 1; PE pages 18–19; TM page 6)
★ READING ABOUT SOCIOLOGY: *Developing a Structured Overview* (Chapter 2; PE pages 40–41; TM page 10)
★ WRITING ABOUT SOCIOLOGY: *Composing an Essay* (Chapter 3; PE pages 62–63; TM page 17)
★ READING ABOUT SOCIOLOGY: *Analyzing Journal Articles* (Chapter 4; PE pages 90–91; TM page 25)

Suggestions for teaching the skills appear on the TM pages mentioned above. The suggestions are clearly identified by the ★ symbol. Each skill is reinforced in the Chapter Review under Exercising Sociological Skills. Answers to the questions in the textbook's skill features appear in the Answers to Developing Sociological Imagination sections of this *Teacher's Manual*.

Introducing the Unit

Organize the class into small groups. Distribute to each group a copy of the following fact sheet.

> Assume that you are part of a 10-member group that is shipwrecked on a deserted tropical island. The island has a plentiful supply of wild fruits and plants, insects, birds, fish, and hardwood trees. Some fresh water can be found in small island pools, but the bulk of the water is contaminated by salt from the ocean. Your group had time to rescue the following items from your sinking ship before escaping in two life rafts:
>
> 2 large fishing knives
> 4 plastic gallon jugs of water
> 1 25-foot rope
> 1 large plastic tarp
> 1 set of binoculars
> 1 can opener
> 20 cans of fruits and vegetables

Instruct each group to establish a list of rules, procedures, and task assignments that would allow the group to survive on the island indefinitely. Allow the groups 20 minutes to complete their lists.

When the groups have finished, have each group share its list with the class. Ask group members to explain how they came to agree on their list and whether they encountered any problems in reaching a consensus.

Explain that for society to operate efficiently, members must work together toward common goals. To ensure that most people cooperate for the common good, societies establish rules of conduct and expectations for behavior. Tell students that the methods societies use to establish and enforce these rules and expectations will be the focus of Unit 1.

References for Teachers

Babbie, E. *The Sociological Spirit: Critical Essays in a Critical Science*. Belmont, CA: Wadsworth, 1988. Brief orientation to sociology as a way of thinking and as a means of empowering oneself to better confront complex social realities.

Coser, Lewis A. *Masters of Sociological Thought*, 2d ed. New York: Harcourt Brace Jovanovich, 1977. Overview of the lives and theories of many of sociology's greatest thinkers.

Encyclopedic Dictionary of Sociology, 4th ed. Guilford, CT: Dushkin, 1991. Reference work that details sociology's language, underlying themes, and academic divisions.

Goodman, Norman. *Introduction to Sociology*. New York: HarperCollins, 1992. Concise overview of sociology presented in an outline format.

Gordon, Milton M. *The Scope of Sociology*. New York: Oxford University Press, 1988. Introduction to the basic principles of sociology.

Levin, W.C. *Sociological Ideas: Concepts and Applications*, 3d ed. Belmont, CA: Wadsworth, 1991. Introductory textbook designed around core concepts and applications.

Macionis, John. *Society: The Basics*. Englewood Cliffs, NJ: Prentice-Hall, 1991. Survey of sociological concepts and issues.

Sedlack, R. Guy, and Stanley, Jay. *Social Research: Theory and Methods*. Needham Heights, MA: Allyn and Bacon, 1992. Introduction to sociological research.

Sociology 92/93: Annual Editions Series. Guilford, CT: Dushkin, 1992. Anthology of articles from a variety of sources that examines sociological issues.

Turner, Jonathan H. *The Structure of Sociological Theory*, 4th ed. Chicago: The Dorsey Press, 1986. Overview of the major theoretical perspectives in sociology.

Readings for Student Enrichment

Adams, Richard. *Watership Down*. New York: Macmillan, 1974. Allegorical examination of the flaws in human society; enables students to analyze group interaction and responses to norms.

Axtell, Roger E., ed. *Do's and Taboos Around the World*, 3d ed. New York: John Wiley and Sons, 1993. Topical presentation of cultural practices found around the world; helps students to understand cultural diversity.

Bradbury, Ray. *Fahrenheit 451*. New York: Ballantine Books, 1987. Futuristic novel in which the government controls the people through censorship; enables students to examine social change and social control.

Capote, Truman. *In Cold Blood*. New York: New American Library, 1988. True story of a violent murder; allows students to examine the consequences of a breakdown in social control.

Golding, William. *Lord of the Flies*. Hauppauge, NY: Barron's Educational Series, 1984. Group of boys stranded on a deserted island create their own power structure; allows students to explore the basic functioning of society.

Hellman, Lillian. "The Children's Hour." In *Six Modern American Plays*. New York: Random House, 1966. Play focusing on a group of children who start a rumor that their teacher has broken one of society's mores; enables students to analyze the social significance of norms.

Lee, Harper. *To Kill a Mockingbird*. New York: Warner Books, 1982. Novel set in the South during the 1930s; allows students to explore the significance of norms and the consequences of norm violations.

Mailer, Norman. *The Executioner's Song*. Boston: Little, Brown & Co., 1979. True story of convicted murderer Gary Gilmore; allows students to examine what happens when social control fails (some portions of this book may not be suitable for all students).

Miller, Arthur. *The Crucible*. New York: Penguin Books, 1976. Play focusing on the Salem witch trials that speaks to society's ability to create scapegoats; allows students to analyze the motives behind the actions of individuals in society.

Nordhoff, Charles, and Hall, James. *Mutiny on the Bounty*. Boston: Little, Brown & Co., 1932. Ship's crew mutinies against a tyrannical captain; allows students to analyze patterns of social interaction that involve conflict.

Orwell, George. *Animal Farm*. New York: New American Library, 1983. Allegorical novel that depicts the power of bureaucracies; helps students recognize the abuse of bureaucratic power.

Orwell, George. *1984*. New York: New American Library, 1983. Pessimistic prediction of society's future; enables students to evaluate norms, values, and social control.

Steinbeck, John. *The Grapes of Wrath*. New York: Penguin Books, 1976. Chronicles the journey of a poverty-stricken family during the Dust Bowl years of the 1930s; enables students to study roles, ingroups, and outgroups.

Steinbeck, John. *The Moon Is Down*. New York: Penguin Books, 1982. Short novel about the efforts of a small town against an invading army; enables students to examine forms of social interaction.

Zindel, Paul. *Pardon Me, You're Stepping on My Eyeball*. New York: Bantam Books, 1983. Story of two teenagers who are different from their peers; helps students analyze how society reacts to people who are different.

Multimedia Materials

The selected materials listed below may be useful during the study of Unit 1. The following abbreviations are used in the list:

c = color	lvd = laser videodisc
b&w = black & white	sim = simulation
f = film	sw = software
fs = filmstrip	g = game
vhs = videocassette	

Chapter 1

A Day in the Life of America (f, vhs; 17 1/2 min.) AM. A day in the life of American society is shown in the images produced by 200 leading photographers from 30 countries around the world.

Introduction to Sociology: The Science of Groups (fs, c; 34 min.) SSSS. Two-part introduction to the field of sociology.

Karl Marx and Marxism (vhs, c; 52 min.) FHS. Introduction to Karl Marx's philosophical and economic theories.

Man as Symbol Maker: Creating New Meanings (fs on vhs; 31 min.) GA. Describes how people have used symbols in art and literature to express basic ideas about themselves and the world.

Marxism: The Theory That Split a World (vhs, c; 26 min.) SSSS. Dramatizes Marx's theories through "interviews" with his wife, a Russian anarchist, and a Latin American revolutionary.

The Social Sciences: What Is Sociology? (fs on vhs; 45 min.) GA. Encourages students to assume the role of sociologist and apply what they have learned to make analyses and predictions.

Technology in America: The Age of Invention (f, vhs; 18 min.) CFV. Describes how the development of new technology in the second half of the nineteenth century changed life in American society.

Why Study Social Studies? (vhs; 30 min.) CSS. Introduces students to the importance and relevance of the major social studies disciplines, including sociology.

Chapter 2

American Tongues (vhs, c; 56 min.) SSSS. Explores the rich diversity of regional dialects found in the United States and illustrates how language can reveal much about a culture (contains brief strong language).

The Amish: A People of Preservation (vhs, c; 28 min.) EBEC. Documentary that focuses on the beliefs and sense of community of the Old-Order Amish in Lancaster, Pennsylvania.

Indians of Early America (vhs, b&w; 22 min.) EBEC. Recreates the activities of North American Indian societies, including a potlatch ceremony.

The Japanese Way of Life (lvd; 25 min.) AM. Journalists Peter Jennings and Jackie Judd examine life in Japan and the relationship between Japan and the United States.

Powwow! (vhs, c; 16 min.) SSSS. Documentary that explores the symbolism underlying Native American cultural practices.

South America: The Andean Region (vhs, c; 21 min.) EBEC. Explores how the environment of the Andes mountain region has influenced life in Colombia, Ecuador, Bolivia, and Chile.

U.S. Regions: Contrasts of Land and People (vhs, c; 30 min.) EBEC. Identifies how climate, geography, time of settlement, and type of settlers determined cultural development in eight U.S. regions.

The Way of the Willow (f, vhs; 30 min.) BF. Documents the cultural and personal problems faced by a family of Vietnamese boat people as they settle into a North American community.

Chapter 3

Africa: Central and Eastern Regions (vhs, c; 15 min.) EBEC. Explores the modern problems brought on by rapid population growth and the development of new industries in these regions.

All the Troubles of the World (vhs; 23 min.) EBEC. Isaac Asimov describes a futuristic world in which a computer controls the earth's economy, science, and inhabitants.

An Essay on War (vhs; 23 min.) EBEC. Explores why we wage war, how we justify it, and how we are affected by it.

Human Values in an Age of Technology (fs on vhs; 33 min.) GA. Explores the impact of technology on individuals and on nations.

The Klan: A Legacy of Hate in America (vhs, c; 29 min.) FIV. Illustrates the concept of ethnocentrism through a graphic examination of the history, ideas, and activities of the Ku Klux Klan.

Native American Myths (vhs, c; 24 min.) EBEC. Explores Native American values, norms, and beliefs through the use of five animated stories based on Native American myths.

Values (vhs; 30 min.) CE. Helps students to focus on values and priorities and illustrates how values may change over the course of a lifetime.

Vietnam: A Television History, 13—Legacies (vhs; 60 min.) FIV. Considers the legacy of the Vietnam War, including veterans' issues and the plight of Vietnamese refugees.

Visions of America (vhs; 58 min.) FHS. Seven American celebrities provide portraits of life and values in the United States.

Chapter 4

Boys and Girls (f, vhs; 26 min.) BF. A young girl fights against the stereotyped role imposed on her by her parents because of her sex. Based on the story by Alice Munro.

Getting Along with Others (vhs; 30 min.) CE. Fast-paced vignettes illustrate techniques for successful interpersonal relations.

Heelotia: A Cross-Cultural Simulation (sim; 24–60 players; 2 class periods) SSSS. Students are assigned to either the imaginary Heelot or Hokie culture and participate in a series of exchanges that teach an appreciation for cultural differences.

The Many Masks We Wear (fs on vhs; 36 min.) GA. Illustrates the concept of the mask in sociological and psychological contexts.

Tradition and Change (fs on vhs, c; 10 min.) SSSS. Uses a global, cross-cultural approach to analyze the conflict between traditional practices and forces for change.

The Turkana (vhs; 60 min.) FIV. Explores life among the East African Turkana cattle herders, nomadic pastoralists in the Rift Valley of northern Kenya.

World Cultures: Puzzles, Games, and Individual Activities (g; 27 photocopy masters) SSSS. Explores the rich diversity of cultures found around the world through a series of games and activities.

CHAPTER 1 *(pages 2–21)*

THE SOCIOLOGICAL POINT OF VIEW

SECTION 1
EXAMINING SOCIAL LIFE

SECTION 2
SOCIOLOGY: THEN AND NOW

Chapter Overview

As sociologist Peter Berger has noted, sociologists do not look at things of which others are unaware, rather they look at everyday events in different ways. By adopting a sociological perspective, sociologists are able to look beyond commonly held beliefs to the hidden meanings behind human actions. Chapter 1 provides students with an introduction to the discipline of sociology and to the sociological perspective. The social science of sociology grew out of the social unrest caused by the rapid social, political, and scientific changes that took place during the seventeenth and eighteenth centuries. At the root of these changes was the Industrial Revolution. Thus it is not surprising that sociology emerged first in France, Germany, and England—the nations most strongly affected by the Industrial Revolution.

The early sociologists attempted to understand the changes brought about by the Industrial Revolution. Most influential among these early sociologists were Auguste Comte, Karl Marx, Herbert Spencer, Emile Durkheim, and Max Weber.

Modern sociologists still are attempting to understand how various factors affect the structure of society and individuals and groups within society. To do this, they generally adopt a theoretical perspective. Three broad theoretical perspectives form the basis of modern sociology. These three theoretical perspectives are the functionalist perspective, the conflict perspective, and the interactionist perspective.

Chapter Objectives

At the conclusion of the chapter, students will be able to

1. Define sociology and the sociological perspective.
2. Explain what it means to possess a sociological imagination, and understand why such an imagination is important.
3. Recognize how sociology's focus differs from and is similar to the focus of each of the other social sciences.
4. Identify the factors that led to the emergence of sociology as a distinct discipline.
5. Discuss the theories and ideas of Auguste Comte, Karl Marx, Herbert Spencer, Emile Durkheim, and Max Weber.

6. Compare and contrast the three main theoretical perspectives in modern sociology.

Introducing the Chapter

There are many misconceptions about sociology and its place in the social sciences. Prior to assigning the reading of Chapter 1, ask the students to write a short essay answering the following three questions: (1) What is sociology? (2) What types of things do sociologists study? (3) Why is it important to study sociology? After they have completed their essays, ask selected volunteers to share their thoughts with the class. Follow up this activity by correctly defining sociology and its subject matter and by stating several reasons why sociology is an important social science.

Chapter 1 Suggested Lesson Plans

Day 1	**Suggested Procedures:** Introducing the Unit; Introducing the Chapter; Section 1 Previewing Key Terms; Introducing the Section **Materials:** PE: pp. 1–8; TM: pp. 1–5
Day 2	**Suggested Procedures:** Section 1 Strategies and Assignments **Materials:** PE: pp. 4–8; TM: pp. 5–6; TRB: Assorted Worksheets
Day 3	**Suggested Procedures:** Section 2 Previewing Key Terms; Introducing the Section; Strategies and Assignments **Materials:** PE: pp. 9–19; TM: pp. 6–7; TRB: Assorted Worksheets
Day 4	**Suggested Procedures:** Closing the Chapter; Assessing the Chapter **Materials:** PE: pp. 20–21; TM: pp. 7–9; TRB: Review Worksheet, Tests, Reteaching Worksheet

SECTION 1 *(pages 4–8)*

EXAMINING SOCIAL LIFE

Section Overview

Sociology—the science that studies human society and social behavior—is one of the related disciplines that make up the social sciences. The other social sciences include anthropology, psychology, economics, political science, and history. The sociological perspective enables us to look below the surface of social life and examine the factors that shape our behavior, our attitudes, and our beliefs. Rather than relying on common sense, which often turns out to be incorrect, sociology teaches us to look at social life in a scientific, systematic way.

Previewing Key Terms

Section 1 contains the following key terms: **sociology, social interaction, phenomenon, sociological imagination, social sciences, anthropology, psychology, social psychology, economics, political science, history**. Ask students to prepare a crossword puzzle using these terms and their definitions. Definitions can be found in Section 1 or in the Glossary. Then have the students exchange papers and complete the puzzles. Students may place the completed puzzles in their study notebooks for later review.

Introducing the Section

Conduct a brainstorming session in which students identify the benefits they hope to derive from learning about sociology. Examples might include learning more about relationships or developing a greater understanding of themselves. When no new ideas are forthcoming, tell students that Section 1 will introduce them to the sociological perspective and the reasons why developing such a perspective will benefit them now and in the future.

Suggested Teaching Strategies

1. **Evaluating Ideas (I)** Conduct a class discussion in which students defend or refute the following statement: "There are many different perceptions of social reality."
2. **Using Sociological Imagination (I)** Define for students what it means to have a sociological imagination. Then describe the following situation: A group of teenagers attend a party where alcohol is being served. After consuming large quantities of alcohol, four of these teenagers decide to leave and drive to another party. Ask students to exercise their sociological imaginations by describing some of the social consequences of this action for (a) the four teenagers; (b) other drivers; (c) the parents of the teenagers; (d) society as a whole.
3. **Working in Groups (II)** After discussing the relationship between sociology and the other social sciences, organize the class into five groups. Have each group interview teachers from one of the following disciplines: anthropology, psychology, economics, political science, history. Group members should elicit information on the focus and subject matter of their assigned discipline. Have selected volunteers from each group report their findings to the class and use this information as the basis of a class discussion comparing the various social sciences.

Suggested Enrichment Activities

1. **Exploring Cross-Cultural Perspectives (I)** Have students complete the appropriate Cross-Cultural Perspectives Worksheet, found in the *Teacher's Resource Binder*.
2. **Analyzing Ideas (III)** Have interested students analyze how social factors and experiences affected the main characters' views of reality and social behavior in one of the following novels: *The Crucible* by Arthur Miller; *Lord of the Flies* by William Golding; *Pardon Me, You're Stepping on My Eyeball* by Paul Zindel.

Suggested Assignments

1. **Stating a Point of View (I)** As homework, have students write a short essay discussing which of the benefits derived from developing a sociological perspective is most personally important to them and why. Ask selected volunteers to read their essays aloud to the class.
2. **Extending Ideas (I)** Have students read the Sociological Research Methods section of the textbook on pages 485–495. Then have students complete the appropriate Developing Research Skills Worksheet, found in the *Teacher's Resource Binder*.
3. **Linking the Past to the Present (II, III)** Have interested students use library sources to locate historical quotations that focus on some aspect of social interaction. Conduct a class discussion in which students evaluate how valid these quotations are in today's society.

Closing the Section

Have students prepare a quiz on the information contained in Section 1. Ask students to write 10 questions on one side of a piece of paper and the answers to these questions on the other side. When the quizzes are complete, have students exchange papers and answer the questions.

Assessing the Section

Have students complete the Section 1 Review.

Answers to Section 1 Review *(page 8)*

Define *sociology:* science that studies human society and social behavior; ***anthropology:*** comparative study of various aspects of past and present cultures; ***psychology:*** social science that deals with the behavior and thinking of organisms; ***economics:*** study of the choices people make in an effort to satisfy their wants and needs; ***political science:*** examination of the organization and operation of governments; ***history:*** study of past events

1. Sociologists tend to focus on groups rather than on individuals because sociology mainly is interested in social interaction—how people relate to one another and influence each other's behavior.
2. **(a)** According to C. Wright Mills, the sociological imagination is the ability to see the connections between the larger world and our personal lives. **(b)** Having a sociological imagination can assist people in their daily lives. First, the sociological imagination can help us to realize that the causes of behavior may be different from what they appear to be on the surface. Second, it can help make us more aware of the fact that our own behavior is the result of social influences—that we have learned our behavior from other people. Third, the sociological imagination can help us look at ourselves and the world around us more objectively. Fourth, it can help us to see beyond our own day-to-day lives by viewing the world through the eyes of others. Finally, it can help us find a balance between our own personal desires and demands and those of our environment.

3. (a) Sociology differs from anthropology in that sociology is most interested in group behavior in complex societies such as the United States. Anthropology traditionally has focused its attention on past cultures and present simple societies. Sociology differs from psychology in that sociology focuses on group behavior rather than on individual behavior. **(b)** Sociology shares many areas of interest with the other social sciences. For example, like economists, sociologists study the effects of economic factors on the lives of various groups in society. Like political scientists, some sociologists study voting behavior, the concentration of political power, and the formation of politically based groups. Sociologists, like historians, also study past events in an attempt to explain contemporary social behaviors and attitudes.

SECTION 2 (pages 9–17)

SOCIOLOGY: THEN AND NOW

Section Overview

The early sociologists attempted to understand the social conditions produced by the Industrial Revolution. With the exception of Max Weber, these early sociologists tended to focus on society as a whole. Auguste Comte, Herbert Spencer, and Emile Durkheim analyzed how society maintains stability over time. Karl Marx, on the other hand, examined the sources of social conflict. Only Max Weber chose to focus on the effects of society on the individual. The three main theoretical perspectives in modern sociology are an outgrowth of these original orientations.

Previewing Key Terms

Section 2 contains the following key terms: **social Darwinism, function, *Verstehen*, ideal type, theory, theoretical perspective, functionalist perspective, dysfunction, manifest function, latent function, conflict perspective, interactionist perspective, symbol, symbolic interaction**. Ask students to create a Word Search puzzle using these terms. Then have them exchange papers and complete the puzzles.

Introducing the Section

Ask students to turn to the Section 2 Review on textbook page 17. Then write the following sentence on the chalkboard: "Based on the review questions, I expect to learn at least 10 things from this section:"

1. _____
2. _____
3. _____
etc.

Ask students to copy the sentence and to fill in the blanks. When the activity has been completed, ask volunteers to discuss their answers with the class. Instruct students to keep their list of items in their study notebooks for later use.

Suggested Teaching Strategies

1. **Organizing Ideas (I)** Have students review the information on Comte, Marx, Spencer, Durkheim, and Weber, and then produce an outline showing the contributions of each person.
2. **Synthesizing Ideas (I, II)** Review the three main theoretical perspectives in sociology and the information covered in the Applying Sociology feature on textbook pages 14–15. Then write the following headings on the chalkboard: Functionalist/Content Analysis; Conflict/Historical Method; Interactionist/ Observation; Functionalist/Survey Method; Conflict/ Statistical Analysis; Interactionist/Case Study. Ask students to give examples of research topics that might be appropriate for each combination. Discuss the rationale for the choices.
3. **Working in Groups (I, II)** Organize the class into small groups and instruct the members of each group to retrieve the lists of items they prepared during the Introducing the Section activity. Have group members read their lists aloud and discuss among themselves how their expectations for learning the section material have been fulfilled.

Suggested Enrichment Activities

1. **Researching Biographies (III)** Have interested students write brief reports on important sociologists, both past and present. Instruct students to identify the theoretical orientations and research interests of each person. Sociologists might include William Graham Sumner, Lester Ward, Robert Park, George Herbert Mead, Talcott Parsons, Robert Merton, and Erving Goffman.
2. **Exploring Multicultural Perspectives (III)** Have interested students conduct library research to learn what life was like in the United States during the Industrial Revolution for one of the following groups: women, African Americans, Asian Americans, Hispanic Americans, Native Americans, children, the elderly. Ask selected volunteers to present what they have learned to the class.

Suggested Assignments

1. **Organizing Ideas (I)** As homework, have students complete the appropriate Graphic Organizer Worksheet, found in the *Teacher's Resource Binder*.
2. **★Reading about Sociology: Using Textbook Features (I)** To reinforce the skill lesson presented on textbook pages 18–19, have students complete the appropriate Critical Skills Mastery Worksheet, found in the *Teacher's Resource Binder*.
3. **Interpreting Ideas (I, II)** Organize the class into small groups and assign each group the task of formulating a list of five elements of society, giving one manifest function and one latent function for each element. Have volunteers from the groups present the lists to the class. Use this information as the basis of a class discussion on functions.

Closing the Section

Close the section by having students complete the appropriate Understanding Sociological Ideas Worksheet, found in the *Teacher's Resource Binder*.

Assessing the Section

Have students complete the Section 2 Review.

Answers to Section 2 Review *(page 17)*

Identify *Auguste Comte:* French philosopher generally considered to be the founder of sociology. Comte believed that the scientific methods used in the natural sciences also could be used to uncover laws that govern the workings of societies; ***Karl Marx:*** German writer and scholar who studied the changing nature of social relations in capitalist societies. Marx believed that the economic basis of society strongly influences the nature of relationships among various groups in society, and was greatly disturbed by the social conditions that resulted from capitalism. He thought that the social problems caused by capitalism would not be solved until ill-treated workers overthrew the people in power; ***Herbert Spencer:*** English scholar who developed a biological model of society based on Charles Darwin's theory of evolution. Spencer's model, referred to as *Social Darwinism,* held that societies are like living organisms that evolve over time, eventually reaching a state of perfection; ***Emile Durkheim:*** French sociologist who studied the problems of social order. Durkheim believed that societies are held together by shared beliefs and values. He was the first sociologist to apply the scientific method to the study of society and to test his theories through statistical analysis; ***Max Weber:*** German economist and sociologist who studied the effects of society on individuals. Weber's method of study required that sociologists put themselves in the place of the people they study in order to see situations through the eyes of the subjects

1. **(a)** Comte is considered the founder of sociology because he was the first person to use the term *sociology* to describe the study of society. **(b)** Comte used the term *social statics* to refer to the processes by which the overall structure of a society remained relatively unchanged over time. He used the term *social dynamics*, on the other hand, to refer to the processes by which elements within society change in a systematic way to allow for social development.
2. Marx believed that open conflict between the ill-treated workers and their capitalist employers was necessary in order to change society in a positive way. Spencer, on the other hand, believed that all of society's problems eventually would disappear as an inevitable part of social evolution. Conflict between parts of the society therefore was necessary for positive social change to occur.
3. Durkheim believed that sociologists should study only those aspects of society that can be directly observed. He therefore did not believe that the thoughts and feelings of individuals are the proper subject matter of sociology. Weber, on the other hand, believed that sociologists should go beyond the

directly observable to study the feelings and thoughts of individuals.
4. **(a)** A theoretical perspective is a general set of assumptions about the nature of phenomena. **(b)** Theoretical perspectives in sociology outline certain assumptions about the nature of social life. The functionalist perspective views society as a set of interrelated parts that work together to produce a stable social system. Functionalists assume that most people agree on what is best for society and will work together to ensure that the social system runs smoothly. The conflict perspective assumes that the conflict that arises over scarce resources leads to valuable social change. Change therefore is an inevitable part of human societies. The interactionist perspective is especially interested in the meanings that individuals attach to their own actions and to the actions of others.

Answers to Developing Sociological Imagination *(pages 18–19)*

Student outlines should contain the following heads and subheads:

The Sociological Point of View
I. Examining Social Life
    A. The Sociological Perspective
    B. Sociology's Place in the Social Sciences
II. Sociology: Then and Now
    A. The Early Years
        1. Auguste Comte
        2. Karl Marx
        3. Herbert Spencer
        4. Emile Durkheim
        5. Max Weber
    B. Current Perspectives
        1. Functionalist Perspective
        2. Conflict Perspective
        3. Interactionist Perspective

Closing the Chapter

Have students complete the Chapter 1 Review Worksheet, found in the *Teacher's Resource Binder*.

Assessing the Chapter

Have students complete the Chapter 1 Review, found on page 20 of the *Pupil's Edition*.

Give students the Chapter 1 Form A Test and, if desired, the Chapter 1 Reteaching Worksheet and Form B Test, found in the *Teacher's Resource Binder*.

Answers to Chapter 1 Review *(page 20)*

Reviewing Sociological Terms

1. social sciences
2. Economics
3. *Verstehen*
4. ideal type
5. social interaction
6. manifest function

Thinking Critically about Sociology

1. **(a)** Spencer used the phrase "survival of the fittest" to refer to the natural and inevitable evolution of societies in which only the best societal elements would survive. The whole world would be upgraded as societal problems faded away. **(b)** Spencer believed that social unrest was a natural part of society that would be eliminated as society moved toward perfection.

2. Functional elements in a society are those things that have beneficial consequences and that enable a society to function smoothly. Dysfunctional elements, on the other hand, disrupt society rather than stabilize it.

3. **(a)** A theory is the systematic explanation of the relationships among phenomena. **(b)** Sociologists who follow the functionalist perspective study the functions of various behavioral patterns, such as the division of household labor, and societal institutions, such as education or religion. Conflict sociologists examine not only violent conflict but also nonviolent competition between societal groups. Conflict sociologists might study relations among various minority groups and disputes between auto workers and auto manufacturers. Symbolic interactionists focus on topics such as the processes through which children learn correct behavior, parent-child relationships, and the formation of the self-concept.

4. **(a)** The functionalist perspective views society as a set of interrelated parts that work together to produce a stable social system. Functionalists assume that most people agree on what is best for society and will work together to ensure that the social system runs smoothly. The conflict perspective assumes that the conflict that arises over scarce resources leads to valuable social change. According to this perspective, change is an inevitable aspect of human societies. The interactionist perspective focuses on how individuals within a society interact with each other. This perspective is especially interested in the meanings that individuals attach to their own actions and to the actions of others. **(b)** Herbert Spencer and Emile Durkheim greatly influenced the functionalist perspective. Durkheim's concept of functions led functionalists to focus on the positive consequences of societal elements. Karl Marx has been a major contributor to the conflict perspective. Conflict theorists are concerned with the control that economically powerful people exercise over the less powerful. The work of Max Weber, particularly his concept of *Verstehen,* has influenced the interactionist perspective. This theoretical perspective focuses on the meanings that individuals attach to actions.

5. Sociology did not emerge as a distinct discipline until the nineteenth century, in France, Germany, and Great Britain. The science of society emerged out of the profound social problems that accompanied industrialization and urbanization. As people left the rural areas to find employment in factories, cities grew rapidly. The rapid growth of cities led to housing shortages and pollution. The number of available jobs could not keep pace with the number of persons looking for employment. Unemployment and crime became major social problems. These problems had a negative impact on individuals. The French and American revolutions occurred as individuals joined to fight for personal freedom and other basic human rights. Another factor influencing the rise of sociology was the development by the natural sciences of methods for studying the physical world in a systematic way. Early sociologists applied these methods to the study of society.

6. By adopting a sociological perspective, we learn to look beyond commonly held beliefs to find hidden meanings behind human actions. A sociological perspective helps make us more aware of the fact that our own behavior is the result of social influences and that we have learned our behavior from other people. This perspective helps us look at ourselves and the world around us more objectively. We learn to see beyond our own day-to-day world by viewing the world through others' eyes. The sociological perspective also helps us find a balance between our own personal desires and demands and those of our environment.

7. A manifest function is the intended and recognized consequence of some element of society. A latent function, on the other hand, is the unintended and unrecognized consequence of some element of society.

Exercising Sociological Skills

1. **(a)** The historical method involves the examination of existing sources from the past, such as diaries, letters, newspapers, magazines, and government records, to learn about patterns in other times. Content analysis also involves the examination of existing sources. This process involves counting the number of times a particular element appears in a given context. The survey method involves the collection of data on attitudes and opinions through the use of written questionnaires or personal interviews. In the observation method, researchers watch and record the behavior of individuals in actual social settings. In some cases, researchers become participants in the situations they are observing. The case study method involves the very detailed analysis of a person, group, event, or social problem. Statistical analysis is a way to summarize and interpret data that have been collected through a variety of methods and is usually done with computers. **(b)** Answers will vary. Any of the methods could be used. For example, content analysis could be used to study newspapers to determine the number of students who participate in and attend sports events. Observation techniques could be used to watch teams practice or to attend pep rallies and sports events. Survey analysis could be used to determine the attitudes of students toward school sports.

2. **(a)** The main purpose of the conventions sponsored by the ASA is to bring together sociologists from around the nation to discuss their most recent research findings. **(b)** The ASA helps sociology teachers in a number of ways, including operating a teaching resources center, sponsoring workshops in which teachers learn effective teaching techniques, providing funds for teacher development and training, and presenting awards to outstanding teachers.

3. The title of the Case Study feature, located on page 7, is "The American Sociological Association." The title of the Applying Sociology feature, found on pages 14–15, is "Using Sociological Methods." The title of the Developing Sociological Imagination feature, located on pages 18–19, is "Using Textbook Features."

Extending Sociological Imagination

1. Answers will vary. For example, the sociologist might look at the characteristics of the homeless to determine what factors lead to this situation and which people are most likely to become homeless. The economist might study the role that government policies play in increasing or decreasing the number of homeless people in society. The psychologist might look at the impact of homelessness on an individual's mental health and well-being. The anthropologist might look at the subculture of the homeless, perhaps examining the survival tips exchanged among homeless persons.

2. Answers will vary.

Answers to Interpreting Primary
Sources *(page 21)*

1. To Mills, the most important concern of sociologists is the application of sociology to the real world and to the daily lives of individuals in the society.

2. Types of questions the sociologist with a sociological imagination must ask are: (1) What is the unique nature of a society? (2) How has the society been changing over time, and what are the unique characteristics of the time period under study? (3) What types of people live in the society, and how does the society shape its citizens?

CHAPTER 2 *(pages 22–43)*

CULTURAL DIVERSITY

SECTION 1
THE MEANING OF CULTURE

SECTION 2
CULTURAL VARIATION

Chapter Overview

Unlike other animals, human beings are not controlled by natural instincts. Thus they are able to adapt to and change their environment. Culture—the shared material and nonmaterial products of human groups—arises from attempts by people to deal with their environment. Chapter 2 examines the components of culture, how culture is transmitted, and how cultural practices vary among and within human groups or societies.

All cultures consist of five basic components. These components are physical objects, symbols, language, values, and norms. Specific examples of material and nonmaterial culture, however, vary from society to society and often from group to group within a society. The scope and nature of cultural variation is of particular interest to sociologists.

Chapter Objectives

At the conclusion of the chapter, students will be able to

1. Define culture, and differentiate between material and nonmaterial culture.
2. Recognize how sociologists distinguish between the terms *culture* and *society*.
3. Identify and discuss the five basic components of culture.
4. Explain how folkways differ from mores.
5. Describe the three levels of culture, and understand how the three levels are interrelated.
6. Assess the significance of the cultural studies completed by George Murdock and Margaret Mead.
7. Define cultural universals and explain why they exist.
8. Discuss cultural variations among societies, and interpret the related issues of ethnocentrism and cultural relativism.
9. Distinguish between subcultures and countercultures.

Introducing the Chapter

The terms *culture* and *society* often are used interchangeably in everyday speech. Sociologists, however, use the terms to refer to two related but separate concepts. Thus it is important for students of sociology to know the proper usage of each term.

Prior to assigning the reading of Chapter 2, ask students to describe what comes to mind when they hear the word *culture*. List their responses on the chalkboard. When doing so, list separately those responses that refer to being a "cultured" person—enjoying classical music, fine art, and literature; dining in expensive restaurants; wearing chic clothing and jewelry; being educated in the "best" schools—from those that refer to the sociological usage of the term. Next ask students to provide definitions of society. Once the responses are on the chalkboard, describe how sociologists distinguish between culture and society, and explain why this distinction is important.

Chapter 2 Suggested Lesson Plans

Day 1	**Suggested Procedures:** Introducing the Chapter; Section 1 Previewing Key Terms; Introducing the Section **Materials:** PE: pp. 22–30; TM: pp. 9–10
Day 2	**Suggested Procedures:** Section 1 Strategies and Assignments **Materials:** PE: pp. 24–30; TM: pp. 10–11; TRB: Assorted Worksheets, Transparency 1

Day 3	**Suggested Procedures:** Section 2 Previewing Key Terms; Introducing the Section; Strategies and Assignments **Materials:** PE: pp. 31–41; TM: pp. 11–12; TRB: Assorted Worksheets
Day 4	**Suggested Procedures:** Closing the Chapter; Assessing the Chapter **Materials:** PE: pp. 42–43; TM: pp. 12–13; TRB: Review Worksheet, Tests, Reteaching Worksheet

SECTION 1 *(pages 24–30)*

THE MEANING OF CULTURE

Section Overview

Culture consists of the shared products of human groups. These products include both physical objects (material culture) and the beliefs, values, and behaviors shared by a group (nonmaterial culture). A society, on the other hand, is a group of mutually interdependent people who have organized in such a way as to share a common culture and feeling of unity. Societies produce culture.

Although the exact nature of cultures varies greatly, physical objects, symbols, language, values, and norms are components common to all cultures. Because cultures are so complex, sociologists study them by dividing them into three levels: culture traits, culture complexes, and culture patterns.

Previewing Key Terms

Section 1 contains the following key terms: **culture, material culture, nonmaterial culture, society, symbol, language, values, norms, folkways, mores, law, culture trait, culture complex, culture pattern**. Have students use the Glossary to find definitions for each of the following groups of terms: culture and society; material culture and nonmaterial culture; symbol and language; values and norms; folkways, mores, and law; culture trait, culture complex, and culture pattern. Then ask selected volunteers to explain how the terms in each grouping are related. Have students take notes during the discussion for later review.

Introducing the Section

Ask a volunteer to turn to the Glossary and read aloud the definitions for the following terms: symbol, language, values, norms. After writing these terms on the chalkboard, tell students to imagine that they are crew members aboard the starship *Enterprise* who have been sent back in time to conduct anthropological research on 1990s American culture. On this basis, have students provide descriptive information that can be written under each of the four headings on the chalkboard. Then tell students that symbols, language, values, and norms,

along with physical objects, are necessary components of all cultures and the focus of Section 1.

Suggested Teaching Strategies

1. **Learning from Graphs (I)** Review the material on levels of culture by placing Transparency 1 on an overhead projector and asking the questions contained in the accompanying teacher's notes. Transparencies and accompanying teacher's notes are found in the *Teacher's Resource Binder*.
2. **Seeing Relationships (I)** To underscore the importance of culture to societies, have students imagine what American society would be like if there were no shared culture. Ask: "What would American society be like if everyone spoke a different language?" Ask similar questions for symbols, norms, and values. Lead students to see that no society can exist without a shared culture.
3. **Working in Groups (I, II)** Organize the class into small groups and have the groups use discarded magazines to create posters with photographs representing the components of American culture. Consider asking some of the groups to make posters that are representative of cultures other than American culture. Have volunteers discuss their posters in class.

Suggested Enrichment Activities

1. **Identifying Ideas (I)** Have students complete the appropriate Critical Skills Mastery Worksheet, found in the *Teacher's Resource Binder*.
2. **Writing Creatively (III)** Have students read the Applying Sociology feature on textbook pages 28–29. Ask interested students to write a similar parody on some other aspect of American culture to present to the class. Have class members try to guess the focus of the parodies.

Suggested Assignments

1. **Applying Ideas (I)** As homework, have students list 20 norms and indicate whether they are folkways or mores. Ask volunteers to read their lists aloud to the class for class discussion.
2. **★Reading about Sociology: Developing a Structured Overview (I)** To reinforce the skill lesson presented on textbook pages 40–41, have students prepare a structured overview of Section 2 of Chapter 2.
3. **Synthesizing Ideas (I, II)** Organize the class into small groups and have each group develop a list of examples of the symbols, language, values, and norms indicative of their school culture. Have volunteers from each group present their lists to the class.

Closing the Section

Close the section by having students complete the appropriate Graphic Organizer Worksheet, found in the *Teacher's Resource Binder*.

Assessing the Section

Have students complete the Section 1 Review.

Answers to Applying Sociology (pages 28–29)

1. Miner's essay is about American culture.
2. Notgnihsaw is George Washington. The Pa-To-Mac is the Potomac River.
3. The shrine refers to the bathroom. The box or chest refers to the medicine cabinet.
4. The mouth ritual is brushing one's teeth. The holy mouth man is the dentist.
5. American culture highly values personal health and hygiene.

Answers to Section 1 Review (page 30)

Identify _!Kung:_ small bands of people who live in the Kalahari Desert in southern Africa. The !Kung hunt and gather their food. They do not raise plants or animals because of the harsh conditions of their physical environment; **_Kwakiutl:_** American Indians who lived in the Pacific Northwest during the eighteenth and nineteenth centuries. The Kwakiutl believed in sharing food and material objects with the people in their tribes who produced less than they did. Although there was competition between individuals in the amount of food and wealth they possessed, the Kwakiutl were not aggressive people; **_Yanomamö:_** group of horticulturalists who live in southern Venezuela and Brazil. The Yanomamö are very competitive and aggressive, so much so that nearly one-third of their males are killed in warfare; **_Napoleon Chagnon:_** anthropologist who has studied the Yanomamö, calling them the Fierce People

1. The term _culture_ refers to all the shared products of human groups, including physical objects, beliefs, values, and behaviors. The term _society_ refers to a group of mutually interdependent people who have organized in such a way as to share a common culture and feeling of unity.
2. The five basic components of culture are physical objects, symbols, language, values, and norms.
3. **(a)** The Kwakiutl valued sharing and cooperation, whereas the Yanomamö value conflict and competition. **(b)** Different values often produce different cultures. The Kwakiutl, for example, valued cooperation and so developed rituals, tools, and other cultural components that revolved around sharing. An example of this was their potlatch, a ritualized feast in which food and objects are shared. The Yanomamö, on the other hand, value conflict and so have developed ceremonies and artifacts revolving around warfare.
4. **(a)** Sociologists examine three levels of culture: traits, complexes, and patterns. Culture traits are individual tools, acts, or beliefs that are related to particular situations or needs. Culture complexes are clusters of interrelated traits. Culture patterns are combinations of a number of culture complexes into interrelated wholes. **(b)** The three levels of culture are related. Footballs, cleats, and rule books, for example, are culture traits. These objects, and many other objects in combination, make up the culture complex of football. Football, tennis, golf, skiing, and many other sports complexes make up the American athletic culture pattern.

SECTION 2 _(pages 31–39)_

CULTURAL VARIATION

Section Overview

Some needs are so basic that all societies must develop culture traits, complexes, and patterns to ensure their fulfillment. These features, common to all societies, are known as cultural universals. Cultural variations, however, are a much more common feature of social life.

For the social scientist, variations in cultural practices have both positive and negative consequences. On the positive side, variations are what make societies interesting to study. On the negative side, diversity gives rise to the problem of ethnocentrism—the tendency to view one's own culture and group as superior. To guard against ethnocentrism, many social scientists adopt the attitude of cultural relativism. Cultural relativism is the belief that cultures should be judged by their own standards.

Cultural variations exist not only among societies, they also exist within societies. Two of the most common sources of variations within societies are subcultures and countercultures.

Previewing Key Terms

Section 2 contains the following key terms: **cultural universals, ethnocentrism, cultural relativism, subculture, counterculture**. Have students look up each of these terms in the Glossary. Next ask the students to write five sentences, each of which should contain one of the terms in the list. Then have selected volunteers read their sentences aloud to the class.

Introducing the Section

To introduce students to the concepts of cultural universals and cultural variation, hold a class discussion in which volunteers identify the cultural groups that make up their family heritages. Ask the class to consider both what these cultural groups have in common and how they differ. Then have students discuss how these various cultural groups have influenced American culture.

Suggested Teaching Strategies

1. **Stating a Point of View (I)** After reviewing the work of George Murdock and Margaret Mead, have students write short reaction papers stating what they believe is the most significant contribution of each person to our understanding of culture.
2. **Understanding Ideas (I)** After defining ethnocentrism, have students list the positive and negative consequences of ethnocentrism.
3. **Analyzing Events (II, III)** Organize the class into small groups and have the groups review the concepts of ethnocentrism and cultural relativism. Ask each group to choose an event in American or world history that was a direct result of ethnocentrism. After

the group has described the event, have group members suggest ways in which practicing cultural relativism might have changed the course of history. Ask volunteers to present their group's ideas to the class for class discussion.

4. **Linking the Past to the Present (III)** Have selected students research how family life in an Israeli kibbutz has changed since the early 1950s. Discuss these changes in class.

Suggested Enrichment Activities

1. **Applying Ideas (I)** Have students complete the appropriate Developing Research Skills Worksheet, found in the *Teacher's Resource Binder*.
2. **Conducting Research (III)** Have interested students prepare research papers on one of the following counterculture groups: skinheads, devil worshippers, drug gangs, terrorists. Ask the students to report their findings to the class.

Suggested Assignments

1. **Exploring Cross-Cultural Perspectives (I)** As homework, have students complete the appropriate Cross-Cultural Perspectives Worksheet, found in the *Teacher's Resource Binder*. Then have the students discuss the reading and their answers in class.
2. **Extending Ideas (II)** Have selected groups of students visit shops in your community that specialize in foods from other nations. Ask students to compile two lists: one containing foods that are generally common in the United States and one containing foods that are generally unfamiliar in the United States. Students should write a short description of the foods on the latter list. The groups may then quiz their classmates on their familiarity with the variety of foods available worldwide.

Closing the Section

Close the section by having students complete the appropriate Understanding Sociological Ideas Worksheet, found in the *Teacher's Resource Binder*.

Assessing the Section

Have students complete the Section 2 Review.

Answers to Section 2 Review *(page 39)*

Identify *George Murdock:* anthropologist who compiled a list of traits common to all cultures. Murdock's research was based on an examination of hundreds of different cultures in the 1940s; ***Margaret Mead:*** anthropologist who conducted a study of cultural variation among small societies in New Guinea. Mead's purpose in the study was to determine whether differences in basic temperament result from inherited characteristics or from cultural influences; ***Arapesh:*** one of the small New Guinea societies studied by Margaret Mead, the Arapesh are cooperative, nonaggressive, and gentle; ***Mundugumor:*** one of the small New Guinea societies studied by Margaret Mead, the Mundugumor, both men and women, are violent, competitive, and jealous

1. **(a)** Cultural universals are features that are common to all human cultures. **(b)** Cultural universals exist because they serve the most basic of all human needs. **(c)** Examples of cultural universals that students might mention include cooking, body adornment, toolmaking, myths and folklore, religion, medicine, family, and language.
2. **(a)** Ethnocentrism is the tendency to view one's own culture and group as superior. **(b)** When ethnocentrism becomes extreme, a culture can stagnate. New influences that might be beneficial for the culture are excluded because they are incorrectly believed to be inferior. **(c)** In mild forms, ethnocentrism is positive because it helps to build unity among the members of the culture.
3. **(a)** Cultural relativism is the belief that cultures should be judged by their own standards. Rather than using the standards of their own cultures, researchers who practice cultural relativism try to understand cultural practices from the viewpoint of the society that is being studied. **(b)** Cultural relativism expands the explanatory power of social scientific studies by providing a wider context in which to view seemingly strange patterns of behavior.
4. **(a)** A subculture is a group with its own unique values, norms, and behaviors that exists within a larger culture. **(b)** A counterculture can be distinguished from a subculture in that the counterculture rejects the values, norms, and behaviors of the larger society, while the subculture does not.

Answers to Developing Sociological Imagination *(pages 40–41)*

The structured overview should match the format shown on textbook page 41.

Closing the Chapter

Have students complete the Chapter 2 Review Worksheet, found in the *Teacher's Resource Binder*.

Assessing the Chapter

Have students complete the Chapter 2 Review, found on page 42 of the *Pupil's Edition*.

Give students the Chapter 2 Form A Test and, if desired, the Chapter 2 Reteaching Worksheet and Form B Test, found in the *Teacher's Resource Binder*.

Answers to Chapter 2 Review *(page 42)*

Reviewing Sociological Terms

1. Artifacts
2. language
3. nonmaterial culture
4. Ethnocentrism
5. material culture
6. cultural universal

Thinking Critically about Sociology

1. **(a)** Values are shared ideas about what is good or bad, right or wrong, desirable or undesirable. Norms

are the shared rules of conduct that tell people how to act in specific situations. Values and norms are related in that norms serve to uphold the values of a society. **(b)** The values of a society help shape the personalities of the population and the types of cultural objects that the society creates. Norms provide guidelines for behavior.

2. **(a)** Answers will vary. For example, students may state that the dominant values of adolescent subcultures include being accepted by one's peers, fitting in with the crowd, and maintaining the appearance of independence from parents. The norms of adolescent subcultures may include dressing like other adolescents and spending time away from parents. **(b)** Answers will vary, but students should identify which of the norms and values they mentioned in the first part of the question conflict with those of the larger society.

3. **(a)** A symbol is anything that stands for something else and has a shared meaning attached to it. **(b)** Words, gestures, images, sounds, physical objects, events, and natural objects can serve as symbols. **(c)** An object becomes a symbol when people recognize that the object conveys a particular meaning.

4. **(a)** According to Harris, the prohibition against killing cows in India can be attributed to the fact that cows are needed to pull the plows for planting, since few Indian farmers have tractors. Additionally, milk is an essential ingredient in the Indian diet. Thus, cows do play an important role in the Indian economy, perhaps even more important than serving as a source of meat. **(b)** Differences between the Arapesh and the Mundugumor can be attributed to the physical environment. The Arapesh live in the mountains. They subsist on food grown in gardens, and food is scarce. The Mundugumor, on the other hand, live in a river valley and have an abundant food supply, which they gather. The scarcity of food among the Arapesh may contribute to their cultural emphasis on cooperation and sharing. The surplus of food among the Mundugumor may be responsible for their emphasis on competition.

5. **(a)** Folkways, mores, and laws are types of norms that differ in terms of their importance for society. Folkways are norms that have little consequence for society, the common customs of everyday living. Mores, on the other hand, have a great moral significance attached to them. Violating the mores of society can have serious negative consequences for the stability of society. Norms that have great moral significance attached to them often are formalized as laws. Laws are important for the stability and smooth operation of society. **(b)** Answers will vary. For example, the rules of table etiquette are folkways. One example of a more is the universal prohibition against cannibalism. One example of a law is the written rule regarding the minimum age at which people can marry.

6. **(a)** Margaret Mead concluded that temperament primarily is the result of cultural factors rather than biological factors. In other words, temperament is learned rather than inherited. **(b)** Mead's conclusion was based on her systematic observation that women and men from the same culture were much more similar to each other than they were to their same-sex counterparts in the other culture. If sex differences were biologically determined, the opposite would have been true.

Exercising Sociological Skills

1. **(a)** No, Miner's description of the Nacirema is not an example of cultural relativism. **(b)** Miner's essay is a humorous attempt to emphasize the need for cultural relativism in studies of other societies. By approaching American society as an outsider would, Miner shows how ethnocentrism can limit the understanding of other cultures.

2. Rabin's research provides some support for the belief that culture influences personality development. The study found that adults who had been raised in a kibbutz were less productive, less satisfied with their marriages, and less attached to their families and friends than were people who had been raised in traditional families. These personality differences reflect the fact that the kibbutz people had been raised in a communal environment that stressed group bonds over individual and family bonds. The observation that kibbutz-raised adults excelled in the military and in athletics may reflect the group orientation of these pursuits.

3. The structured overview should match the format of the structured overview on text page 41.

Extending Sociological Imagination

1. Answers will vary, but students should be sure to address the elements against which the group was rebelling, and discuss the major norms and values of the group.

2. Answers will vary, but students should be sure to discuss both the differences and the similarities between the United States and the societies they have chosen to research.

3. Answers will vary. For example, students might describe the culture pattern of education in American society. This pattern would include the culture traits of books, pencils, chalkboards, students, and so on. These culture traits would combine into culture complexes such as requirements for graduation, testing procedures, and student-teacher relationships.

Answers to Interpreting Primary Sources *(page 43)*

1. The mother believes that the delivery of pills will bring sickness to her family.

2. The mother believes sickness is caused by interpersonal factors, that is, by one person's desire to cause sickness in the other person. The druggist, on the other hand, undoubtedly attributes illness to biological factors.

3. Knowing that Chinese druggists send raisins for good luck along with prescriptions enables us to understand why the Chinese woman expected the same treatment from the American druggist. If we did not practice cultural relativism, we would think that the woman's expectation was strange, since giving raisins is not something normally practiced by American druggists.

CHAPTER 3 *(pages 44–65)*

CULTURAL CONFORMITY AND ADAPTATION

SECTION 1
THE AMERICAN VALUE SYSTEM

SECTION 2
SOCIAL CONTROL

SECTION 3
SOCIAL CHANGE

Chapter Overview

All societies must establish norms and values. It is not enough, however, simply to establish the norms and values. Societies also must ensure that these norms and values are enforced. Societies accomplish this through internalization and the use of sanctions. The enforcement of norms and values through internalization and sanctions is called social control.

Even when social control is effective, societies still undergo change. The major sources of social change are values and beliefs, technology, population, diffusion, the physical environment, and wars and conquests. The major sources of resistance to social change are ethnocentrism, cultural lag, and vested interests.

Chapter Objectives

At the conclusion of the chapter, students will be able to

1. Identify and describe the traditional American values discussed in the textbook chapter.
2. Assess the positive and negative consequences of the new American value of self-fulfillment.
3. Define social control, and discuss internalization and sanctions—the two basic methods of social control.
4. Recognize and describe the sources of social change.
5. Explain why individuals and groups tend to resist social change.

Introducing the Chapter

Write the following statement on the chalkboard: "Every society must have norms, and these norms must be enforced." Then instruct students to make lists of norms that they are faced with in their daily lives and to indicate the ways in which these norms are enforced. Next ask students to rank these norms in order of importance. Have the students share their lists with the class. Be sure that students justify their rankings when sharing the lists. Discuss whether the rankings and the strictness of the enforcement appear to be correlated. After discussing the lists, assign the reading of Chapter 3.

Chapter 3 Suggested Lesson Plans

Day 1	**Suggested Procedures:** Introducing the Chapter; Section 1 Previewing Key Terms; Introducing the Section **Materials:** PE: pp. 44–51; TM: pp. 14–15
Day 2	**Suggested Procedures: Section** 1 Strategies and Assignments **Materials:** PE: pp. 46–51; TM: pp. 15–16; TRB: Worksheet
Day 3	**Suggested Procedures:** Section 2 Previewing Key Terms; Introducing the Section; Strategies and Assignments **Materials:** PE: pp. 52–54; TM: pp. 16–17; TRB: Worksheet
Day 4	**Suggested Procedures:** Section 3 Previewing Key Terms; Introducing the Section; Strategies and Assignments **Materials:** PE: pp. 55–63; TM: pp. 17–18; TRB: Assorted Worksheets
Day 5	**Suggested Procedures:** Closing the Chapter; Assessing the Chapter **Materials:** PE: pp. 64–65; TM: pp. 18–19; TRB: Review Worksheet, Tests, Reteaching Worksheet

SECTION 1 *(pages 46–51)*

THE AMERICAN VALUE SYSTEM

Section Overview

In a now-classic study, sociologist Robin Williams outlined a set of 15 values that are central to the American way of life. Among these values are personal achievement, work, morality, humanitarianism, efficiency, practicality, progress, material comfort, equality, democracy, and freedom. In recent years, sociologists have noted the emergence of several new values. The most significant of these new values is self-fulfillment.

Previewing Key Terms

Section 1 contains the following key terms: **self-fulfillment, narcissism**. Have students find definitions for each of these terms in the Glossary. Then hold a class discussion centering on how these terms might relate to the American value system.

Introducing the Section

Discuss with students the fact that many politicians in recent years have urged as part of their campaigns a return to "traditional American values." Then conduct a brainstorming session in which students consider what values might be considered traditionally American. When no new ideas are forthcoming, tell students that sociologist Robin Williams has compiled a list of such values, which they will read about in Section 1.

Suggested Teaching Strategies

1. **Summarizing Ideas (I)** After reviewing Section 1, have students list the 11 values outlined by Robin Williams and explain each value in his or her own words.
2. **Working in Groups (II, III)** Organize the class into small groups and have each group choose one of the 11 traditional values discussed in the section. Have the members of each group work together to create a piece of art that illustrates the value chosen by their group. Art may take the form of a song, a poem, a painting, a collage, a dance, and so on.
3. **Linking the Past to the Present (II, III)** Ask students to watch two television situation comedies that focus on family life. One program should be a rerun from the 1950s or 1960s. The other program should be current. Have students identify the values depicted in each of the programs. Use the programs as the basis of a class discussion on changing values.

Suggested Enrichment Activities

1. **Evaluating Ideas (I, II)** Organize interested students into two groups and have them debate the following statement in front of the class: "All Americans should hold the same values."
2. **Dramatizing Sociology (II, III)** Have interested students prepare and present brief skits showing examples of narcissism in American society.

Suggested Assignments

1. **Conducting a Poll (I)** As homework, have students conduct a poll in which they ask 10 people (friends, family, neighbors) the following question: "Which traditional American value do you believe is most important to the American way of life?" Have students present their findings to the class, and ask a volunteer to tally and rank the results. Use the rankings as the basis of a class discussion.
2. **Practicing Geography Skills (II)** Have students read the Applying Sociology feature on textbook pages 48–49. Then have the students determine the geographic location of each culture mentioned in the feature.
3. **Researching Biographies (III)** Have interested students research the life and work of sociologist Robin Williams.

Closing the Section

Close the section by having students complete the appropriate Graphic Organizer Worksheet, found in the *Teacher's Resource Binder*.

Assessing the Section

Have students complete the Section 1 Review.

Answers to Applying Sociology *(pages 48–49)*

Student answers should match the following: *bed,* Near East; *covers: cotton,* India, *linen,* Near East, *silk,* China; *spinning and weaving,* Near East; *moccasins,* the Americas; *pajamas,* India; *soap,* Gauls; *shaving,* Sumer, ancient Egypt; *chair,* Asia; *shoes: leather,* Egypt, *pattern,* Mediterranean; *glass,* Egypt; *rubber,* Central America; *umbrella,* Southeast Asia; *felt,* Asia; *coin,* Lydia; *pottery,* China; *steel,* India; *fork,* Italy; *spoon,* Rome; *orange,* Mediterranean; *cantaloupe,* Persia; *watermelon,* Africa; *coffee,* Abyssinia; *cows, milking,* Near East; *sugar,* India; *waffles,* Scandinavia; *wheat,* Asia; *maple syrup,* North America; *chicken,* Indo-China; *pigs,* Asia; *meat smoking,* Europe; *alphabet,* Semites; *paper,* China; *printing,* Germany; *God,* Israel; *language,* Indo-Europe

Answers to Section 1 Review *(page 51)*

Define *self-fulfillment:* commitment to the full development of one's personality, talents, and potential; ***narcissism:*** extreme self-centeredness

Identify *Robin Williams:* sociologist who conducted a major study in 1970 to identify the central values in American society, and outlined a list of 15 such values; ***Christopher Lasch:*** sociologist who concluded that the increasing emphasis on personal fulfillment in our society has given rise to narcissism, or extreme self-centeredness; ***Daniel Yankelovich:*** psychologist and survey researcher who believes that the increased emphasis on self-centeredness is beneficial in that it represents an emphasis on self-improvement and a movement away from satisfaction based on material gain

1. Robin Williams outlined the following traditional American values. *Personal achievement:* high value placed on successful competition, particularly in the occupational realm; *work:* virtue attributed to people who show discipline and dedication to their work, regardless of the rewards involved; *morality and humanitarianism:* behaviors, attitudes, and attributes are categorized as right or wrong and such categorizations are used to guide behavior. Americans also willing to provide aid to those who are not as well-off; *efficiency and practicality:* high value placed on the ability to solve problems and to get things done in the most direct way; *progress and material comfort:* strong belief in the inevitability of progress, defined largely in terms of material comfort and personal convenience, through science and technology; *equality and democracy:* strong belief that all people should—and do—have equal opportunities for success. Extends to the right of all citizens to be equally represented in government by leaders they have helped to select; *freedom:* strong belief in the importance of individual freedom from direct government interference and in the ability to make personal decisions.
2. Every society develops norms that are built around preserving the society's fundamental values. In this way, values lend stability to society. However, values inevitably lead to conflict because not all individuals agree as to what are the most important values.

3. (a) The new value of self-fulfillment is the growing emphasis placed on the development of one's own talents and abilities to the fullest extent. **(b)** Lasch believes that Americans often carry self-fulfillment to unhealthy levels, whereas Yankelovich believes that self-fulfillment represents a healthy shift away from material rewards and toward self-improvement. **(c)** Bell believes that the emphasis on self-fulfillment undermines older values of hard work and moderation and threatens the stability of capitalism. Etzioni, like Bell, believes the new value of self-fulfillment will have a negative impact on the American economy. He also believes it will undermine the family and education.

SECTION 2 (pages 52–54)

SOCIAL CONTROL

Section Overview

For a society to run smoothly, norms must be enforced. Societies enforce norms through two basic means: internalization and sanctions. Internalization is the process by which a norm become a part of an individual's personality, thereby conditioning the individual to conform to society's expectations. Sanctions are rewards or punishments used to enforce conformity to norms.

Sanctions in the form of rewards are called positive sanctions, while sanctions in the form of punishments or threats of punishments are called negative sanctions. In addition to being positive or negative, sanctions can be formal or informal. Formal sanctions are rewards or punishments that are given by some formal organization or regulatory body. Informal sanctions are spontaneous expressions of approval or disapproval given by individuals or groups. The enforcing of norms through internalization and sanctions is called social control.

Previewing Key Terms

Section 2 contains the following key terms: **internalization, sanctions, positive sanction, negative sanction, formal sanction, informal sanction, social control**. Have students prepare a matching test using these terms and their definitions, found in the Glossary or in Section 2. Answers should appear on the back of the paper. Then have students exchange their papers and complete the tests. Finally, have students place their tests in their study notebooks for later review.

Introducing the Section

Review for students the definition of the term *norms*. Then ask: "What are the norms, or shared rules of conduct, that operate within your friendship groups?" Have a volunteer write these norms on the chalkboard as students call them out. Then, for each norm listed on the chalkboard, have students explain how members of their friendship groups ensure that everyone in the group follows that norm. Tell students that society, like friendship

groups, cannot run smoothly unless norms are enforced, and that the ways in which norms are enforced is the focus of Section 2.

Suggested Teaching Strategies

1. **Seeing Relationships (I)** After reviewing the information on internalization and sanctions, have students compile a list of 10 to 20 norms, ranging from folkways to mores (including laws). Then have students identify some of the formal and informal positive and negative sanctions that society uses to enforce these norms. List the norms and sanctions on the chalkboard as they are discussed.
2. **Learning from Photographs (I)** Have students examine the photographs on textbook page 54. Ask: "How do these six people act as agents of social control?" As an extension exercise, have students identify other political, religious, and social leaders who are authority figures.
3. **Using Sociological Imagination (I, II)** Organize the class into small groups. Tell each group to imagine that they are responsible for establishing the values, norms, and sanctions for a new society. Have each group prepare lists of their society's major values; the norms that correspond to those values; and the positive, negative, formal, and informal sanctions that would be needed to enforce the norms. Have the groups share their lists with the class.

Suggested Enrichment Activities

1. **Extending Ideas (I)** Have students complete the appropriate Developing Research Skills Worksheet, found in the *Teacher's Resource Binder*.
2. **Developing Interviewing Skills (III)** Have interested students interview school administrators, faculty, and students concerning the sanctions used in your school to enforce norms and possible alternative sanctions that might be employed. Students may use the information to write a report or an article for the school newspaper.

Suggested Assignments

1. **Stating a Point of View (I)** As homework, have students write a short essay in response to the following question: Which is more effective in controlling the behavior of teenagers—positive sanctions or negative sanctions? Instruct students to include the reasons why they have taken their particular points of view. Ask volunteers to read their essays aloud to the class for class discussion.
2. **Conducting Historical Research (III)** Ask interested students to research the formal and informal sanctions that were used to punish wrongdoers in colonial America. Have students compare this information to modern-day sanctions.

Closing the Section

Close the section by having students write a short essay describing what life might be like in a society free of norms. Have volunteers read their essays aloud to the class.

Assessing the Section

Have students complete the Section 2 Review.

Answers to Section 2 Review *(page 54)*

Define *internalization:* process by which a norm becomes a part of an individual's personality, thereby conditioning the individual to conform to society's expectations; *sanctions:* rewards or punishments used to enforce conformity to social norms; *social control:* enforcing of society's norms through either internalization or sanctions

1. Norms are enforced in society through internalization and sanctions. Internalization is the process by which the norms of society become part of an individual's personality. Once a person has internalized society's norms, these norms tend to be followed without question. Sanctions are rewards and punishments designed to encourage conformity to the norms of society.
2. **(a)** A positive sanction is a reward given to individuals who follow norms that is designed to encourage them to continue following the norms. **(b)** A negative sanction is a punishment or threat of punishment given to individuals who fail to follow norms in an attempt to discourage them from further violation of those norms. **(c)** Examples of positive sanctions range from encouraging pats on the back and smiles to trophies and monetary rewards. Negative sanctions include frowns and cross words to fines and imprisonment.
3. **(a)** A formal sanction is a sanction issued by a formal organization or regulatory body, such as the government or a corporation. An informal sanction, on the other hand, is a spontaneous expression of approval or disapproval given by an individual or group. **(b)** Positive formal sanctions include diplomas, merit raises, and medals. Positive informal sanctions include thank-you cards, friendly smiles, and applause. Negative formal sanctions include parking fines, expulsion from school, and imprisonment. Negative informal sanctions include insults and frowns.
4. The norms of society must be enforced if social behavior is to occur in patterned, predictable ways. If norms were not enforced, societal chaos and confusion would result.

SECTION 3 *(pages 55–61)*

SOCIAL CHANGE

Section Overview

All cultures change over time. Among the most significant sources of social change are values and beliefs, technology, population, diffusion, the physical environment, and wars and conquests. Cultural change, however, never occurs without some opposition. Among the reasons that people resist cultural change are ethnocentrism, cultural lag, and vested interests.

Previewing Key Terms

Section 3 contains the following key terms: **ideology, social movement, technology, discovery, invention, diffusion, ethnocentrism, cultural lag**. Ask each student to prepare a crossword puzzle using these terms and their definitions. Definitions can be found in Section 3 or in the Glossary. Then have the students exchange papers and complete the puzzles. Students may then place the puzzles in their study notebooks for later review.

Introducing the Section

Begin by asking a volunteer to read aloud the definition of social change given in the Glossary. Then have the class debate the following statement: "All cultures change over time." When no new ideas are forthcoming, tell students there are many reasons why social change is inevitable, some of which they will read about in Section 3. Also tell them that such change never occurs without some opposition.

Suggested Teaching Strategies

1. **Analyzing Ideas (I)** After reviewing the six factors that promote social change, have students provide specific examples of each of the sources of social change. Then ask students to suggest some of the social consequences of each of these examples. (For example, technology: example—invention of compact discs; consequence—disappearance of record albums from music stores.) List the examples and their consequences on the chalkboard as they are mentioned. Use the list as the basis of a discussion of the far-reaching consequences of changes in any aspect of society.
2. **★Writing about Sociology: Composing an Essay (I)** After reviewing the Developing Sociological Imagination feature on textbook pages 62–63, discuss with the class the reasons why people resist social change. Then instruct students to compose an essay in response to the following directive: Based on the information provided in the class discussion and in your textbook, describe what sociologists mean by ethnocentrism, cultural lag, and vested interests and then discuss how these factors produce resistance to social change.
3. **Exploring Multicultural Perspectives (III)** Have interested students conduct library research to find specific historical examples of how ethnocentrism has blocked the social, political, or economic progress of minority groups in American society. Ask students to present their findings to the class.

Suggested Enrichment Activities

1. **Exploring Cross-Cultural Perspectives (I)** Have students complete the appropriate Cross-Cultural Perspectives Worksheet, found in the *Teacher's Resource Binder*.
2. **Conducting a Debate (I, II)** Have interested students debate the following statement in front of the class: "Computers have negatively affected people's right to privacy in the United States."

Suggested Assignments

1. **Reading for Detail (I)** As homework, have students complete the appropriate Critical Skills Mastery Worksheet, found in the *Teacher's Resource Binder*.
2. **Locating Information (I)** Have students scan newspapers and magazines for an article that focuses on attempts for social change occurring in nations other than the United States. Instruct students to write a synopsis of the article, including the change that is being sought and any resistance to that change.
3. **Making Oral Presentations (III)** Have interested students prepare and make oral presentations on the social changes brought about in the United States by World War I, World War II, or the Vietnam War.

Closing the Section

Close the section by having students complete the appropriate Understanding Sociological Ideas Worksheet, found in the *Teacher's Resource Binder*.

Assessing the Section

Have students complete the Section 3 Review

Answers to Section 3 Review *(page 61)*

Define *ideology:* system of beliefs or ideas that justifies some social, moral, religious, political, or economic interests held by a group or by a society; ***social movement:*** long-term conscious effort to promote or prevent social change; ***technology:*** knowledge and tools that people use to manipulate their environment for practical purposes; ***diffusion:*** process of spreading culture traits from one society to another

1. **(a)** The six sources of social change are values and beliefs, technology, population, diffusion, the physical environment, and wars and conquests. **(b)** Changes in underlying values and beliefs bring about social change as people attempt to sway others to the new values and beliefs. Technology brings about social change as people use new tools and knowledge to manipulate their environment. Population changes also may bring about social change by increasing or decreasing the need for housing, energy, and social services and by affecting the economy of an area. Diffusion brings about social change by spreading the culture of one society to other societies. The physical environment may cause social change as people learn to deal with natural disasters such as earthquakes, tornadoes, floods, and droughts. Wars and conquests, because they may destroy property, affect the work force, and kill human beings, also bring social change.
2. Discovery occurs when people recognize new uses for existing elements in the world or begin to understand existing elements in new ways. Invention, on the other hand, occurs when people use existing knowledge to create something that did not previously exist.
3. **(a)** The three factors that produce resistance to social change are ethnocentrism, cultural lag, and vested

interests. **(b)** Ethnocentrism, the tendency to view one's own culture or group as superior, causes resistance to the adoption of beliefs or practices of other cultures. Cultural lag refers to the fact that people are more willing to accept new elements of material culture than they are to accept new beliefs and values. Vested interests refers to the fact that people who benefit from current cultural practices and social organization will resist social change.

Answers to Developing Sociological Imagination *(pages 62–63)*

1. The terms are school system, education, competition, Utes, and achievement.
2. **(a)** The subject is the differences between the school system and the Utes in terms of the role of education, competition, and achievement. **(b)** The main ideas are the views concerning the role of education and competition held by the school system and the Utes and the ways in which these two groups measure achievement.
3. Reread; contrast; discuss
4. Student responses should match the format shown on textbook page 41.
5. Answers will vary, but student essays should reflect the directive given.

Closing the Chapter

Have students complete the Chapter 3 Review Worksheet, found in the *Teacher's Resource Binder*.

Assessing the Chapter

Have students complete the Chapter 3 Review, found on page 64 of the *Pupil's Edition*.

Give students the Chapter 3 Form A Test and, if desired, the Chapter 3 Reteaching Worksheet and Form B Test, found in the *Teacher's Resource Binder*.

Answers to Chapter 3 Review *(page 64)*

Reviewing Sociological Terms

1. invention
2. Technology
3. diffusion
4. discovery
5. Ideology

Thinking Critically about Sociology

1. **(a)** Answers will vary. For example, students may list the rise of the airline industry, easy worldwide transportation, and the opening of new jobs as cultural changes brought about by the airplane. **(b)** Answers will vary. For example, students may list the rise of the automobile industry, a reduced reliance on horses as a source of transportation, and the opening of new jobs as cultural changes brought about by the automobile.
2. The physical environment may affect cultural change in a number of ways. A change in climate or weather patterns, for instance, may affect farm crops and thus

trading patterns with other regions. Additionally, when a change in available resources such as fuel occurs, societies must adapt by reducing their reliance on the cultural artifacts that depend on the resource. Finally, when natural disasters occur, there may be irreparable damage in the material culture and the society may take steps to prevent similar damage in the future.

3. Answers will vary. For example, two traditional American values that seem to be contradictory are the emphasis on hard work for its own sake, regardless of monetary reward, and the emphasis on personal achievement as reflected in personal power, wealth, and prestige.

4. Wars and conquests may bring about cultural change in a number of ways, both positive and negative. On the positive side, wartime innovations in medical technology, communications, and transportation can be introduced into civilian life. On the negative side, wars and conquests can disrupt cultural patterns by breaking up families, destroying buildings, and producing shortages in consumer goods as the economy shifts to the production of military equipment. Defeated governments also are subject to dramatic changes in legal and economic policies.

5. **(a)** Answers will vary. For example, the government may use negative formal sanctions such as audits by the Internal Revenue Service, parking tickets, imprisonment, executions, exiles, and driving license revocations. **(b)** Answers will vary. For example, the government may use positive formal sanctions such as military medals, income tax deductions for dependents, monuments, holidays, and postage stamps named in honor of valued citizens.

6. Population changes may affect many aspects of life in communities, such as the demand for schools, medical services, roads, food, and stores. Such changes also may affect the economy by changing the demand for goods and services, as well as the labor supply and demand. Changes in the average age of the population also have an impact on the society and culture. A society with a large pool of children, for example, has an increased need for baby food and other baby products, elementary schools, high schools, and colleges. A society with a large pool of elderly citizens, on the other hand, has an increased need for services and agencies geared toward the elderly.

7. Answers will vary. For instance, one example of cultural lag is the reluctance of many clerical workers to learn to use computerized office machines. The role of vested interests in resisting social change can be seen in the negative reaction of the American Medical Association to nationalized health care. An example of ethnocentrism can be seen in the emphasis of American broadcasters on the performance of American athletes during the Olympics.

Exercising Sociological Skills

1. Answers will vary, but students should list 10 American culture traits and indicate where they originated.

2. **(a)** Assimilation is the blending of culturally distinct groups into a single group with a common culture and identity. **(b)** The American educational institution is designed to instill the value of competition in students. It encourages competition through testing, grading, and sports events. The primary goal of education is to prepare students to be successful in the occupational world. Ute society, on the other hand, does not value competition. Achievement is based on effort, commitment, and personal satisfaction. Jobs in the Ute community are such that workers can easily transfer from one job to another. Preparation for occupational competition consequently is irrelevant to the Utes.

3. **(a)** The fast-food hamburger restaurant arose in the United States as a result of four factors. First, scientific procedures allowed farmers to increase the availability of beef for consumption. Second, the growth of suburban living and outdoor barbecues encouraged Americans to consume large quantities of beef. A third factor was the entrance of large numbers of women into the work force. This reduced the amount of time women spent in the home and encouraged an increased reliance on restaurants. And finally, the availability and low cost of hamburgers made them an attractive alternative to home cooking. **(b)** The fast-food hamburger restaurant provides the two-wage-earner family with the opportunity to dine without the drudgery involved in cooking at home.

Extending Sociological Imagination

1. Answers will vary. For example, positive formal sanctions used by schools to control behavior may include honor rolls and leadership awards. Negative formal sanctions may include demerits, detention, physical punishment, and expulsion. Informal positive sanctions may include praises and smiles from a teacher and being called on in class more frequently. Informal negative sanctions may include being sent to the principal's office, being ignored, and being reprimanded in front of the class.

2. Answers will vary, but ensure that students make proper use of the content analysis technique when analyzing the television programs.

Answers to Interpreting Primary Sources (page 65)

1. There are several reasons for the emergence of beef as America's favorite meat. First, changes in the production of beef made it cheaper and more readily available. Second, the movement of large numbers of Americans to the suburbs increased the popularity of outdoor cooking. And third, changes in women's roles involving an increase in female labor force participation and a decrease in time spent on domestic labor increased the frequency of eating out in fast-food restaurants. Beef is a major product used in outdoor barbecuing and in fast-food restaurants.

2. Fast-food restaurants sell 200 hamburgers per second to American consumers. Each year, this amounts to 6.7 billion hamburgers, worth $10 billion.

3. Answers will vary. For example, students may discuss the increased risk of heart attack and stroke that accompany a diet high in beef, and the increased need for workers in the fast-food industry.

CHAPTER 4 *(pages 66–93)*

SOCIAL STRUCTURE

SECTION 1
BUILDING BLOCKS OF SOCIAL STRUCTURE

SECTION 2
THE STRUCTURE OF GROUPS AND SOCIETIES

SECTION 3
TYPES OF SOCIAL INTERACTION

SECTION 4
THE STRUCTURE OF FORMAL ORGANIZATIONS

Chapter Overview

Social structure is what gives society its enduring characteristics and what makes patterns of human interaction predictable. Sociologists define social structure as the network of interrelated statuses and roles that guides human interaction.

The human interaction that is the focus of role behavior takes place within groups and within the context of society. Among the types of groups recognized by sociologists are primary groups, secondary groups, reference groups, ingroups, and outgroups. Sociologists generally recognize three major categories of societies: preindustrial, industrial, and postindustrial. Preindustrial societies are further subdivided into hunting and gathering, pastoral, horticultural, and agricultural societies.

Just as groups and societies can take many forms, interaction also can take several forms. Among the most common forms of social interaction are exchange, competition, conflict, cooperation, and accommodation.

In industrial and postindustrial societies, large secondary groups that have been formed to achieve specific goals are common. Sociologists refer to these groups as formal organizations. Many formal organizations are structured in the form of bureaucracies. According to sociologists, bureaucracies have both positive and negative consequences for society and for individuals within society.

Chapter Objectives

At the conclusion of the chapter, students will be able to

1. Define social structure, and describe the characteristics of its two major components.
2. Define social institution.
3. Define group, and describe the features of group structure and the characteristics of the most common types of groups.

4. Identify the various types of societies recognized by sociologists, and compare and contrast the characteristics of these societies.
5. Identify the five types of social interaction that take place in societies, and recognize the consequences of each type of interaction.
6. Define formal organization and bureaucracy, and discuss the characteristics of bureaucracies.

Introducing the Chapter

Write the following quotation by Lionel Tiger and Robin Fox on the chalkboard: "We are none of us truly isolated; we are connected to one another by a web of regularities and by a host of shared, deep-seated certainties." Ask students to write short, in-class essays on what they think this statement means. Discuss the essays in class before assigning the reading of Chapter 4.

Chapter 4 Suggested Lesson Plans

Day 1	**Suggested Procedures:** Introducing the Chapter; Section 1 Previewing Key Terms; Introducing the Section **Materials:** PE: pp. 66–70; TM: pp. 20–21
Day 2	**Suggested Procedures:** Section 1 Strategies and Assignments **Materials:** PE: pp. 68–70; TM: pp. 21–22
Day 3	**Suggested Procedures:** Section 2 Previewing Key Terms; Introducing the Section; Strategies and Assignments **Materials:** PE: pp. 71–79; TM: pp. 22–23; TRB: Assorted Worksheets
Day 4	**Suggested Procedures:** Section 3 Previewing Key Terms; Introducing the Section; Strategies and Assignments **Materials:** PE: pp. 80–82; TM: pp. 23–24; TRB: Worksheet
Day 5	**Suggested Procedures:** Section 4 Previewing Key Terms; Introducing the Section; Strategies and Assignments **Materials:** PE: pp. 83–91; TM: pp. 24–25; TRB: Transparency 2, Assorted Worksheets
Day 6	**Suggested Procedures:** Closing the Chapter; Assessing the Chapter **Materials:** PE: pp. 92–93; TM: pp. 25–26; TRB: Review Worksheet, Tests, Reteaching Worksheet
Day 7	**Suggested Procedures:** Closing the Unit; Assessing the Unit **Materials:** PE: p. 94–95; TM: pp. 26–28; TRB: Review Worksheet, Tests, Reteaching Worksheet

SECTION 1 (pages 68–70)

BUILDING BLOCKS OF SOCIAL STRUCTURE

Section Overview

Social structure—the network of interrelated statuses and roles that guides human interaction—provides society with a relatively stable framework that promotes continuity. As the definition indicates, statuses and roles are the two major components of social structure.

Individuals occupy many different statuses and perform many different roles. When sociologists study statuses, they focus on ascribed statuses, achieved statuses, and master statuses. When sociologists examine roles, they focus on things such as reciprocal roles, role expectations, role performance, role sets, role conflict, and role strain.

Sociologists often examine social structure on the group level. When social structure is examined on the societal level, however, attention is focused on social institutions.

Previewing Key Terms

Section 1 contains the following key terms: **social structure, status, role, ascribed status, achieved status, master status, reciprocal roles, role expectations, role performance, role set, role conflict, role strain, social institution**. Have students prepare riddles, using the key terms as answers. For example: "I am a socially defined position in a group or in a society. What am I?" *(a status)* Tell students to write their riddles on one side of the paper and the answers on the other side. Completed sets of riddles can be exchanged among students and answered. Then have students put their papers in their study notebooks for later review.

Introducing the Section

Write the following statement on the chalkboard: "Human behavior is totally unpredictable." Have students discuss whether they agree or disagree with this statement and ask them to give reasons for their responses. Then tell students it is the predictability of human behavior that lends stability to society and makes interaction possible. This predictability is an outcome of social structure, which is the focus of Section 1.

Suggested Teaching Strategies

1. **Creating a Chart (I)** After the class has read Section 1, ask students to prepare charts depicting 10 statuses they now occupy. Have students use the following column headings: Status, How Acquired (ascribed or achieved), Associated Roles, Reciprocal Roles, Role Expectations, Role Performance, Sources of Role Conflict, Sources of Role Strain. Have students indicate which of these statuses they would consider to be their master statuses. Discuss the charts in class.

2. **Extending Ideas (I)** To reinforce the concept of reciprocal roles, have students make a list of 10 reciprocal role groupings not discussed in the textbook. Have students explain how the corresponding roles guide the pattern of interaction between the related statuses.

3. **Working in Groups (I, II)** Organize the class into small groups. Then assign each group one of the social institutions mentioned in the section and have the groups collect magazine photographs that depict the statuses and roles associated with their assigned social institution. Have group members discuss the photographs in class.

Suggested Enrichment Activity

Dramatizing Sociology (I, II) Have interested students write and perform short skits illustrating common examples of role strain and role conflict. Have class members critique the performances.

Suggested Assignments

1. **Conducting a Poll (I)** As homework, have students read the definition of master status to five people (friends, neighbors, or family members) and ask the following question: "What do you consider to be your master status?" Have students present their findings to the class, and ask a volunteer to tally and rank the results. Use the rankings as the basis of a class discussion on the concept of master statuses.

2. **Exploring Multicultural Perspectives (III)** Have interested students conduct library research to find biographies or autobiographies of members of minority groups whose lives were strongly affected by an ascribed or achieved status. Students should analyze how the people were affected and present their analyses to the class.

Closing the Section

Close the section by having students examine the photograph on textbook page 69. Ask: "What are the ascribed and achieved statuses that the grandmother and the granddaughter are likely to hold?" For each status mentioned and written on the chalkboard, have students suggest the roles that accompany it.

Assessing the Section

Have students complete the Section 1 Review.

Answers to Section 1 Review *(page 70)*

Define *social structure:* network of interrelated statuses and roles that guides human interaction; ***master status:*** status that plays the greatest role in shaping a person's life and determining his or her social identity; ***role:*** behavior—the rights and obligations—expected of someone occupying a particular status; ***reciprocal role:*** corresponding roles that define the pattern of interaction between related statuses; ***role set:*** different roles attached to a single status; ***social institution:*** system of statuses, roles, values, and norms that is organized to satisfy one or more of the basic needs of society

1. (a) A status is a socially defined position in a group or in a society. (b) An ascribed status is one that is assigned to an individual at birth. It is outside an individual's control and is unchangeable. An achieved status, on the other hand, is a position that is attained as a direct result of the individual's own behavior.

2. Role expectations are the socially determined behaviors expected of a person performing a role. Role performance, on the other hand, is the person's actual role behavior.

3. Role conflict occurs when fulfilling the role expectations of one status make it difficult to fulfill the role expectations of another status. Role strain, on the other hand, occurs when a person has difficulty meeting the role expectations of a single status.

SECTION 2 (pages 71–79)

THE STRUCTURE OF GROUPS AND SOCIETIES

Section Overview

Sociologists examine human interaction within the context of groups and society. Groups can be differentiated on the basis of the length of time they remain together, organizational structure, and size. Among the most common types of groups are primary groups, secondary groups, reference groups, ingroups, and outgroups. Sociologists also are interested in social networks.

Sociologists generally recognize three broad categories of societies: preindustrial, industrial, and postindustrial. Preindustrial societies are further subdivided into hunting and gathering, pastoral, horticultural, and agricultural societies. Sociologists often use the concepts of mechanical solidarity, organic solidarity, *Gemeinschaft,* and *Gesellschaft* to distinguish between preindustrial societies and industrial societies.

Previewing Key Terms

Section 2 contains the following key terms: **group, aggregate, social category, dyad, triad, small group, primary group, secondary group, reference group, ingroup, outgroup, social network, subsistence strategy, division of labor, preindustrial society, industrial society, postindustrial society, hunting and gathering society, pastoral society, horticultural society, agricultural society, barter, urbanization, mechanical solidarity, organic solidarity, *Gemeinschaft, Gesellschaft*.** Ask students to choose 10 of the key terms in the list and create a Word Search puzzle using each of the terms. Then have students exchange papers and complete the puzzle. Students then may place the puzzles in their notebooks for later review.

Introducing the Section

Tell students that they are going to practice their outlining skills in this section. First, ask a volunteer to copy the headings and subheadings in Section 2 on the chalkboard. Then have the class provide the important details that should appear under each item in the outline. Have students copy the final outline into their notebooks for later review.

Suggested Teaching Strategies

1. **Classifying Relationships (I)** After discussing the nature of groups with the class, have students compile lists of their primary group, secondary group, reference group, ingroup, and outgroup relationships. Use the lists as the basis of a class discussion.

2. **Comparing Ideas (I)** To help students understand how preindustrial and industrial societies differ, ask volunteers to explain the concepts of mechanical solidarity, organic solidarity, *Gemeinschaft,* and *Gesellschaft.* Then have students identify what they believe to be the negative and positive aspects of living in the types of societies described by Emile Durkheim and Ferdinand Tönnies.

3. **Working in Groups (II, III)** Organize the class into four small groups and assign each group one of the following societies: hunting and gathering, pastoral, horticultural, or agricultural. Tell the groups that they are to conduct research to find a real-life example of their assigned society and gather information on that society. They are to use this information to make a theater presentation to the class entitled "A Day in the Life of the _____ Society." All members of the group are to participate in the theater, which may include music, drama, posters, narration, costumes, props, etc. Have the class critique the presentations for sociological accuracy.

Suggested Enrichment Activities

1. **Using Source Materials (I)** Have students complete the appropriate Developing Research Skills Worksheet, found in the *Teacher's Resource Binder.*

2. **Making Oral Presentations (II, III)** Have students read the Case Study feature on textbook page 75. Then have interested students conduct research on the volunteer organizations mentioned in the feature and make oral presentations to the class.

Suggested Assignments

1. **Summarizing Ideas (I)** As homework, have students summarize the major characteristics of the four types of preindustrial societies and of industrial and postindustrial societies.

2. **Linking the Past to the Present (II, III)** Have interested students use library sources to locate historical quotations that focus on some aspect of group interaction. Conduct a class discussion in which students identify what type of group is being discussed and evaluate how valid these quotations are in today's society.

Closing the Section

Close the section by having students complete the appropriate Graphic Organizer Worksheet, found in the *Teacher's Resource Binder.*

Assessing the Section

Have students complete the Section 2 Review.

Answers to Section 2 Review *(page 79)*

Define *dyad:* group with two members; *triad:* three-member group; *small group:* group with few enough members that everyone is able to interact on a face-to-face basis; *social network:* web of relationships that is formed by the sum total of a person's interactions with other people

1. **(a)** A group is a set of two or more people who interact on the basis of shared expectations and who possess some degree of common identity. **(b)** Three of the most common features used to distinguish among groups are the length of time they remain together, their organizational structure, and their size.
2. A primary group has a small number of members who interact over a relatively long period of time in a direct and personal way. The relationships are intimate, the communication is deep, the structure is informal, and personal satisfaction is of primary importance. A secondary group is characterized by impersonal and temporary interactions. Relationships tend to be casual and limited in personal involvement, and the group tends to be organized around specific tasks. A reference group is one with whom an individual identifies and whose attitudes and values the individual adopts. An ingroup is a group an individual belongs to and with whom the individual identifies. An outgroup is a group an individual does not belong to and with whom the individual does not identify.
3. Hunting and gathering societies are characterized by the daily collection of plants and animals as the main form of subsistence, frequent geographic mobility, small size, nonspecialized division of labor, and an egalitarian distribution of goods and services. Pastoral societies are characterized by the domestication of animals as the basis of subsistence, frequent geographic mobility, control over food supply surplus giving rise to economic stratification, and specialized economic and political institutions. Horticultural societies are characterized by the growing of vegetables in garden plots as the basis of subsistence, development of semipermanent or permanent villages, better developed economic and political institutions, and rudimentary specialization of roles. Agricultural societies are characterized by agriculture enhanced through the use of draft animals as the basis of subsistence, specialized tools and irrigation, permanent settlements, very large populations, efficient farming that frees people to work in nonfarm occupations, specialization of occupations, specialized government and military institutions, and a sharply defined stratification system. Industrial societies are characterized by the engagement of the majority of workers in the manufacture of goods rather than food, production based on the use of machinery, large, urban populations, specialized jobs, and separate institutions. Postindustrial societies are characterized by an economic emphasis on the production of information and the provision of services, a reliance on science and education for providing and maintaining a high quality of life, and an emphasis on the rights of individuals and personal fulfillment.
4. **(a)** Mechanical and organic solidarity are terms used by Durkheim to refer to the "glue" that holds societies together. Mechanical solidarity refers to the process whereby small societies are held together by the similarity of values and tasks. Organic solidarity, on the other hand, arises out of mutual need. The increased job specialization characteristic of industrial societies means that individuals cannot provide for all of their needs. Society thus is held together by the interdependence of people. **(b)** Characteristics that distinguish *Gemeinschaft* and *Gesellschaft* societies are the degree of emotional closeness among societal members and the motives behind relationships. *Gemeinschaft* refers to societies in which most members know each other and share a strong sense of belonging. *Gesellschaft,* on the other hand, refers to societies in which most relationships are impersonal and temporary and based on needs rather than on close emotions.

SECTION 3 *(pages 80–82)*

TYPES OF SOCIAL INTERACTION

Section Overview

Interaction can take many forms. Some forms of interaction help to stabilize the social structure. Other forms help to promote social change. Among the most common forms of social interaction are exchange, competition, conflict, cooperation, and accommodation.

Previewing Key Terms

Section 3 contains the following key terms: **exchange, reciprocity, exchange theory, competition, conflict, cooperation, accommodation**. Have students write a paragraph in which they use the key terms listed to describe social interaction. Completed paragraphs then can be shared with the class.

Introducing the Section

Ask a volunteer to turn to the Glossary and read the definitions for the terms *exchange, competition, conflict, cooperation,* and *accommodation.* Write these terms on the chalkboard. Then ask students to provide examples from family life that illustrate each one of these concepts. Tell students that sociologists have identified these concepts as the most common forms of social interaction and that they can be used to analyze any number of social settings. Then have students read Section 3.

Suggested Teaching Strategies

1. **Interpreting Ideas (I)** While discussing the five types of social interaction, ask students to provide

examples from your classroom setting that illustrate each type of interaction.

2. **Dramatizing Sociology (I, II)** After discussing the various forms of accommodation, organize the class into four groups. Have each group prepare and present a skit on one of the forms of accommodation. Have the class guess which form of accommodation each group is trying to illustrate.

3. **Debating Ideas (I, II)** Have selected volunteers debate the following statement in front of the class: "Social life can be explained as the attempt to maximize rewards while minimizing costs."

Suggested Enrichment Activities

1. **Building Vocabulary Skills (I)** Have students complete the appropriate Critical Skills Mastery Worksheet, found in the *Teacher's Resource Binder*.

2. **Linking the Past to the Present (III)** Have interested students prepare reports on historic events in which specific forms of accommodation were used in efforts to end conflicts. Examples might include strike settlements or truces between warring parties. Ask students to present their findings to the class.

Suggested Assignments

1. **Developing a Structured Overview (I)** As homework, have students develop a structured overview of the types of social interaction, following the guidelines presented on textbook pages 40–41.

2. **Solving Problems (I, II)** Have students write short essays in which they develop an imaginative scenario depicting a conflict situation between two people or two groups. Ask volunteers to read their essays to the class and have class members state their views concerning how best to resolve these conflicts.

Closing the Section

Tell each student to bring in a newspaper article that depicts one of the types of social interaction discussed in the section. Ask volunteers to read portions of their articles to the class and have the class guess which type of interaction is being depicted.

Assessing the Section

Have students complete the Section 3 Review.

Answers to Section 3 Review *(page 82)*

Define *reciprocity:* idea that if you do something for someone, they owe you something in return; ***exchange theory:*** theory that holds that people are motivated by self-interests in their interactions with other people

Identify *Georg Simmel:* sociologist who identified four sources of conflict: wars, conflict within groups, legal disputes, and clashes over ideology

1. The five most common forms of social interaction are exchange, competition, conflict, cooperation, and accommodation. Exchange involves interaction that is undertaken in an attempt to receive a reward or a return for the action. Competition occurs when two or more people or groups oppose each other to achieve a goal only one can reach. Conflict is the deliberate attempt to control by force, oppose, harm, or resist the will of another person or persons. Cooperation occurs when two or more people or groups work together to achieve a goal. Accommodation is interaction that involves giving a little to get a little.

2. The four forms of accommodation are compromise, truce, mediation, and arbitration. A compromise occurs when two parties both give up something to come to a mutual agreement. A truce brings the conflict to a halt until a compromise can be reached. In mediation, a third party is brought in to act as an advisor and to help the parties reach an agreement. In arbitration, a third party makes a decision that is binding on both parties.

SECTION 4 *(pages 83–89)*

THE STRUCTURE OF FORMAL ORGANIZATIONS

Section Overview

Sociologists have a special term to designate a large, complex secondary group that has been established to achieve specific goals. They call such a group a formal organization. Many formal organizations are structured as bureaucracies. According to Max Weber, bureaucracies arise in industrial societies because of an increasing tendency toward rationalization. The model of bureaucracies created by Max Weber still is in use by sociologists today.

Previewing Key Terms

Section 4 contains the following key terms: **formal organization, bureaucracy, rationalization, voluntary association, iron law of oligarchy**. Write these terms on the chalkboard. Then have students develop a definition for each term, based on what they think it means. Write the definitions on the chalkboard and ask a volunteer to record them on a piece of paper. After students have read Section 4, ask them to revise the definitions based on the material presented in the section.

Introducing the Section

Begin the section by asking the following question: "Everyone who has ever dealt with bureaucracies seems to have complaints about them. Why is this?" After students have made their complaints known, ask: "If everyone has complaints about bureaucracies, why do bureaucracies exist?" Lead students to the conclusion that bureaucracies are the most efficient way for large numbers of people to achieve specific goals. Then tell students that Section 4 will examine the characteristics of bureaucracies and explain why they are highly efficient organizations.

Suggested Teaching Strategies

1. **Identifying Ideas (I)** Discuss with the class what Weber meant by rationalization. Then have each student compile a list of 15 examples of rationalization in American society. Share the lists in class.
2. **Learning from Graphs (I)** Review the material on formal organizations by placing Transparency 2 on an overhead projector and asking the questions contained in the accompanying teacher's notes. Transparencies and accompanying teacher's notes are found in the *Teacher's Resource Binder*.
3. **★Reading about Sociology: Analyzing Journal Articles (II, III)** To reinforce the skill lesson presented on textbook pages 90–91, have students analyze a journal article that explores either the advantages or disadvantages of bureaucracies.

Suggested Enrichment Activities

1. **Exploring Cross-Cultural Perspectives (I)** Have students complete the appropriate Cross-Cultural Perspectives Worksheet, found in the *Teacher's Resource Binder*.
2. **Practicing Interviewing Skills (I, II)** Ask a member of a voluntary association to make a presentation to the class concerning the goals and activities of his or her group. Have students draw up a list of questions beforehand to ask the speaker. Later, have the students use this information to compare the bureaucratic structure of voluntary associations and more formal organizations.

Suggested Assignments

1. **Drawing Conclusions (I)** As homework, have students choose a bureaucracy with which they are familiar and identify how closely this bureaucracy meets the five characteristics outlined in Weber's model of bureaucracies.
2. **Solving Problems (I, II)** Ask interested students to review the criticisms of bureaucracies discussed on textbook pages 85 and 88. Then have the students make suggestions about what can be done to improve the effectiveness of bureaucracies.
3. **Writing a Book Report (III)** Have interested students prepare book reports on *The Peter Principle* by Laurence J. Peter.

Closing the Section

Close the section by having students complete the appropriate Understanding Sociological Ideas Worksheet, found in the *Teacher's Resource Binder*.

Assessing the Section

Have students complete the Section 4 Review.

Answers to Applying Sociology *(pages 86–87)*

1. Answers will vary, but students should present their points of view and explain why they have reached these conclusions.
2. Answers will vary, but students should clearly state their positions in response to the questions.

Answers to Section 4 Review *(page 89)*

Define *formal organization:* large, complex secondary group that has been established to achieve specific goals; *rationalization:* process by which every feature of human behavior becomes subject to calculation, measurement, and control; *voluntary association:* nonprofit association formed to pursue some common interest; *iron law of oligarchy:* tendency for organizations to become increasingly dominated by small groups of people

1. **(a)** A bureaucracy is a ranked authority structure that operates according to specific rules and procedures. **(b)** Weber's model of bureaucracies includes: (1) a specialized division of labor; (2) a ranking of authority roles; (3) employment based on formal qualifications; (4) strict adherence to rules, regulations, and procedures that guide operations; and (5) specific lines of promotion and advancement.
2. Researchers first discovered the importance of primary group relationships in formal organizations in the late 1920s. At this time, a series of experiments were designed to examine the effect of work conditions on productivity. In the course of the studies, sociologists studied the interaction among a group of workers. Rather than working as fast as possible to maximize their own individual gain, the workers jointly determined the day's output for the group as a whole. Informal sanctions were used by group members to ensure strict conformity to the group's productivity standards.
3. One criticism of bureaucracies is that they eventually lose sight of their original goals and become preoccupied with maintaining their own existence as an end it itself. A second criticism is that workers develop bureaucratic personalities. Rules come to replace common sense. Third, too much time is spent on paperwork and not enough on task solving. A fourth criticism of bureaucracies is that they tend to become oligarchies, with power concentrated in the hands of a few people. The fifth criticism of bureaucracies is that too much attention is given to simply looking busy. The work expands to fill the time.

Answers to Developing Sociological Imagination *(pages 90–91)*

Answers will vary, but students should prepare their analyses in accord with the guidelines presented in the feature.

Closing the Chapter

Have students complete the Chapter 4 Review Worksheet, found in the *Teacher's Resource Binder*.

Assessing the Chapter

Have students complete the Chapter 4 Review, found on page 92 of the *Pupil's Edition*.

Give students the Chapter 4 Form A Test and, if desired, the Chapter 4 Reteaching Worksheet and Form B Test, found in the *Teacher's Resource Binder*.

Answers to Chapter 4 Review *(page 92)*

Reviewing Sociological Terms

1. social structure
2. Role strain
3. small group; dyad; triad
4. status
5. role conflict
6. group

Thinking Critically about Sociology

1. Answers will vary. Examples of reciprocal roles include: sister-brother, performer-audience, neighbor-neighbor, doctor-patient, sender-receiver.
2. **(a)** The types of societies discussed differ primarily in terms of subsistence strategy, which refers to the ways in which societies use technology to provide for the needs of their members. This means of classifying societies allows them to be placed on a continuum from simple to complex. At one end of the continuum are societies with very simple divisions of labor and at the other end are those with highly specialized divisions of labor. **(b)** Mechanical solidarity, organic solidarity, *Gemeinschaft,* and *Gesellschaft* refer to the factors and processes that provide cohesion in a society.
3. **(a)** The four requirements for the existence of groups are two or more people, interaction among the people, shared experiences, and a sense of common identity. **(b)** Answers will vary.
4. **(a)** The most common forms of social interaction are exchange, competition, conflict, cooperation, and accommodation. Exchange occurs whenever people, groups, or societies interact in an attempt to receive a reward or return for something they have provided. Competition occurs when two or more people or groups attempt to achieve a goal that only one can have. Conflict occurs when one person or group sets out in intentional opposition to another. Cooperation occurs when two people or groups jointly pursue a goal of mutual value. Accommodation is a situation in which the parties reach a compromise—a situation of balance between conflict and cooperation. **(b)** Answers will vary, but students should provide one example of each type of interaction.
5. **(a)** Answers will vary, but students should select a formal organization and explain how it meets the characteristics described by Weber. **(b)** Answers will vary, but students should state which of the criticisms leveled against bureaucracies apply to the bureaucracies they have chosen.

Exercising Sociological Skills

1. Answers will vary, but students should explain how they would structure a bureaucracy.
2. The elderly form a number of social networks. One such network is formed with the family. Within this network, the elderly person receives affection, comfort, help, and support in exchange for gifts, babysitting, affection, and advice. Another social network provides the elderly with the opportunity to socialize, to share feelings, and to offer mutual assistance and advice. The elderly also form social networks within the community. They perform volunteer services in a number of organizations, lending valuable skills to those in need. Many elderly also are employed part-time in a number of different programs.
3. Answers will vary, but students should analyze the journal articles they have chosen according to the guidelines presented in the feature.

Extending Sociological Imagination

1. Answers will vary, but students should specify how members of the groups they have chosen separate themselves from members of outgroups.
2. Answers will vary, but students should create photo essays illustrating how achieved statuses and ascribed statuses differ.

Answers to Interpreting Primary Sources *(page 93)*

1. Cultural networks are the informal communication systems that exist in bureaucracies. Such networks are the primary means through which information is passed up and down the corporate hierarchy.
2. The real business of corporations occurs behind the scenes, in the informal interactions among coworkers, not in formal meetings.
3. First, cultural networks can help reinforce the basic values of the corporation. Second, they create and maintain legends of corporate heroes, which act as sources of inspiration for workers. Third, they can facilitate change in the corporation by decreasing informal resistance. Finally, they help executives increase their power by informally generating support among workers.

Closing the Unit

Have students complete the Unit 1 Review Worksheet, found in the *Teacher's Resource Binder.*

Assessing the Unit

Have students complete the Unit 1 Review, found on page 95 of the *Pupil's Edition.*

Give students the Unit 1 Form A Test and, if desired, the Unit 1 Reteaching Worksheet and Form B Test, found in the *Teacher's Resource Binder.*

Answers to Unit 1 Review *(page 95)*

Reviewing Sociological Ideas

1. **(a)** Sociology is the science that studies human society and social behavior. **(b)** Sociology emerged as a separate field of study as a result of the profound social problems that accompanied industrialization and urbanization. **(c)** Having a sociological imagination means having the ability to see the connections between the larger world and one's personal life.
2. **(a)** *Verstehen* is the empathetic understanding of the meanings others attach to their actions. **(b)** The interactionist perspective would be most likely to use *Verstehen* as a research method.

3. **(a)** Mechanical solidarity results in a society when a small group of people share the same values and perform the same tasks. Organic solidarity arises in a society when people become so specialized in their tasks that they can no longer provide for all of their own needs. **(b)** *Gemeinschaft* refers to societies in which most members know one another. In these societies, relationships are close and activities center on the family and community. *Gesellschaft* refers to societies in which most social relations are based on need rather than on emotion.

4. **(a)** Culture refers to the shared products of human groups. These products include both physical objects and the beliefs, values, and behaviors shared by the group. **(b)** The five components of culture are physical objects, symbols, language, values, and norms. **(c)** Sociologists study three levels of culture: traits, complexes, and patterns. Traits are individual tools, acts, or beliefs that are related to particular needs. Complexes are combinations of culture traits. Culture patterns are combinations of culture complexes.

5. **(a)** The basic values that form the foundation for American culture are personal achievement, work, morality and humanitarianism, efficiency and practicality, progress and material comfort, equality and democracy, and freedom. **(b)** The newly emerging American value is self-fulfillment.

6. **(a)** Society is a group of mutually interdependent people who have organized in such a way as to share a common culture and feeling of unity. **(b)** The two major components of social structure are statuses and roles. A status is a socially defined position in a group or in a society. A role is the behavior—the rights and obligations—of someone occupying a particular status.

7. **(a)** A formal organization is a large, complex secondary group that has been established to achieve certain goals. **(b)** A voluntary association is a nonprofit association formed to pursue some common interest. **(c)** A bureaucracy is a ranked authority structure that operates according to specific rules and procedures. **(d)** The iron law of oligarchy is the tendency of organizations to become increasingly dominated by small groups of people.

Synthesizing Sociological Ideas

1. **(a)** The functionalist perspective views society as a set of interrelated parts that work together to produce a stable social system. The conflict perspective assumes that the inevitable conflict that arises over scarce resources leads to valuable social change. The interactionist perspective focuses on how individuals within a society interact with one another. **(b)** Functionalists would view adolescence as a period of anticipatory socialization for adulthood. They would focus on the leadership roles that arise among peer groups. Conflict theorists might look at the conflict between adolescents and their parents as the young people fight for independence. Symbolic interactionists might focus on the specialized language used by adolescents.

2. **(a)** Values are shared beliefs about what is good or bad, right or wrong, desirable or undesirable. Norms are the shared rules of conduct that tell people how to act in specific situations. Values and norms are related in that norms serve to uphold the values of a society. **(b)** Societies use positive and negative sanctions (rewards and punishments) to enforce norms.

3. **(a)** A group is a set of two or more people who interact on the basis of shared expectations and who possess some degree of common identity. **(b)** The four requirements for the existence of groups are two or more people, interaction among the people, shared expectations, and a sense of common identity.

4. **(a)** The six sources of social change are values and beliefs, technology, population, diffusion, the physical environment, and wars and conquests. Changes in underlying values and beliefs bring about social change as people attempt to sway others to the new values and beliefs. Technology brings about social change as people use new tools and knowledge to manipulate their environment. Population changes also may bring about social change by increasing or decreasing the need for housing, energy, and social services and by affecting the economy of an area. Diffusion brings about social change by spreading the culture of one society to other societies. The physical environment may cause social change as people learn to deal with natural disasters such as earthquakes, tornadoes, floods, and droughts. Wars and conquests, because they may destroy property, affect the work force, and kill human beings, also bring social change. **(b)** The three factors that produce resistance to social change are ethnocentrism, cultural lag, and vested interests. Ethnocentrism, the tendency to view one's own culture or group as superior, causes resistance to the adoption of beliefs or practices of other cultures. Cultural lag refers to the fact that people are more willing to accept new elements of material culture than they are to accept new beliefs and values. Vested interests refers to the fact that people who benefit from current cultural practices and social organization will resist social change.

5. **(a)** A role set consists of the different roles attached to a single status. **(b)** The often contradictory expectations within role sets can lead to role conflict and role strain. **(c)** Role conflict is the situation that occurs when fulfilling the expectations of one role makes it difficult to fulfill the expectations of another role. Role strain, on the other hand, is the situation that occurs when a person has difficulty meeting the expectations of a single role.

6. **(a)** Cultural universals, common features that are found in all human cultures, exist because they serve basic human needs. **(b)** Variations among and within cultures exist because the specific nature of cultural traits varies among and within cultures. **(c)** Cultural diversity sometimes leads to ethnocentrism, the belief that one's own culture or group is superior. To guard against ethnocentrism, sociologists adopt the attitude of cultural relativism, the belief that cultures should be judged by their own standards.

7. **(a)** The five most common types of groups are primary groups, secondary groups, reference groups, ingroups, and outgroups. **(b)** Primary groups continue over a relatively long period of time, are

informally organized, and are small. Secondary groups are temporary, formal, and can be quite large. Reference groups, ingroups, and outgroups can be either long-term or temporary, formally or informally organized, and large or small in size.

8. **(a)** The five characteristics of bureaucracies outlined in Weber's model are a division of labor, a ranking of authority, employment based on formal qualifications, rules and regulations, and specific lines of promotion and advancement. **(b)** Answers will vary, but students should take a stand in relation to the directive posed.

Applying Sociological Imagination

1. Answers will vary.
2. Answers will vary.
3. Answers will vary.

UNIT 2 *(pages 96–201)*

THE INDIVIDUAL IN SOCIETY

Unit Overview

Unit 2 explores how individuals become functioning members of society and what happens when people do not conform to societal expectations. The unit begins with an examination of the socialization process. In the next two chapters, the social characteristics of adolescence and adulthood are presented. The unit closes with a discussion of deviance and crime.

Unit Goals

At the end of the unit, students should be able to

1. Identify the factors that affect personality development and the emergence of the self, including the roles played by various agents of socialization.
2. Compare and contrast theories of socialization.
3. Explain how adolescence emerged as a distinct stage of the life cycle.
4. Describe the characteristics of adolescence, focusing on topics such as dating, sexual behavior, drug use, and suicide.
5. Recognize and describe the stages of adult male and female development.
6. Assess the nature of work in terms of adult roles.
7. Discuss development in the later years.
8. Explain the nature and functions of deviance, crime, and the criminal justice system in the United States.
9. Compare and contrast the various theories concerning deviance and crime.

Unit Skills

Four skills are developed in Unit 2.

★ READING ABOUT SOCIOLOGY: *Comparing Sociological Perspectives* (Chapter 5; PE pages 116–117; TM page 35)

★ INTERPRETING THE VISUAL RECORD: *Interpreting Tables* (Chapter 6; PE pages 144–145; TM page 41)
★ INTERPRETING THE VISUAL RECORD: *Understanding Graphs* (Chapter 7; PE pages 170–171; TM page 47)
★ THINKING ABOUT SOCIOLOGY: *Interpreting Statistics* (Chapter 8; PE pages 196–197; TM page 52)

Suggestions for teaching the skills appear on the TM pages mentioned above. The suggestions are clearly identified by the ★ symbol. Each skill is reinforced in the Chapter Review under Exercising Sociological Skills. Answers to the questions in the textbook's skill features appear in the Answers to Developing Sociological Imagination sections of this *Teacher's Manual.*

Introducing the Unit

Conduct the class in a manner that will surprise students. For example, dress in an unexpected manner—either very formally or very informally or in clothes that do not match in color or in style. Next adopt a teaching style that differs greatly from your normal style. For instance, employ an extremely belligerent or lackadaisical tone. Then, without explaining why you are acting strangely, begin lecturing on a topic that is inappropriate for the class. You might, for example, lecture on biology or math or history. Ignore all protests from the students.

Once the class becomes truly annoyed, stop your act and explain to the class that we all come to expect certain behaviors in certain situations. When people violate these expectations, social order begins to break down. Tell students that in Unit 2, they will examine the ways in which people become functioning members of society and the consequences of deviating from societal expectations.

References for Teachers

Bigelow, William, and Diamond, Norman. *The Power in Our Hands: A Curriculum on the History of Work and Workers in the United States.* New York: Monthly Review Press, 1988. Set of 16 reproducible classroom activities focusing on work and workers.

Burkitt, Ian. *Social Selves: Theories of the Social Formation of Personality.* Newbury Park, CA: Sage Publications, 1992. Good introduction to the theories of personality development.

Cox, H.G. *Later Life: The Realities of Aging,* 2d ed. Englewood Cliffs, NJ: Prentice-Hall, 1988. An interdisciplinary discussion of major trends and developments in the field of gerontology.

Crime Victimization in City, Suburban, and Rural Areas. Washington, DC: U.S. Department of Justice, 1992. Presents statistical data on crime victims.

Durkheim, Emile. *Suicide.* Glencoe, IL: The Free Press, 1964. Originally published in 1897. The classic sociological study into the nature of suicide.

Hyde, Margaret, and Forsyth, Elizabeth Held. *The Violent Mind.* New York, Franklin Watts, 1991. Uses case studies to examine the nature and prevalence of violence in American society.

Juvenile Justice, 1992 Annual Report. Washington, DC: U.S. Department of Justice, 1993. Presents statistical data on juvenile crime and delinquency in the United States.

Meltzer, Milton. *Crime in America.* New York: Morrow Books, 1990. A cross-disciplinary examination of crime and criminals.

Pavalko, Ronald M. *Sociology of Occupations and Professions.* Itasca, IL: F.E. Peacock, 1988. A sociological examination of the world of work.

Pontell, Henry N. *Social Deviance: Readings in Theory and Research.* Englewood Cliffs, NJ: Prentice-Hall, 1993. Scholarly anthology of readings on deviance.

Readings for Student Enrichment

Brown, Gene. *Violence on America's Streets: Headliner Series.* Brookfield, CT: Millbrook Press, 1992. Draws upon contemporary newspaper headlines to examine crime; enables students to gain insight into the criminal justice system.

Dolan, Edward, and Scariano, Margaret. *The Police in American Society.* New York: Franklin Watts, 1988. Examines the role of the police in society from both a historical and a contemporary perspective; gives students a broad picture of the police and police work.

Go Ask Alice. New York: Avon, 1982. The diary of an adolescent drug abuser; enables students to examine some of the serious stresses of adolescence.

Jankowski, Martín Sánchez. *Islands in the Street: Gangs and American Urban Society.* Berkeley, CA: University of California Press, 1991. Presents results of interviews with gang members from around the country; gives students sociological insight into the nature of gang life.

Miller, Arthur. *The Crucible.* New York: Penguin Books, 1976. A play about the Salem witch trials; allows students to examine the issue of deviance from the perspective of labeling theory.

Schneider, Meg. *Popularity Has Its Ups and Downs.* New York: Messner, 1991. Motivational guide that teaches students to appreciate themselves and their friends without tying their self-esteem to the opinions of others; helps students build self-confidence.

Swarthout, Glendon. *Bless the Beasts and the Children.* New York: Pocket Books, 1984. The story of a group of misfit boys who learn about themselves and each other as they attempt to rescue a herd of buffalo; enables students to explore what happens when "fitting in" takes on primary importance.

Turgenev, Ivan S. *Fathers and Sons.* New York: Bantam Books, 1982. A short Russian novel that examines differences between generations in the nineteenth century; allows students to explore socialization through the life span.

Multimedia Materials

The selected materials listed below may be useful during the study of Unit 2. The following abbreviations are used in the list:

c = color	lvd = laser videodisc
b&w = black & white	sim = simulation
f = film	sw = software
fs = filmstrip	g = game
vhs = videocassette	

Chapter 5

Coping with Peer Pressure (vhs, c; 15 min.) FHS. Teaches students how to cope with peer pressure by looking ahead to the consequences of their actions and being honest with themselves.

Fitting In: A New Look at Peer Pressure (vhs; 25 min.) FM. Provides students with skills for dealing with negative peer pressure, building self-esteem, and promoting positive peer pressure.

Growing Up in the Great Depression (vhs, f; 28 min.) CFV. Five adults who survived the Great Depression talk about how growing up during that time shaped their development and their lives.

How to Live with Your Parents and Survive (fs on vhs; 14 min.) GA. Bill Cosby and Art Buchwald present humorous sketches about the relationships of parents and children.

I Don't Know What to Do: Decision-Making Skills (vhs; 45 min.) GA. Scenarios guide students step by step through various decision-making situations.

The Impact of Television (vhs; 20 min.) EBEC. Uses sequences from popular television shows to illustrate how we are affected by television.

The Lottery (vhs; 18 min.) GA. Dramatization of Shirley Jackson's powerful story that ultimately speaks to the place of the individual in society.

Social Primates (vhs; 38 min.) EBEC. Two-part video that teaches students how to analyze social behavior by observing the behavior of rhesus monkeys and human children.

Television and Human Behavior (vhs, c; 26 min.) SSSS. Discusses a wide variety of topics concerning the influence of television on human behavior.

Chapter 6

AIDS: Nobody Is Immune (vhs; 15 min.) GA. AIDS experts and victims lead a discussion that illustrates the fact that everyone is vulnerable to this deadly disease.

An Anorexic's Tale: The Brief Life of Catherine (vhs, c; 80 min.) FHS. Docudrama of Catherine Dunbar's seven-year battle against anorexia.

Choices: Learning about AIDS (lvd; 20 min.) EBEC. Addresses the complex issues of morality, religion, and basic human needs in the context of AIDS education.

Coping with Pressures (vhs, c; 30 min.) ZM. Juvenile probation officer turned comedian Michael Pritchard uses small-group dialogues to help teenagers learn to deal with life's pressures.

The Date (vhs; 20 min.) EBEC. Uses comedy to explore what men and women expect from one another in dating situations.

Drinking: This Buzz Is Not for You (vhs; 30 min.) CE. Uses documentary and narrative footage to illustrate the problems encountered by young people who drink to excess.

Not My Kid (vhs; 97 min.) SVE. George Segal and Stockard Channing star in this dramatization of a teenager's struggle with drug abuse.

Second Wind (vhs; 50 min.) GA. Students and adults discuss the pressures that might result in attempts at suicide; also discusses suicide prevention techniques that can be used with people in crisis.

Sexually Transmitted Diseases (vhs, f; 15 min.) AM. Explains how STDs are contracted, describes common symptoms, and emphasizes the importance of seeking medical attention.

Substance Abuse: Decisions, Decisions (sw; 30 student booklets) SSSS. Software program that allows students to take on the role of an innocent teenager who unexpectedly gets caught up in a drug-related predicament.

Teen Contraception (vhs, lvd, f; 13 min.) AM. Straight-forward discussion of AIDS, sexually transmitted diseases, and contraception methods.

Wasted (vhs; 22 min.) FIV. Profiles teenagers who have lived through substance abuse and the parents who must cope with this situation.

Chapter 7

The Art of Job Negotiation (vhs; 16 min.) EBEC. Guides students through the interview process and shows them how to market their skills and abilities.

Grandparents (vhs; 29 min.) GA. Teenagers, adults, and young children share stories about their grandparents, illustrating the bond between the generations.

Investigating the World of Work (vhs; 30 min.) CE. Suggests specific techniques to help students narrow down their potential career choices.

Japan: Economic World Power (vhs; 16 min.) EBEC. Illustrates how the Japanese work ethic helped Japan become an economic world power.

The Japan They Don't Talk About (vhs; 52 min.) FIV. NBC News White Paper examines how Japanese workers cope with extremely long workdays, cramped and expensive housing, and other problems.

Jobs for the 21st Century (vhs; 63 min.) GA. Discusses the fields and industries that are expected to offer the greatest opportunities in the year 2000.

Preparing for the Jobs of the 1990s: What You Should Know (vhs; 56 min.) GA. Teaches students how to choose a career that can keep pace with our changing technology.

The Robot Revolution (vhs; 19 min.) EBEC. Explores the potential of robots for improving human life and their threat to the labor force as they enter the workplace.

The Transformation of Mabel Wells (vhs; 12 min.) GA. Mabel Wells, a complaining elderly woman, finds her home filled with cards and gifts after a long hospital stay.

Women at Work: Change, Choice, Challenge (vhs; 19 min.) EBEC. Seven women discuss their attitudes toward work, their reasons for their career choices, and their views of their work-family relationships.

Chapter 8

Cancelled Lives: Letters from the Inside (vhs, c; 41 min.) SSSS. Documentary in which celebrities read excerpts from letters written by prison inmates to their friends and family members.

Crime, Punishment . . . and Kids (vhs; 52 min.) FIV. Explores the fine line between the public's right to safety from juvenile offenders and the ideal of reforming these offenders.

Gangs: Decisions and Options (vhs; 17 min.) NY. Presents three young people from different back-grounds who wrestle with their decision to join a youth gang or reject membership; deals with the difficult issues of low self-esteem, dysfunctional families, and gang violence.

Juvenile Law (vhs; 24 min.) GA. Illustrates the differences between criminal procedures and juvenile law.

Police Patrol (sim; 20–35 players; 1, 3, or 5 50–min. periods) SSSS. Simulation that allows students to explore their attitudes toward police officers and authority, while broadening their understanding of the police officer's job.

Teen Violence (lvd; 29 min.) CMFV. Documentary about inner city teenagers that examines the effectiveness of violence prevention strategies.

Teenagers and Serious Crime: Here and Now (vhs, c; 12 min.) SSSS. Examines the pros and cons of capital punishment for some juvenile crimes.

The Vandals (vhs; 25 min.) GA. Harry Reasoner examines the social causes of vandalism.

CHAPTER 5 *(pages 98–119)*

SOCIALIZING THE INDIVIDUAL

SECTION 1
PERSONALITY DEVELOPMENT

SECTION 2
THE SOCIAL SELF

SECTION 3
AGENTS OF SOCIALIZATION

Chapter Overview

Unlike the behavior of other animals, the behavior of humans is not heavily influenced by instincts. Humans, instead, become functioning members of society through socialization. Socialization is an interactive process through which individuals learn the basic skills, values, beliefs, and behavior patterns of their society. Because human behavior is socially determined, people exhibit a wide range of behaviors and personality traits. Chapter 5 examines the factors that shape personality development and the social forces that work to mold people into functioning members of society in spite of their individual differences.

Chapter Objectives

At the conclusion of the chapter, students will be able to

1. Define personality, and explain why personality development is a subject of debate.
2. Evaluate the influences of heredity and environment on the development of personality.

3. Assess the effects that isolation in childhood has on personality development.
4. Describe how our sense of self emerges, and discuss the theories that have been put forth to explain the process of socialization.
5. Identify and describe the most important agents of socialization in the United States.
6. Define resocialization, and explain the relationship between total institutions and the concept of resocialization.

Introducing the Chapter

Until relatively recently, a discussion among sociologists of personality development often led to a heated debate over the influences of nature (heredity) versus the influences of nurture (environment and social learning). While most contemporary sociologists stress the importance of social factors in the development of personality, the effect of nature on human behavior still is of interest to sociobiologists.

Before assigning the reading of Chapter 5, have students write short position papers that address the following question: "Are babies born with the basic personalities that they will keep throughout their lives, or do they develop personalities through experience and interaction with other people?" Then have students place their position papers in their study notebooks for use later in the chapter.

Chapter 5 Suggested Lesson Plans

Day 1	**Suggested Procedures:** Introducing the Unit; Introducing the Chapter; Section 1 Previewing Key Terms; Introducing the Section **Materials:** PE: pp. 96–108; TM: pp. 29–32
Day 2	**Suggested Procedures:** Section 1 Strategies and Assignments **Materials:** PE: pp. 100–108; TM: pp. 32–34; TRB: Assorted Worksheets
Day 3	**Suggested Procedures:** Section 2 Previewing Key Terms; Introducing the Section; Strategies and Assignments **Materials:** PE: pp. 109–111; TM: pp. 34–35; TRB: Worksheet
Day 4	**Suggested Procedures:** Section 3 Previewing Key Terms; Introducing the Section; Strategies and Assignments **Materials:** PE: pp. 112–117; TM: pp. 35–36; TRB: Assorted Worksheets
Day 5	**Suggested Procedures:** Closing the Chapter; Assessing the Chapter **Materials:** PE: pp. 118–119; TM: pp. 36–37; TRB: Review Worksheet, Tests, Reteaching Worksheet

SECTION 1 (pages 100–108)

PERSONALITY DEVELOPMENT

Section Overview

Personality is the sum total of behaviors, attitudes, beliefs, and values that are characteristic of an individual. Until fairly recently, a heated debate in the social sciences centered on whether nature (heredity) or nurture (environment and social learning) gives rise to personality and social behavior. While admitting that heredity plays a role in personality development, most contemporary sociologists stress the importance of social factors. Social scientists point to the developmental problems faced by children who are raised in isolation as evidence of the importance of social factors in influencing the development of personality.

Previewing Key Terms

Section 1 contains the following key terms: **personality, heredity, instinct, sociobiology, aptitude**. Have students look up each term in the Glossary, and then write a paragraph that discusses personality development. Although each term listed above should be used in the paragraph, students should indicate these terms only with numbered blanks. The correct answer for each number may be put on the back of the paper. When students have finished their paragraphs, have them exchange papers and fill in the blanks with the correct terms.

Introducing the Section

Have students retrieve the position papers they prepared for the Introducing the Chapter activity. Then ask selected volunteers to read their position papers aloud to the class. Use the papers as the basis of a class discussion of the influences of heredity and environment on human behavior. Then tell students that Section 1 will introduce them to the sociological perspective on personality development.

Suggested Teaching Strategies

1. **Seeing Relationships (I)** Define personality and then discuss with the class the influence of birth order, parental characteristics, the cultural environment, and heredity on personality development. Next ask each student to prepare a written description of how his or her own personality development has been influenced by these four factors. If desired, the students' papers can be used as the basis for a discussion of the nature versus nurture debate.
2. **Using Sociological Imagination (I)** After reviewing the material on isolation in childhood, have students write an imaginative short story about a world in which all newborn children are raised by robots in a separate newborn facility. Ask volunteers to read their stories to the class for class discussion.

3. **Exploring Multicultural Perspectives (I)** Have students consider the following question: "How has your own race, ethnic background, religion, or gender influenced your personality development and view of the social world?" Ask volunteers to share their ideas with the class for class discussion.
4. **Working in Groups (II, III)** Organize the class into small groups and have the members of each group identify themselves as first-born, middle-born, or last-born children of their families. Then have the groups conduct library research and compile lists of 7–10 personality traits that have been found to be characteristic of each birth position. Have the groups discuss how closely their personality traits correspond to the lists of traits they have compiled.

Suggested Enrichment Activities

1. **Exploring Cross-Cultural Perspectives (I)** Have students complete the appropriate Cross-Cultural Perspectives Worksheet, found in the *Teacher's Resource Binder*.
2. **Practicing Interviewing Skills (II)** Have interested students interview health-care workers who are assigned to neonatal intensive-care units to determine the workers' views on the importance of human contact during the first months of life. Ask the students to report their findings to the class.

Suggested Assignments

1. **Conducting a Poll (I)** As homework, have students ask five people (friends, neighbors, family members) the following question: "Which do you believe has a greater influence on personality development—heredity or the environment?" Instruct students to take notes on the reasons why the interviewees have answered a certain way. Then, in class, tally the responses and have students compare the results of the poll with the results of sociological research.
2. **Writing a Case Study (I)** Have students complete the appropriate Developing Research Skills Worksheet, found in the *Teacher's Resource Binder*.
3. **Making Oral Presentations (II, III)** Have interested students research a game or sport that is popular in a foreign nation. Instruct students to prepare a short paper for oral presentation to the class that describes the rules and procedures of the game or sport and explains why these rules and procedures are important in the socialization of that nation's youth.

Closing the Section

To close the section, have students write short essays summarizing the nature versus nurture debate.

Assessing the Section

Have students complete the Section 1 Review.

Answers to Applying Sociology (pages 106–107)

1. b
2. c

3. c
4. d
5. c
6. b

Answers to Section 1 Review (page 108)

Define *personality*: sum total of behaviors, attitudes, beliefs, and values that are characteristic of an individual; ***instinct*:** unchanging, biologically inherited behavior pattern; ***sociobiology*:** systematic study of the biological basis of all social behavior; ***aptitude*:** capacity to learn a particular skill or acquire a particular body of knowledge

Identify *John B. Watson*: American psychologist who believed that personality and behavior can be attributed to environmental factors and social learning; ***Edward O. Wilson*:** leading sociobiologist who believes that the various cultural characteristics and behavioral traits are rooted in the genetic makeup of humans; ***IK*:** people of the mountainous region of northern Uganda who, prior to World War II, hunted and gathered their food. After WW II, they were displaced when the government turned their land into a national park. The Ik were resettled and, as a result of food shortages and the disruption accompanying the relocation, underwent profound social and psychological changes; ***Kingsley Davis*:** sociologist who studied Anna and Isabelle, two children raised in isolation. His studies indicate that human personality is produced by the cultural environment; ***Rene Spitz*:** psychologist who studied the effects of institutional confinement on children living in orphanages. His work with orphans showed the importance of human interaction for children's development

1. **(a)** Heredity is the transmission of genetic characteristics from parents to children. **(b)** The nature versus nurture debate centers around the source of personality and social behavior. People who hold to the nature side of the debate believe that personality and social behavior are a direct result of heredity. Nature supporters, on the other hand, attribute personality and social behavior to social learning and environmental factors.
2. The principal factors that influence personality and social behavior are birth order, parental characteristics, the cultural environment, and heredity. Birth order refers to the order in which a person is born into his or her family, which may produce different personality traits. The characteristics of one's parents, such as age, level of education, religious orientation, economic status, and occupational background, create an environment that can affect personality development. The cultural environment determines the basic types of personalities that are typical of members of a culture. Heredity refers to the transmission of genetic characteristics from parents to children, and so sets limits on what is possible.
3. The factors accounting for the different levels of success in teaching Anna, Isabelle, and Genie to function normally probably were the type and amount of human contact they had during their early years. The

child who made the most progress after being discovered had had the benefit of close physical contact with her mother.

4. Few of the institutionalized children studied by Spitz could walk by themselves, dress themselves, or use a spoon. Only one of the children could speak in complete sentences. Spitz attributed these developmental deficiencies to a lack of close human contact.

SECTION 2 (pages 109–111)

THE SOCIAL SELF

Section Overview

Individuals are transformed into participating members of society through interaction with their social and cultural environments. This interactive process through which individuals learn the basic skills, values, beliefs, and behavior patterns of society is called socialization.

A number of theories exist to explain how individuals become socialized and develop a sense of self. Among these theories are those put forth by John Locke, Charles Horton Cooley, and George Herbert Mead.

Previewing Key Terms

Section 2 contains the following key terms: **socialization, self, looking-glass self, role-taking, significant others, generalized other, I, me**. Have students prepare a matching test using these terms and their definitions, found in the Glossary or in Section 2. Answers should appear on the back of the paper. Then have students exchange their papers and complete the tests. Finally, have students place their tests in their study notebooks for later review.

Introducing the Section

Introduce the class to the concept of the social self by showing the film *Social Primates,* which teaches students how to analyze social behavior by observing the behavior of rhesus monkeys and human children (rental information can be found in the introductory section of this *Teacher's Manual*). Then tell students that Section 2 will introduce them to three theories that have been put forth to explain how individuals become socialized and develop a sense of self.

Suggested Teaching Strategies

1. **Evaluating Ideas (I)** After reviewing Locke's theory of socialization, have the class debate Locke's belief that he could shape a newborn infant into any type of person he wanted through socialization.
2. **Seeing Relationships (I)** Have students make lists of the significant others in their lives. When they have completed their lists, instruct them to write next to each person's name an example of how that person has assisted in their socialization. Use the lists as a basis for class discussion.

3. **Linking the Past to the Present (II, III)** Have interested students use library sources to locate historical quotations that focus on the socialization of children. Conduct a class discussion in which students evaluate how valid these quotations are in today's society.

Suggested Enrichment Activities

1. **Dramatizing Sociology (I, II)** Have interested students write and present short skits illustrating the concepts of the "I" and the "me" and their integration in adulthood.
2. **Conducting an Observational Study (II, III)** Have groups of interested students conduct research on Mead's three-stage process of role-taking, using either detached observation or participant observation. The first group should study the process of imitation among children under the age of three. The second group should examine the characteristics of play among preschool children. And the third group should examine game playing among school-age children. Caution students to ask permission of parents, teachers, or daycare workers before they begin their research. Have the groups report their observations to the class.

Suggested Assignments

1. **Organizing Ideas (I)** As homework, have students complete the appropriate Graphic Organizer Worksheet, found in the *Teacher's Resource Binder*.
2. **Drawing Conclusions (I, II)** Have students visit a toy store and examine 15 toys or games available for preschoolers. Ask them to list the toys that show only boys on the cover or wrapping material, the ones that show only girls, and the ones that show a gender mix. Have students perform a content analysis of their lists to determine if there is a difference in socialization patterns for boys and girls. Use the lists as the basis of a class discussion.

Closing the Section

Close the section by having students prepare a quiz on the information contained in Section 2. Ask students to write 10 questions on one side of a piece of paper and the answers to these questions on the other side. When the quizzes are complete, have students exchange papers and answer the questions.

Assessing the Section

Have students complete the Section 2 Review.

Answers to Section 2 Review (page 111)

Define socialization: interactive process through which individuals learn the basic skills, values, beliefs, and behavior patterns of the society; **self:** conscious awareness of possessing a distinct identity that separates us from other members of society; **significant others:** specific people, such as parents, brothers, sisters, other relatives, and friends, who have a direct influence on our socialization; **generalized other:** internalized attitudes, expectations, and viewpoints of society that we use to guide our behavior and reinforce our sense of self

Identify *John Locke:* English philosopher who believed that human beings are born without a personality but develop one through interaction with others; *Charles Horton Cooley:* American social psychologist who developed the concept of the looking-glass self, which refers to the interactive process through which we develop an image of ourselves based on how we imagine we appear to others; *George Herbert Mead:* American sociologist who extended Cooley's theory of socialization and development of the self with the concept of role-taking, a process involving imitation, play, and games

1. Locke believed that individuals are born without personalities and that they acquire their personalities as a result of social experiences. Because of this, Locke believed that human beings can be molded into any type of character.
2. **(a)** The looking-glass self refers to the interactive process by which we develop an image of ourselves based on how we imagine we appear to others. **(b)** The development of the looking-glass self is a three-step process. First, we image how we appear to others. Second, based on their reactions to us, we attempt to determine whether others view us as we view ourselves. Third, we use our perceptions of how others judge us to develop feelings about ourselves.
3. **(a)** Role-taking is taking or pretending to take the role of others. **(b)** Role-taking is a three-step process. In the first stage, children can only imitate the actions of other people. This is a preparatory stage for role-taking. In the next stage (about age three), children begin to play and act out the roles of specific people. By the time they reach school age, children begin to participate in organized games that require them to anticipate the actions and expectations of others.
4. According to Mead, the two components of the self are the I and the me. The I is the spontaneous, unsocialized, and self-centered part. The me, on the other hand, is the socialized self. The I component dominates in childhood but loses power as a result of socialization. Both the I and the me are necessary components of the self.

SECTION 3 *(pages 112–115)*

AGENTS OF SOCIALIZATION

Section Overview

The views of Locke, Cooley, and Mead are theoretical explanations of the socialization process. It also is important to consider some specific forces and situations that shape socialization experiences. In sociological terms, the specific individuals, groups, and institutions that provide the situations in which socialization can occur are called agents of socialization. In the United States, the primary agents of socialization include the family, peer groups, the school, and the mass media. In addition, religion, organizations, jobs, and total institutions serve as agents of socialization for many people.

Previewing Key Terms

Section 3 contains the following key terms: **agents of socialization, peer group, mass media, total institution, resocialization**. Have students look up each term in the Glossary. Then have them write on a piece of paper what is important about each term with regard to socialization. Finished papers may be shared with the class, and then placed in the students' study notebooks for later review.

Introducing the Section

Write the term "agents of socialization" on the chalkboard, and have students speculate as to what the term might mean. Then ask students to consider what people, groups, and institutions might be considered agents of socialization. Tell them that Section 3 will introduce them to agents of socialization and explain how these people, groups, and organizations aid in the socialization process.

Suggested Teaching Strategies

1. **Solving Problems (I)** Show a film on peer pressure from the list given in the beginning of this unit. Use the film as the basis of a discussion of the ways in which students can overcome negative peer pressure and build self-esteem.
2. **Working in Groups (I, II)** Organize the class into eight groups and assign each group one of the following agents of socialization: the family, peer groups, the school, the mass media, religion, organizations, jobs, and total institutions. Instruct each group to develop a summary of how its particular agent of socialization contributes to the socialization process. Caution the groups to include specific examples and definitions of important terms. Have the groups present their conclusions to the class.
3. **Analyzing Fairy Tales (II, III)** Discuss with the class Bruno Bettleheim's view of the function of fairy tales. Then have interested students analyze specific fairy tales, describing how these tales contribute to children's socialization. Have students present their findings to the class.
4. **★Reading about Sociology: Comparing Sociological Perspectives (III)** Review with the class the Developing Sociological Imagination feature that appears on textbook pages 116–117. Then have students locate two magazine articles that present different views on the impact of television violence. Have students compare these articles by following the steps outlined in the feature.

Suggested Enrichment Activities

1. **Distinguishing Between Fact and Opinion (I)** Have students complete the appropriate Critical Skills Mastery Worksheet, found in the *Teacher's Resource Binder.*
2. **Making Oral Presentations (II, III)** Assign interested students to research and make oral presentations on the resocialization that takes place in prisons, military boot camps, psychiatric hospitals, or other total institutions.

Suggested Assignments

1. **Organizing Ideas (I)** As homework, have students create a piece of art that illustrates one of the agents of socialization discussed in the section. Art may take the form of a song, a poem, a painting, a collage, a dance, and so on. Have students display their pieces of art in the classroom or perform them for the class.
2. **Debating Ideas (I, II)** Assign students the task of watching one full hour of children's cartoons on television. Instruct them to keep a tally of the number and kind of violent incidents that appear in the cartoons during the hour. As a class, combine the individual tallies and have volunteers debate the following statement: "Television teaches young children to be violent."

Closing the Section

Close the section by having students complete the appropriate Understanding Sociological Ideas Worksheet, found in the *Teacher's Resource Binder*.

Assessing the Section

Have students complete the Section 3 Review.

Answers to Section 3 Review *(page 115)*

Define *agents of socialization:* specific individuals, groups, and institutions that provide the situations in which socialization can occur; ***resocialization:*** break with past experiences and the learning of new values and norms

1. The primary agents of socialization are the family, the peer group, the school, and the mass media. The family is the most important agent of socialization in virtually every society. It is within the family that children learn how to behave in acceptable ways, to develop close emotional ties, and to internalize the norms and values of society. Peer groups are composed of individuals of roughly equal age and social characteristics. The socialization that occurs within the peer group is informal and unstructured. Peer groups are particularly important in adolescence and early adulthood. The school is another important agent of socialization. In addition to teaching academic subjects, the school transmits cultural values such as patriotism, responsibility, and good citizenship. Finally, the mass media, which include newspapers, magazines, books, television, radio, and films, is an influential agent of socialization. Of the various forms of mass media, television probably has the most influence on socialization. The negative aspects of mass media involvement in socialization is a topic of continued debate.
2. Total institutions differ from other agents of socialization in that they primarily are concerned with resocialization, that is, forcibly changing an individual's personality and social behavior. The idea is to disrupt the individual's sense of self so that the individual will conform to new patterns of behavior. Examples of total institutions include prisons, monasteries, military boot camps, and psychiatric hospitals.

Answers to Developing Sociological Imagination *(pages 116–117)*

Answers will vary, but students should create charts similar in nature to that shown on textbook page 117.

Closing the Chapter

Have students complete the Chapter 5 Review Worksheet, found in the *Teacher's Resource Binder*.

Assessing the Chapter

Have students complete the Chapter 5 Review, found on page 118 of the *Pupil's Edition*.

Give students the Chapter 5 Form A Test and, if desired, the Chapter 5 Reteaching Worksheet and Form B Test, found in the *Teacher's Resource Binder*.

Answers to Chapter 5 Review *(page 118)*

Reviewing Sociological Terms

1. socialization
2. instinct
3. heredity
4. resocialization
5. aptitude
6. personality

Thinking Critically about Sociology

1. **(a)** A self is a conscious awareness of possessing a distinct identity that separates us from other members of society. **(b)** According to Locke, every newborn child is a *tabula rasa,* or clean slate, on which anything can be written. In other words, personality development and the sense of self are totally dependent on one's social experiences. Cooley believed that personality development is influenced by the development of the looking-glass self, an interactive process by which we develop an image of ourselves based on how we imagine we appear to others. According to Cooley, the development of the looking-glass self is a three-stage process. First, we imagine how we appear to others. Second, based on their reactions to us, we try to determine whether others view us as we view ourselves. Third, we use our perceptions of how others view us to develop feelings about ourselves. Mead extended Cooley's theory to include taking the role of the other. This role-taking is at the base of the socialization process because it allows us to anticipate what others expect of us and to see ourselves through the eyes of others. According to Mead, our significant others are the people with whom we first experience role-taking. As we grow older, we internalize the attitudes, expectations, and viewpoints of society, the "generalized other." Through role-playing, a sense of self composed of the "I" and the "me" develops. The I is the unsocialized self and the me is the socialized self. The me comes to power as we bring our actions in line with the expectations of others.
2. **(a)** The nature supporters of the early twentieth century believed that much of human behavior is instinctual in origin. Contemporary sociobiologists believe

that most of social life is determined by biological factors. **(b)** The views of nature supporters and contemporary sociobiologists are similar in that they attribute most of social life to biological factors.

3. **(a)** The cultural environment shapes personality development through the transmission of values and norms considered appropriate for the members of the culture. **(b)** When the hunting and gathering Ik were relocated to barren land by the Ugandan government, their typical personalities changed from being cooperative and family-like to being competitive and hostile.

4. **(a)** Agents of socialization are the specific individuals, groups, and institutions that provide the situations in which socialization can occur. **(b)** Television is a powerful influence on society. It has the power to shape public opinion and to influence the awareness of prevailing social patterns. In this respect, it can have both negative and positive effects on socialization. On the negative side, television presents viewers with countless acts of violence. It also presents an image of society based on white, middle-class values, often ignoring or portraying in a negative light groups that differ from this image. On the positive side, television expands our world by bringing many novel experiences into the home that we otherwise would not experience.

5. Studies of children raised in isolation indicate that social and psychological development are determined by the cultural environment.

6. Social scientists recognize several contributions of heredity to personality development. First, heredity determines physical characteristics, such as body build, skin color, and eye color. Heredity also determines certain aptitudes, the capacity to learn particular skills or acquire particular knowledge. Finally, heredity provides humans with certain needs, but culture determines acceptable ways of meeting these needs. In essence, heredity places limits on what is possible in personality development.

7. **(a)** Cooley believed that the sense of self is influenced by the development of the looking-glass self, an interactive process whereby we develop an image of ourselves based on how we imagine we appear to others. According to Cooley, the development of the looking-glass self is a three-stage process. First, we imagine how we appear to others. Second, based on their reactions to us, we try to determine whether others view us as we view ourselves. Third, we use our perceptions of how others view us to develop feelings about ourselves. **(b)** According to Cooley, this process continues throughout our lives. We continually refine our self-images as we alter our interpretations of the way we think others view us.

Exercising Sociological Skills

1. Answers will vary, but students should explain how Tibet's cultural and physical environments have affected socialization in that country.

2. **(a)** Fairy tales can help children conquer the problems of growing up. They teach children that there are good and bad aspects associated with every situation and that unavoidable difficulties in life must be confronted directly. **(b)** Fairy tales are effective because they engage children's imagination and allow them to explore their darkest fears.

3. Students' charts should match the format presented on textbook page 117.

Extending Sociological Imagination

1. Answers will vary, but students should compare the birth order traits portrayed on a television program with those predicted in the scientific research.

2. Students' pictures will vary, but should show children engaged in each of the three steps of the role-taking process described by Mead.

Answers to Interpreting Primary Sources *(page 119)*

1. Genie would walk up to people, even those she did not know, and touch their clothes or other belongings. She also would stand very close to people with her face very close to theirs, violating their personal space.

2. Such behavior makes people uncomfortable because it violates fundamental norms of human interaction between strangers.

3. Socialization simplifies interaction by providing norms that regulate behavior, making human behavior and social interaction predictable and patterned.

CHAPTER 6 *(pages 120–147)*

THE ADOLESCENT IN SOCIETY

SECTION 1
ADOLESCENCE IN OUR SOCIETY

SECTION 2
TEENAGERS AND DATING

SECTION 3
PROBLEMS OF ADOLESCENCE

Chapter Overview

Adolescence—the period between the normal onset of puberty and the beginning of adulthood—is not a universal stage of the life cycle. In many preindustrial societies, young people pass directly from childhood to adulthood once they have performed the necessary puberty rites. Even in industrialized societies, adolescence is a fairly recent phenomenon. In the United States, for example, adolescence did not exist prior to the Civil War.

In the United States and other industrialized societies, dating plays a major role in adolescent life. Although dating is the means through which marriage partners are selected, eventual marriage is not the only function of dating. Dating also serves as a form of recreation, a mechanism for psychological fulfillment, and a means of status attainment.

The characteristics of adolescence that mark it as a distinct stage of the life cycle give rise to many pressures and problems. In recent years, social scientists have devoted considerable attention to the examination of these pressures and problems. Among the topics being examined are the influences on and consequences of early sexual activity, the effects of drug and alcohol use, and the factors contributing to the increase in teenage suicide.

Chapter Objectives

At the conclusion of the chapter, students will be able to

1. Define adolescence and puberty.
2. Identify the factors that have led to the development of adolescence as a distinct stage of the life cycle in the United States.
3. Recognize and describe the five general characteristics of adolescence.
4. Distinguish between courtship and dating, and identify the factors that led to the development of dating.
5. Explain the functions of dating, and discuss the characteristics of traditional and contemporary dating.
6. Describe some of the social problems facing teenagers in the United States.

Introducing the Chapter

Prior to assigning the reading of Chapter 6, write the following questions on the chalkboard:

1. What does it mean to be an adolescent?
2. What are your greatest fears at this stage of your life?
3. How important is dating to you, and why?
4. What are the most significant social problems facing teenagers today?

Have students write short answers to these questions on a piece of paper, and use the answers as the basis of a class discussion on adolescence in the United States.

Chapter 6 Suggested Lesson Plans

Day 1	**Suggested Procedures:** Introducing the Chapter; Section 1 Previewing Key Terms; Introducing the Section **Materials:** PE: pp. 120–127; TM: pp. 37–39
Day 2	**Suggested Procedures:** Section 1 Strategies and Assignments **Materials:** PE: pp. 122–127; TM: p. 39; TRB: Transparency 3, Assorted Worksheets
Day 3	**Suggested Procedures:** Section 2 Previewing Key Terms; Introducing the Section; Strategies and Assignments **Materials:** PE: pp. 128–135; TM: pp. 39–41

Day 4	**Suggested Procedures:** Section 3 Previewing Key Terms; Introducing the Section; Strategies and Assignments **Materials:** PE: pp. 136–145; TM: pp. 41–42; TRB: Transparency 4, Assorted Worksheets
Day 5	**Suggested Procedures:** Closing the Chapter; Assessing the Chapter **Materials:** PE: pp. 146–147; TM: pp. 42–43; TRB: Review Worksheet, Tests, Reteaching Worksheet

SECTION 1 *(pages 122–127)*

ADOLESCENCE IN OUR SOCIETY

Section Overview

All young people experience puberty—the physical maturing that makes an individual capable of sexual reproduction. Adolescence, on the other hand, is a relatively recent creation of industrialized societies.

Three factors have been particularly important in the development of adolescence as a distinct stage of the life cycle in the United States. These factors are mandatory education and the pursuit of higher education, the exclusion of youth from the labor force through child labor laws and job training requirements, and the development of the juvenile justice system.

Adolescence is marked by five general characteristics. First, adolescence is a time of biological growth and development. Second, the status of young people during adolescence is undefined. Third, adolescence is a period of increased decision making. Fourth, adolescence is a time of great pressure from a variety of sources. And finally, adolescence is a time of finding oneself.

Previewing Key Terms

Section 1 contains the following key terms: **adolescence, puberty, anticipatory socialization**. Ask students the following question: "What is the difference between adolescence and puberty?" After several volunteers have suggested answers to the question, have students look up the definitions of these terms in the Glossary. Then ask: "What role does anticipatory socialization play in adolescence?" Lead students to the conclusion that anticipatory socialization is preparation for taking on adult roles.

Introducing the Section

Tell students to imagine what their lives would be like if adolescence was not considered a separate stage of the life cycle. Ask: "How would your life be different from what it is today if all people in the United States were considered to be adults at the age of 13?" Then tell students that adolescence is a relatively recent creation of industrialized societies, and that they will learn in Section 1 how the concept of adolescence came about in our society.

Suggested Teaching Strategies

1. **Interpreting Ideas (I)** Discuss with the class the five characteristics of adolescence. Then ask students to write essays focusing on their own experiences in relation to these characteristics.
2. **Understanding Tables (I)** Place Transparency 3, which focuses on extracurricular activities, on an overhead projector and ask the questions contained in the accompanying teacher's notes. Transparencies and accompanying teacher's notes are found in the *Teacher's Resource Binder*.
3. **Interpreting Photographs (I, II)** Instruct students to turn to textbook page 123 and examine the photographs on that page. Then have students list three things they have learned about child labor from their examination of the photographs. Ask volunteers to share their ideas with the class and have students speculate about what working conditions were like for the youngsters portrayed. Interested students may elect to conduct library research on the subject and make presentations to the class.

Suggested Enrichment Activities

1. **Exploring Cross-Cultural Perspectives (I)** Have students complete the appropriate Cross-Cultural Perspectives Worksheet, found in the *Teacher's Resource Binder*.
2. **Using the Historical Method (III)** If an art museum is nearby, or if your school library has books that contain reproductions of paintings from different historical periods, have interested students analyze paintings that show the daily lives of young people at different points in history. Instruct students to prepare a general description of each painting and a list of the characteristics of childhood that can be determined from studying the painting. Have students present their findings to the class.

Suggested Assignments

1. **Developing an Outline (I)** As homework, have students complete the appropriate Critical Skills Mastery Worksheet, found in the *Teacher's Resource Binder*.
2. **Summarizing Information (I)** Have students read and then summarize the Case Study feature on textbook page 125.
3. **Conducting Research (III)** Have interested students conduct library research on the development of the American juvenile justice system.

Closing the Section

Close the section by having students write a short essay in response to the following question: "Which of the characteristics of adolescence presents the most problems for today's teenagers?" Ask volunteers to read their essays aloud to the class for class discussion.

Assessing the Section

Have students complete the Section 1 Review.

Answers to Section 1 Review *(page 127)*

Define *adolescence:* period between the normal onset of puberty and the beginning of adulthood; ***puberty:*** physical maturing that makes an individual capable of sexual reproduction; ***anticipatory socialization:*** learning the rights, obligations, and expectations of a role in preparation for assuming that role at a future date

1. Three factors have been important in the development of adolescence as a separate stage in the life cycle. The first factor is mandatory education laws. These laws require that students remain in school until at least age 16. This requirement means in effect that young people remain dependent on their families until at least that age. The second factor is protective labor legislation that denies employment in industries that engage in interstate commerce to people under 16. The inability to take paid employment adds to the dependency of the adolescent. The third factor is the juvenile justice system, which distinguishes between children and adults in its treatment of criminal offenders.
2. The five general characteristics of adolescence are biological growth and development; indefinite social status; increased decision making; increased pressure; and the search for self.
3. Answers will vary. For example, students may note that factors such as social class, cultural background, and family characteristics can affect the timing of the transition from adolescence to adulthood. People from working-class backgrounds, for instance, are less likely to attend college so may begin working at earlier ages. Thus, working-class children leave the adolescent stage at an earlier age than middle-class children who attend college.

SECTION 2 *(pages 128–135)*

TEENAGERS AND DATING

Section Overview

Dating plays a central role in adolescent life in modern society. This has not always been the case, however. Prior to the Industrial Revolution, courtship was the primary form of social interaction between unmarried members of the opposite sex. Dating differs from courtship in that the intended purpose of courtship is eventual marriage. Dating, on the other hand, serves many functions other than mate selection. Among the various functions of dating are recreation, socialization, psychological fulfillment, and status attainment.

Prior to the 1960s, responsibility for arranging a date fell to the male. He was expected to contact his intended dating partner, suggest a time and place for the date, select an activity, and pay for any expenses that arose. Although this traditional dating pattern still exists, new dating patterns have emerged since the 1960s. Today, dates often are not prearranged. Instead, a couple will break away from a group activity on the spur of the moment. In addition, dates can be initiated by either males or females, and it is acceptable for either or both partners to pay the expenses of the date.

Previewing Key Terms

Section 2 contains the following key term: **homogamy**. Have a volunteer turn to the Glossary and read the definition of this term to the class. Then have students consider the following question: "Which of these two sayings do you believe is true in terms of dating—'opposites attract' or 'birds of a feather flock together'?"

Introducing the Section

Introduce the section by showing the film *The Date,* which uses comedy to explore what men and women expect from one another in dating situations (rental information can be found in the introductory section of this *Teacher's Manual*). Ask students to evaluate the validity of the film in terms of their own and their peers' dating experiences. Then tell students that Section 2 will introduce them to the sociological perspective on teenagers and dating.

Suggested Teaching Strategies

1. **Recognizing Cause and Effect (I)** Have students read the information on the emergence of dating and write a short summary identifying the causative factors in the rise of casual dating. As an extension exercise, have students consider how dating today would be different if telephones and automobiles had never been invented.
2. **Contrasting Ideas (I, II)** After students have read the section, ask them to identify the characteristics of traditional dating. (Have students draw information from the discussion of Willard Waller's study, as well as from the discussion of traditional dating patterns.) As students identify a characteristic, write it on the chalkboard. Once the list is complete, ask students to contrast these characteristics with the characteristics of current dating patterns. Use the two lists as the basis of a class discussion.
3. **Expressing Viewpoints (I, II)** Ask students to consider the following questions: (a) At what age should young people be allowed to start dating? (b) At what point, if any, does dating shift from being casual to serious during adolescence? (c) How is this shift marked? Use the students' answers as the basis of a class discussion.

Suggested Enrichment Activities

1. **Dramatizing Sociology (I, II)** Ask interested students to write and perform short skits showing what typical dates might have been like prior to the 1960s. Have the class compare these "typical" dates to dating practices today.
2. **Making Oral Presentations (III)** Ask interested students to conduct research on dating patterns in other

cultures. Have the students make oral presentations of their findings to the class.

Suggested Assignments

1. **Organizing Ideas (I)** As homework, have students write an imaginative short story entitled "The 'Perfect' First Date." Ask volunteers to read their stories aloud to the class for class discussion.
2. **Conducting a Content Analysis (III)** Have students complete the activity outlined in the Applying Sociology feature on textbook pages 132–133.

Closing the Section

Close the section by organizing the class into five small groups and assigning each group one of the following five functions of dating: mate selection, recreation, socialization, psychological fulfillment, status attainment. Tell each group that they are to prepare a strong argument identifying the reasons why their assigned function is the most important function of dating. Have a representative from each group present the group's ideas to the class and then have the class vote on which argument was most persuasive.

Assessing the Section

Have students complete the Section 2 Review.

Answers to Applying Sociology *(pages 132–133)*

Answers will vary, but students' charts should resemble the chart on textbook page 133.

Answers to Section 2 Review *(page 135)*

Define *homogamy:* tendency for individuals to marry people who have social characteristics similar to their own

1. **(a)** Courtship differed from dating in that its purpose was marriage rather than simple recreation. Courtship was formal rather than casual, and was closely controlled by the parents of the young people. Typically, the young man asked the young woman's parents for permission to court her. Parents assumed that this was an indication of his intention to marry their daughter. Courtship usually occurred in the young woman's home under supervision of the parents or a chaperone. Dating, on the other hand, also may lead to marriage, but its main purpose is recreation. **(b)** Dating emerged in the United States as a result of several social changes associated with the process of industrialization. As Americans moved from farms to cities, young people had more leisure time and less parental supervision. Additionally, the rise of coeducation meant that young people had more opportunities to interact with members of the opposite sex. Cars and telephones also made dating more common. These inventions gave young people the freedom to arrange dates without parental intervention. Finally, changes in women's social and political status in the 1920s made it more acceptable for unmarried women and men to spend time alone together.

2. Dating serves five major functions: recreation; socialization; fulfillment of basic psychological needs; attainment of social status; and a context within which to find marriage mates.

3. Traditional dating patterns followed rather rigid rules. Young men were responsible for arranging the date and for paying the costs of the date. Most dates revolved around limited activities such as movies or sports events. Dates typically had to be arranged several days in advance. Individuals who did not have dates on weekends were considered social misfits by other young people. Contemporary dating, on the other hand, tends to be more spontaneous. Dates are not always arranged in advance. Often two people who go out with a group of mutual friends will pair off and go somewhere together. Women as well as men can initiate dates and it is acceptable for the partners to share the expenses of the date.

SECTION 3 (pages 136-143)

PROBLEMS OF ADOLESCENCE

Section Overview

Caught between the relative safety of childhood and the supposed independence of adulthood, teenagers face important developmental tasks—carving out an identity, planning for the future, becoming more independent, and developing close relationships. Most teenagers accomplish these tasks with a minimum of trauma. Others, however, do not, For these teenagers, life at times seems overwhelming.

Concern over the problems associated with adolescence has caused an explosion in scientific research on the adolescent stage of development. Among the issues being examined by social scientists are the influences on and consequences of early sexual activity, the effects of drug use, and the factors contributing to the increase in teenage suicide.

Previewing Key Terms

Section 3 contains the following key terms: **drug, social integration**. Have a volunteer turn to the Glossary and read the definition of social integration aloud to the class. Then ask: "Why do you think the term 'social integration' is important in a section on the problems of adolescence?" After students have answered the question, direct the class to read the definition in context on textbook pages 140–141.

Introducing the Section

Have students recount stories they have heard from their parents, grandparents, or other adults about what life was like for teenagers of earlier generations. Then ask: "Is it more difficult to be a teenager today? Why or why not?" When no more comments are forthcoming, tell students that Section 3 will focus on some of the serious social problems facing teenagers in American society today.

Suggested Teaching Strategies

1. **Seeing Relationships (I)** After reviewing the information on teenage sexuality, have students identify the negative consequences of early sexual activity. Then show the film *AIDS: Nobody is Immune* (rental information can be found in the introductory section of this *Teacher's Manual*). Ask: "How serious a threat is AIDS to today's teenagers?" Lead students to see that everyone is vulnerable to this deadly disease.

2. **Understanding Tables (I)** Place Transparency 4, which focuses on drug use among high school seniors, on an overhead projector and ask the questions contained in the accompanying teacher's notes. Transparencies and accompanying teacher's notes are found in the *Teacher's Resource Binder*.

3. **Working in Groups (II, III)** Organize the class into three groups. Assign each group one of the following three topic areas: teenage sexual behavior, teenage drug use, or teenage suicide. Have each group collect and summarize current newspaper and magazine articles on their topic area. Then ask individuals from each group to read the summaries to the class. Use the summaries as a basis for class discussion.

Suggested Enrichment Activities

1. **Recognizing Inferences (I)** Have students complete the appropriate Developing Research Skills Worksheet, found in the *Teacher's Resource Binder*.

2. **Developing Interviewing Skills (III)** Ask interested students to interview personnel at various agencies geared toward helping teenagers deal with the problems of adolescence. Interviews should focus on the causes and solutions to specific problems (unwanted pregnancies, exposure to AIDS, alcoholism, crack use, or teenage suicide, for example). Have students report their findings to the class.

Suggested Assignments

1. **Using Sociological Imagination (I)** As homework, have students write an imaginative essay in which they describe what the teenage years will be like for their children. Have volunteers read their essays aloud to the class.

2. **Solving a Crossword Puzzle (I)** Have students complete the appropriate Understanding Sociological Ideas Worksheet, found in the *Teacher's Resource Binder*.

3. **★Interpreting the Visual Record: Interpreting Tables (I)** After reviewing the Developing Sociological Imagination feature on textbook pages 144–145, have students complete the Practicing the Skill section on page 145.

Closing the Section

Close the section by having students complete the appropriate Graphic Organizer Worksheet, found in the *Teacher's Resource Binder*.

Assessing the Section

Have students complete the Section 3 Review.

Answers to Section 3 Review *(page 143)*

Define *drug:* any substance that changes mood, behavior, or consciousness; ***social integration:*** degree of attachment people have to social groups or to society as a whole

1. **(a)** The rate of sexual activity among unmarried teenage girls between the ages of 15 and 19 increased from 29 percent in 1970 to 48 percent in 1990. **(b)** Generally, teenagers from low-income, one-parent families are more likely to have sexual relations at early ages. Similarly, nonreligious teenagers tend to hold more permissive attitudes toward sexuality and are more sexually active than are teenagers who actively practice their religion. Also, teenagers whose friends are sexually active have a greater likelihood of being sexually active themselves, and early sexual activity is associated with other risk-taking behaviors such as drug use and delinquency. The consequences of early sexual activity include a high risk of pregnancy and exposure to sexually transmitted diseases, including AIDS.
2. **(a)** The use of drugs, other than inhalants, has been in general decline among teenagers in recent years, but the United States still has the highest rate of drug use among teenagers of any industrialized nation. **(b)** Since 1979, the percentage of American teenagers who believe that drugs such as marijuana, cocaine, and cigarettes are harmful has increased significantly. Also, disapproval ratings among teenagers have increased significantly for marijuana and cigarettes. Disapproval ratings have remained fairly constant over the years for LSD, cocaine, heroin, amphetamines, barbiturates, and alcohol.
3. Sociologists believe that suicide can be understood by studying the structure of the society. A key element of social structure in regard to suicide rates is social integration—the degree to which individuals feel attached to groups within a society or to the society as a whole. Societies with very high and very low levels of social integration have higher suicide rates. In the former, individuals are so group-oriented that they will give up their own lives if they believe that it is in the best interest of the group. In the latter, suicide occurs because norms governing behavior become weak and unclear and some people find it difficult to live under these conditions. Teenagers sometimes are unsettled by the changes in expected and acceptable behavior that occurs with the transition to adulthood. Some teenagers choose suicide as the way of coping with uncertainty.

Answers to Developing Sociological Imagination *(pages 144–145)*

1. The purpose of the table is to show the unemployment rate among categories of teenagers aged 16 to 19.
2. The column headings indicate that the categories of teenagers being examined are males, females, whites, African Americans, and Hispanic Americans. The left-hand label indicates that the unemployment rate is being examined for the years 1986 through 1992.

3. The units of measurement used in the tables are percentages.
4. The data indicate that the unemployment rate for African Americans and Hispanic Americans has been significantly higher than that for whites in each of the years studied. The data also indicate that the unemployment rate for males tends to be slightly higher than the rate for females.
5. The most significant finding from the data is that African American teenagers, and to a lesser extent Hispanic American teenagers, consistently experience a high rate of unemployment. The data also show that the unemployment rate for teenagers declined steadily through the latter part of the 1980s, but rose again beginning in 1990.

Closing the Chapter

Have students complete the Chapter 6 Review Worksheet, found in the *Teacher's Resource Binder.*

Assessing the Chapter

Have students complete the Chapter 6 Review, found on page 146 of the *Pupil's Edition.*

Give students the Chapter 6 Form A Test and, if desired, the Chapter 6 Reteaching Worksheet and Form B Test, found in the *Teacher's Resource Binder.*

Answers to Chapter 6 Review *(page 146)*

Reviewing Sociological Terms

1. Puberty
2. homogamy
3. Anticipatory socialization
4. Adolescence
5. social integration

Thinking Critically about Sociology

1. Answers will vary, but students should address both parts of the question asked in regard to television programs.
2. **(a)** Willard Waller found that dating on the Pennsylvania State campus in the late 1920s and early 1930s had little to do with courtship or mate selection. The objectives of dating during that time apparently centered on excitement and status attainment. Dating partners were chosen on the basis of characteristics that determined social status (such as appearance and popularity) rather than on characteristics that made a good spouse. **(b)** More recent sociological research has failed to support Waller's conclusion that dating has little to do with mate selection. The recent research has found that recreation and status attainment are important in mate selection as well as in casual dating and that people look for the same characteristics in a dating partner that they look for in a marriage partner.
3. The Industrial Revolution contributed to the rise of dating in the following ways: (1) The amount of leisure time available to young people increased as they were freed from farm work. (2) Parental supervision over the activities of young people decreased

as the parents were employed outside the home. (3) Coeducational public schools increased the opportunity for interaction between the sexes. (4) The availability of telephones and automobiles gave young people the freedom to arrange dates and be together away from supervision.

4. The structured overview should match the format shown on textbook page 41.

5. **(a)** The relationship continuum refers to the development of commitment between dating partners as they move from casual dating to steady dating to engagement and, eventually, to marriage. **(b)** In the early stages of the relationship continuum, recreation and status attainment may be the most important functions of dating. As the degree of commitment in the relationship increases, the socialization and psychological fulfillment functions may become more important.

6. **(a)** According to the table on page 126, academic clubs have the highest rate of student participation. **(b)** According to the same table, African American students have the highest rate of participation in the school band.

7. **(a)** Traditional dating patterns were rigid, male controlled, and couple oriented. Contemporary patterns tend to be more spontaneous, egalitarian, and group centered. **(b)** Answers will vary.

Exercising Sociological Skills

1. Answers will vary, but students should provide content analyses of five short stories that have adolescents as main characters.

2. Television and films have played a major role in blurring the differences between adults and children. These media do this by providing children with access to adult situations and adult views on life.

3. The table on page 139 provides information concerning trends in drug use among high school seniors for every year since 1979. The data in the table reveal that, with the exception of inhalants, drug use among adolescents has been in general decline.

Extending Sociological Imagination

1. Answers will vary, but students should report on the social factors that affect teenage suicide rates.

2. Answers will vary, but students should research laws relating to juveniles, and compare the disposition of juveniles and adults in courts of law and the prison system.

Answers to Interpreting Primary Sources (page 147)

1. Concerning the causes of eating disorders, one theory holds that some young women feel abnormally pressured to be as thin as the "ideal" portrayed by the media. Another theory holds that defects in key chemical messengers in the brain contribute to the disorders' development or persistence.

2. Physical problems caused by eating disorders include fatigue, seizures, irregular heartbeat, thinner bones, damage to the stomach and esophagus, gum recession, and erosion of tooth enamel. Other effects include skin rashes, broken blood vessels in the face, and irregular menstrual cycles.

CHAPTER 7 *(pages 148–173)*

THE ADULT IN SOCIETY

SECTION 1
EARLY AND MIDDLE ADULTHOOD

SECTION 2
THE WORLD OF WORK

SECTION 3
THE LATER YEARS

Chapter Overview

Socialization does not end with childhood and adolescence. It continues throughout the life span. At every age, we are faced with new experiences and new demands that affect how we view ourselves and society. Our first paid job, marriage, our first child, a place of our own, various triumphs and disappointments, retirement, and our approaching death in old age add new dimensions to our sense of self and our relationships with others.

Social scientists are interested in the ways in which people adapt to the changing roles and statuses that accompany each stage of adult development. Topics of special importance in the area of adult development include how male development differs from and is similar to female development during early and middle adulthood, the world of work, and development during later life.

Chapter Objectives

At the conclusion of the chapter, students will be able to

1. Explain Daniel Levinson's theory of adult male development.
2. Explain Irene Frieze's theory of adult female development.
3. Discuss the nature of work in the United States.
4. Define labor force, and describe the changing composition of the labor force in the United States.
5. Identify the characteristics of life in later adulthood.

Introducing the Chapter

Prior to assigning the reading of Chapter 7, write the following statement on the chalkboard: "Socialization is a lifelong process." Next write the following headings high on the chalkboard: Early Adulthood (ages 17 through 39), Middle Adulthood (ages 40 through 59), and Late Adulthood (ages 60 and over). Under each heading make a column for males and a column for females. Ask the class to indicate 5 to 10 new experiences or demands that are common to each age category. Some experiences or demands will apply to men, others will apply to women, and many will apply to both. Use the lists as the basis of a class discussion on why socialization is a lifelong process. At the end of the session, have students copy the lists into their study notebooks for use later in the chapter.

Chapter 7 Suggested Lesson Plans

Day 1	**Suggested Procedures:** Introducing the Chapter; Section 1 Previewing Key Terms; Introducing the Section **Materials:** PE: pp. 148–155; TM: pp. 43–44
Day 2	**Suggested Procedures:** Section 1 Strategies and Assignments **Materials:** PE: pp. 150–155; TM: pp. 44–45; TRB: Assorted Worksheets
Day 3	**Suggested Procedures:** Section 2 Previewing Key Terms; Introducing the Section; Strategies and Assignments **Materials:** PE: pp. 156–161; TM: pp. 45–47; TRB: Worksheet
Day 4	**Suggested Procedures:** Section 3 Previewing Key Terms; Introducing the Section; Strategies and Assignments **Materials:** PE: pp. 162–171; TM: pp. 47–48; TRB: Transparency 5, Assorted Worksheets
Day 5	**Suggested Procedures:** Closing the Chapter; Assessing the Chapter **Materials:** PE: pp. 172–173; TM: pp. 48–49; TRB: Review Worksheet, Tests, Reteaching Worksheet

SECTION 1 *(pages 150–155)*

EARLY AND MIDDLE ADULTHOOD

Section Overview

Because life patterns differ somewhat for men and women, some social scientists have chosen to focus on a single sex when examining adult development. Daniel Levinson and his colleagues, for instance, have explored the developmental process of adult males. On the basis of interviews with 40 men between the ages of 35 and 45, Levinson has distinguished three eras in adult male development: early adulthood, middle adulthood, and late adulthood. Each of these eras is divided into a series of transitional and stable periods.

Irene Frieze, on the other hand, has proposed a slightly different developmental sequence for women. According to Frieze, marriage and children play a major role in the adult life of women. In recognition of this fact, Frieze

suggests a three-stage developmental process for women: leaving the family, entering the adult world, and reentering the adult world once the children reach school age.

Previewing Key Terms

Section 1 contains the following key terms: **life structure, early adulthood, middle adulthood, late adulthood, novice phase, mentor**. Have students prepare riddles, using the key terms as answers. For example: "I am the era of adulthood spanning the ages 40 through 59. What am I?" *(middle adulthood)* Tell students to write their riddles on one side of the paper and the answers on the other side. Completed sets of riddles can be exchanged among students and answered. Then have students put their papers in their study notebooks for later review.

Introducing the Section

Have students retrieve the lists they prepared during the Introducing the Chapter activity. Tell students to take a few minutes to review the lists and recall the class discussion of socialization as a lifelong process. Then instruct students to use this information to write one paragraph that characterizes adult male development and one paragraph that characterizes adult female development. Ask volunteers to read their paragraphs aloud to the class, and have the class discuss the differences and similarities between male and female development. Then tell students that Section 1 will introduce them to theories that have been proposed to explain the adult development of men and women.

Suggested Teaching Strategies

1. **Setting Goals (I)** Have students take out a sheet of paper and write the following headings across the top of the page: Ages 17 Through 39; Ages 40 Through 59; Ages 60 and Over. Instruct students to write down five goals they hope to achieve during each phase of life, and a brief statement as to how they will go about achieving each goal. Have volunteers share their goals with the class, and ask the class to consider the following questions: Do the goals of men and women differ? Do all people in the class seem to share the same goals? Why or why not?

2. **Working in Groups (I, II)** After discussing Levinson's theory of adult male development, organize the class into five groups—one group for each of the first five periods of male development. Ask each group to interview several men whose ages place them within the group's assigned period. Based on their interviews, have the group construct a life structure for each subject and determine whether that life structure supports or contradicts Levinson's findings. Discuss the findings in class.

3. **Using Sociological Imagination (I, II)** After discussing Frieze's theory of adult female development, organize the class into three groups—one group for each phase of development. Ask each group to hypothesize what affect changing work patterns, delayed marriage, delayed parenthood, and single

parenthood might have on the characteristics of their phase. Have each group report their ideas to the class.

Suggested Enrichment Activities

1. **Organizing Ideas (I)** Have students complete the appropriate Graphic Organizer Worksheet, found in the *Teacher's Resource Binder*.
2. **Making Oral Presentations (III)** Select seven interested students to prepare oral presentations on material from the seven sections of the book *Passages: Predictable Crises of Adult Life* by Gail Sheehy.

Suggested Assignments

1. **Classifying Ideas (I)** As homework, have students complete the appropriate Critical Skills Mastery Worksheet, found in the *Teacher's Resource Binder*.
2. **Interpreting Primary Sources (I)** Ask students to read the Interpreting Primary Sources feature on textbook page 173 and then answer the source review questions.

Closing the Section

Close the section by asking students to consider the following question: "With all of the changes that have been occurring in women's roles in recent years, can women's development now be better explained by Levinson's theory rather than Frieze's theory?"

Assessing the Section

Have students complete the Section 1 Review.

Answers to Section 1 Review *(page 155)*

Define *life structure:* combination of statuses, roles, activities, goals, values, beliefs, and life circumstances that characterize an individual; ***novice phase:*** first three periods of the early adulthood era; ***mentor:*** someone who fosters an individual's development by believing in the person, sharing the person's dreams, and helping the person achieve these dreams

Identify *Daniel Levinson:* psychologist who conducted a long-term study to determine the developmental stages through which men pass during adulthood; ***Becoming One's Own Man:*** conscious effort by men in their 30s to establish their own identities; ***Irene Frieze:*** researcher who studied adult female development

1. **(a)** The three eras of adulthood are early adulthood (ages 17 through 39), middle adulthood (ages 40 through 59), and late adulthood (ages 60 and over). **(b)** The first stage in men's development is the early adult transition (ages 17 through 22). The most important tasks facing men in this period are leaving home and emotionally separating from parents. The second stage is entering the adult world (ages 23 through 27). During this stage, young men are expected to explore a variety of relationships and career opportunities and to become responsible members of society. The third stage is the age 30 transition (ages 28 through 32), a time when men examine the choices they have made,

reevaluate their commitments, and often make changes in what directions their lives will take. The fourth stage is the settling down period (ages 33 through 39). During this period, men try to establish themselves in society, usually in the work world, form true commitments to family, friends, and other valued roles and relationships, and establish their own identities apart from mentors. The fifth stage is the mid-life transition (ages 40 through 44), characterized by self-examination. Men come to realize that their earlier dreams were beyond fulfillment and reformulate them along more realistic lines.

2. The three phases of adult female development are leaving the family, entering the adult world, and reentering the adult world. The first period of adulthood for women begins with leaving the family home, becoming emotionally independent from parents, and making a life plan. In many cases, the life plan is largely determined by marriage. The emphasis on marriage distinguishes women's development from men's development. The second phase of women's development involves entering the adult world. In the United States today, many women work before marriage and continue to do so after marriage. Among about half of these women, however, work stops temporarily with the birth of children. This interruption of employment is another distinguishing factor of women's adult development. The final stage begins when women reenter the work world or reevaluate their life roles once children reach school age.

SECTION 2 *(pages 156–161)*

THE WORLD OF WORK

Section Overview

For both men and women, participation in the labor force plays a significant role during early and middle adulthood. In recent decades, the composition of the labor force has undergone many changes. Among these changes are increased participation by women, increased participation by minority workers, and better educated workers.

Being unemployed is one of the most difficult experiences of adulthood. The unemployment rate in the United States varies by factors such as age, sex, race, and cultural background. Adding to problems of unemployment are changes in the types of jobs held by American workers. In recent years, the economy has shifted away from manufacturing and toward the provision of services and the processing of information. It is expected that this trend will continue into the future.

Previewing Key Terms

Section 2 contains the following key terms: **labor force, profession, unemployment, unemployment rate**. Have students look up each of these terms in the Glossary. Then instruct them to write four sentences about the world of work, each sentence containing one of the key terms. Students should place their sentences in their study notebooks for later review.

Introducing the Section

Have students write a short essay entitled "What I Expect from My Future Career." Have volunteers read their essays aloud to the class, and have the class consider the following questions: "Do high school students seem to share the same expectations about their future careers? Why or why not?" "How realistic do these expectations appear to be?" Then have students place their essays in their study notebooks for use later in the section, and assign the reading of Section 2.

Suggested Teaching Strategies

1. **Working in Groups (I, II)** Organize the class into nine groups and give each group a slip of paper with one of the nine occupational categories written on it. Caution the groups to share this information only with the members of their own group. Tell the groups that they are to write five riddles describing the type of work done by people who fall into their occupational category. For example: "I cut down the trees used to make paper and furniture. Who am I, and what is my occupational category?" (lumberjack—farming, forestry, and fishing) Then have the groups, alternating groups one riddle at a time, read a riddle for the class to answer.
2. **Conducting Research (I, II)** After reviewing the information in the section, invite the manager of an employment agency to speak to the class about job prospects for the near and distant future. Have students prepare a list of questions to ask the speaker. As a follow-up assignment, ask interested students to research the educational requirements, work setting, salary, and duties associated with specific jobs. Have these students report their findings to the class.
3. **Developing Interviewing Skills (III)** Ask students to read the Applying Sociology feature on textbook pages 160–161. Then have students conduct interviews, following the guidelines presented in the feature.

Suggested Enrichment Activities

1. **Classifying Information (I)** Have students complete the appropriate Developing Research Skills Worksheet, found in the *Teacher's Resource Binder*.
2. **Seeing Relationships (III)** Have interested students research the ways in which the shift from a manufacturing economy to a service economy has affected employment opportunities in the 1980s and 1990s. Instruct students to examines issues such as job layoffs, the need for worker retraining, changing educational requirements, and high- and low-growth occupations.

Suggested Assignments

1. **Evaluating Ideas (I)** Have students retrieve the essays entitled "What I Expect from My Future Career" that were written for the Introducing the Section

activity. Ask them to think of what they have learned during the study of Section 2 as they reread their essays. Then, as homework, have students determine whether, if they wrote these essays now, the essays would change in any way. If so, what would change and why? Finally, have students edit their original essays to reflect what they have learned from the section.
2. **Using Sociological Imagination (I)** Ask students to consider what jobs today did not exist 25 years ago. Then have them write a paragraph describing a new job they think will exist 25 years in the future. Ask volunteers to read their paragraphs aloud to the class.

Closing the Section

Close the section by having students prepare a 10-question quiz on the material in the section. Students should write their questions on one side of the page and the answers on the other side. Then have them exchange papers and complete the quiz. If students have difficulty with any of the material covered in the questions, ask volunteers to provide clarification.

Assessing the Section

Have students complete the Section 2 Review.

Answers to Section 2 Review *(page 159)*

Define *labor force:* all individuals 16 years of age and older who are employed in paid positions or who are seeking paid employment; ***profession:*** high-status occupation that requires specialized skills obtained through formal education; ***unemployment:*** situation that occurs when people do not have jobs but are actively seeking employment; ***unemployment rate:*** percentage of the civilian labor force that is unemployed but actively seeking employment

1. Several major changes have occurred in the composition of the labor force in recent years. First, the proportion of the labor force made up of women has increased dramatically and is now over 45 percent. Second, the percentage of the work force made up of minorities has been on the rise. Finally, the average educational attainment level of the work force has been increasing.
2. Examples given by students should be taken from the listing of occupational categories found on textbook pages 157–158.
3. The following are among the most important determinants of job satisfaction: having health insurance and other benefits; having interesting work; having job security; having the opportunity to learn new skills; being able to work independently; and having a job that helps other people.
4. **(a)** In 1900, 40 percent of workers were involved in farming, another 40 percent were employed in manufacturing, and the remaining 20 percent were involved in professional, clerical, or service jobs. Today, less than 3 percent of workers are involved in farming, less than 30 percent are involved in non-farm physical labor, and more than 70 percent work

in professional, office, sales, and service jobs. **(b)** According to the Bureau of Labor Statistics, the occupations that will have the greatest percentage increase from now until the year 2000 are as follows: registered nurses; truck drivers; waiters and waitresses; receptionists and information clerks; secondary school teachers; computer systems analysts and programmers; child care workers; accountants and auditors; home health aides; lawyers; marketing, advertising, and public relations workers; physicians; automotive mechanics; medical secretaries; and electricians.

Answers to Applying Sociology *(pages 160–161)*

Answers will vary, but students should conduct interviews with several people to find out about their work, and interpret these findings carefully.

SECTION 3 *(pages 162–169)*

THE LATER YEARS

Section Overview

Because people now are living longer, it has become impossible to view the late adulthood era as a single period of development. Life at age 65 is very different from life at age 85. Thus gerontologists have placed the elderly population into three categories: the young-old, the middle-old, and the old-old. Developmental issues vary depending on which stage of late adulthood is under consideration.

Previewing Key Terms

Section 3 contains the following key terms: **gerontology, social gerontology, young-old, middle-old, old-old, Alzheimer's disease, dependency, life expectancy**. Ask students to create a Word Search puzzle using these terms. Then have them exchange papers and complete the puzzles.

Introducing the Section

Introduce the section by showing the film *Grandparents*, in which teenagers, adults, and young children share stories about their grandparents. Then tell students to imagine that it is the year 2060 and they are watching a film in which their own grandchildren are sharing stories about them. Have students write the stories they imagine their grandchildren will tell.

Suggested Teaching Strategies

1. **Summarizing Ideas (I)** After reviewing the developmental issues of late adulthood, have students summarize this information for each of the three older age groups discussed in the section.
2. **Understanding Charts (I)** Place Transparency 5, which focuses on adapting patterns in later adulthood, on an overhead projector and ask the questions

contained in the accompanying teacher's notes. Transparencies and accompanying teacher's notes are found in the *Teacher's Resource Binder*.
3. **Understanding Ideas (I)** Ask students to read the Case Study feature on textbook page 167 and then answer the following questions: (a) What is the expected role behavior of widows? (b) In what ways does widowhood differ for working-class and middle-class women?

Suggested Enrichment Activities

1. **Exploring Cross-Cultural Perspectives (I)** Have students complete the appropriate Cross-Cultural Perspectives Worksheet, found in the *Teacher's Resource Binder*.
2. **Conducting Library Research (III)** Ask interested students to write research reports on some aspect of one of the following developmental issues of late adulthood: adjustment to retirement, physical and mental functioning, or dealing with dependency and death. Have the students share their reports with the class.

Suggested Assignments

1. **Practicing Content Analysis (I)** As homework, have students perform a content analysis on an evening's worth of television commercials. Instruct them to record the number of commercials shown, the number of commercials that contain elderly characters, and the types of products being advertised in the commercials containing elderly characters. Tell students to use this information to write a paragraph describing how advertisers characterize the elderly. Have volunteers read their paragraphs aloud to the class and have the class debate the validity of this characterization.
2. **★Intrepreting the Visual Record: Understanding Graphs (I)** After discussing the material covered in the Developing Sociological Imagination feature on textbook pages 170–171, have students complete the Practicing the Skill section on page 171.

Closing the Section

Close the section by having students complete the appropriate Understanding Sociological Ideas Worksheet, found in the *Teacher's Resource Binder*.

Assessing the Section

Have students complete the Section 3 Review.

Answers to Section 3 Review *(page 169)*

Define *gerontology:* scientific study of the processes and phenomena of aging; ***social gerontology:*** study of the nonphysical aspects of aging; ***Alzheimer's disease:*** organic condition that results in the progressive destruction of brain cells; ***dependency:*** shift from being an independent adult to being dependent on others for physical and financial assistance

1. **(a)** Gerontologists place the aged population into three groups: the young-old, the middle-old, and the

old-old. **(b)** The young-old are ages 65 through 74, the middle-old are ages 75 through 84, and the old-old are ages 85 and older.

2. For the young-old, adjustment to retirement is one of the most important developmental issues. Issues surrounding mental and physical decline and death are of greater importance to the middle-old and the old-old.

3. **(a)** One of the opportunities associated with late adulthood is the greater availability of leisure time. Many older people use the time to travel and to develop hobbies that they had not had time for earlier in their lives. Other older adults become active in politics or start a second career as a volunteer or part-time worker. **(b)** Planning ahead for retirement helps people take advantage of the opportunities available in late adulthood. Planning for retirement involves financial planning, broadening one's interests, developing hobbies, taking care of one's health, and improving one's physical fitness.

Answers to Developing Sociological Imagination *(pages 170–171)*

1. bar graph
2. Marital Status of Men and Women Aged 65 and Over
3. Percent; Single, Married, Widowed, Divorced
4. Among people aged 65 and over, far more men than women are married. In this same age group, far more women than men are widowed.

Closing the Chapter

Have students complete the Chapter 7 Review Worksheet, found in the *Teacher's Resource Binder*.

Assessing the Chapter

Have students complete the Chapter 7 Review, found on page 172 of the *Pupil's Edition*.

Give students the Chapter 7 Form A Test and, if desired, the Chapter 7 Reteaching Worksheet and Form B Test, found in the *Teacher's Resource Binder*.

Answers to Chapter 7 Review *(page 172)*

Reviewing Sociological Terms

1. profession
2. social gerontology
3. Life expectancy
4. unemployment rate

Thinking Critically about Sociology

1. **(a)** People change jobs much more frequently than they change careers. Workers under 35 look for a job once every 18 months, while those over 35 do so once every three years. People who have careers, on the other hand, change fields only three to five times during their lives. **(b)** Changing careers means that workers go into a new field for which their previous experience does not qualify them. Changing jobs, on the other hand, means changing employers but may not involve changing to a radically different type of work. Even if it does, however, the retraining involved is not as extensive as would be required for a change of career.

2. **(a)** The three largest occupational sectors indicated by the table on page 157 are managers and professionals; technical, sales, and administrative support; and operators, fabricators, and laborers. **(b)** The three smallest sectors as indicated by the table are service occupations; precision, production, craft, and repair; and farming, forestry, and fishing.

3. **(a)** The three phases of adult female development are leaving the family, entering the adult world, and entering the adult world again. **(b)** Among women, the life planning that occurs in the first stage often is centered around marriage. For men, planning typically is centered around work. In the second stage, about half of all American women who have children leave the labor force temporarily. Men rarely do so. Finally, women enter the adult world again when they once again begin to plan life goals. Generally, this occurs in the early 30s. Women going through this stage are similar to men in their 20s. Ironically, many wives start gearing up for careers at the point when their husbands may be de-emphasizing their careers.

4. **(a)** As an individual ages, body cells begin to die. Muscles and tissues shrink, the skin develops wrinkles, and the entire body begins to lose weight. Strength and endurance begin to decrease. The nervous system functions more slowly and less accurately. Hair turns to gray or white as root cells produce less pigment. Most people, however, remain mentally alert. **(b)** Earlier research assumed that loss of intellectual ability was an inevitable part of the aging process. The earlier research conclusions were based on intelligence tests that were given to people of all ages. Young people always scored higher on tests. Psychologists now realize that two factors may have been distorting the earlier research. First, the intelligence tests were relevant primarily to young people and may have contained items less familiar to older adults. And second, young people tend to have more formal education than the elderly. Psychologists now are beginning to compare an individual's scores at different points in time. This provides a more accurate indicator of the changes in intellectual abilities that accompany aging.

5. Sociological research reveals that the loss of the work role affects a much smaller number of retired people than generally is believed. Most people adjust to not working within the first three months of their retirement. Retirement generally does not produce a sudden drop in psychological well-being. Those people who have trouble adjusting typically are those who feel they did not accomplish their work goals or those who have not developed nonwork-related interests. Additionally, people who are forced to retire are less satisfied with retirement than are those who retire voluntarily. Research has found that satisfaction with retirement is associated with good health and financial security.

6. The structured overview should match the format shown on textbook page 41.

7. (a) The first personality type identified by the Kansas City study is the integrated personality. Three adapting patterns associated with this are the reorganizers, the focused, and the disengaged. The second personality type is the armored personality, which includes two types of adapting patterns: the holders and the constructors. The third personality type is the passive-dependent personality. The typical adapting patterns for this type are the succorance-seeking pattern and the apathy pattern. The final personality type is the unintegrated personality. The primary adapting pattern for this personality is the disorganized adapting pattern. **(b)** People with integrated personalities tend to find a high level of satisfaction in retirement regardless of their particular adapting style. Those people with armored personalities find adjustment to retirement more difficult. People with passive-dependent personalities can find some satisfaction if they have someone on whom to depend. Adapting to old age is most difficult for those people with unintegrated personalities.

8. The nature of work in the United States has changed from primarily manufacturing to primarily the provision of services. The composition of the American labor force has changed in three important ways: First, the proportion of women has increased. Second, the proportion of minorities has increased. Third, the average educational attainment of the labor force has increased.

Exercising Sociological Skills

1. (a) Positive statements: "It's fulfilling"; "work is an essential part of being alive"; "I want it to be just right." Negative statements: "The pressure. The constant rush to get things done"; "you never see the end result of it"; "there never seemed to be any end to it." **(b)** An enjoyable job is one that is challenging, that engages the worker. It is one in which the worker can control his or her pace and can see the end product of his or her efforts.

2. The characteristics of widowhood discussed in the feature include a crisis of identity, economic problems, and, often, loneliness. Middle-class women tend to do better financially but are more likely to experience an identity crisis.

3. The graph on textbook page 157 is a bar graph. The bar graph is entitled "Unemployment Rate by Social Category, 1992." The vertical axis is divided into sex, race, and age categories. The horizontal axis shows the unemployment rate in percents. Between the sexes, unemployment is higher for males. Among the races, unemployment is highest for African Americans. The age group 20–24 has the highest unemployment rate.

Extending Sociological Imagination

Answers will vary, but students' charts should be modeled after the chart shown on textbook page 171.

Answers to Interpreting Primary Sources *(page 171)*

Women described their lives in terms of the people with whom they had had relationships. Men, on the other hand, talked of their career accomplishments.

CHAPTER 8 *(pages 174–199)*

DEVIANCE AND SOCIAL CONTROL

SECTION 1
DEVIANCE

SECTION 2
CRIME

Chapter Overview

Deviance and crime are everyday events in modern society. High levels of deviance are disruptive to society. Low levels, however, can serve positive functions. Deviance can help to unify the group, clarify norms, diffuse tension, identify problems, and provide jobs.

Crime is a special category of deviance. Crimes can be grouped into five categories: violent crime, crime against property, victimless crime, white-collar crime, and organized crime. Although violent crimes are a small percentage of all crimes, they produce the most fear in members of society.

Once a crime is committed and reported, it falls under the jurisdiction of the criminal justice system. The main components of the criminal justice system are the police, the courts, and corrections.

Chapter Objectives

At the conclusion of the chapter, students will be able to

1. Define deviance, and identify the social functions of deviance.
2. Discuss the theories that have been developed to explain deviance.
3. Define crime, and explain why there are problems with the collection of crime statistics.
4. Identify five general categories of crime, and recognize which crimes fall into each general category.
5. Describe the characteristics of the American criminal justice system.

Introducing the Chapter

Prior to assigning the reading of the chapter, ask students to give examples of deviant acts. As students name the acts, write them on the chalkboard. Without indicating that you are doing so, place criminal acts in one column and noncriminal acts in another column. Once the lists are complete, count the number of acts in each list. Most likely, the list of criminal acts will be the longer list. Point out that crime and deviance are not synonymous. Crime is only one form of deviance.

Next, define deviance and stress the fact that deviance is socially determined. The social nature of deviance can be reinforced by citing cross-cultural or historical variations in what is considered deviant. Note that in the United States, for instance, it is acceptable for women to dress in a wide range of clothes, freedom to criticize the government is a guaranteed right, and the defense of democracy is a sign of patriotism. In many Middle East nations, on the other hand, there are strong norms against women wearing Western-style clothes. Similarly, criticizing the government in totalitarian nations often is considered a criminal offense. And in some non-democratic nations, such as the People's Republic of China, pro-democracy demonstrators are considered to be enemies of the state.

Chapter 8 Suggested Lesson Plans

Day 1	**Suggested Procedures:** Introducing the Chapter; Section 1 Previewing Key Terms; Introducing the Section **Materials:** PE: pp. 174–186; TM: pp. 49–50
Day 2	**Suggested Procedures:** Section 1 Strategies and Assignments **Materials:** PE: pp. 176–186; TM: pp. 50–51; TRB: Transparency 6, Assorted Worksheets
Day 3	**Suggested Procedures:** Section 2 Previewing Key Terms; Introducing the Section; Strategies and Assignments **Materials:** PE: pp. 187–197; TM: pp. 51–53; TRB: Transparency 7, Assorted Worksheets
Day 4	**Suggested Procedures:** Closing the Chapter; Assessing the Chapter **Materials:** PE: pp. 198–199; TM: pp. 53–54; TRB: Review Worksheet, Tests, Reteaching Worksheet
Day 5	**Suggested Procedures:** Closing the Unit; Assessing the Unit **Materials:** PE: pp. 200–201; TM: pp. 54–56; TRB: Review Worksheet, Tests, Reteaching Worksheet

SECTION 1 *(pages 176–186)*

DEVIANCE

Section Overview

Because there are so many norms existing in society, occasional violations are unavoidable. But not all norm violations are considered deviant acts. It is society that decides which acts will be labeled as deviant.

Several theories have been developed to explain deviant behavior. Each theory takes a slightly different perspective. Among the major theories of deviance are cultural-transmission theory, structural-strain theory, control theory, conflict theory, and labeling theory.

Previewing Key Terms

Section 1 contains the following key terms: **deviance, stigma, cultural-transmission theory, differential association, structural-strain theory, anomie, control theory, labeling theory, primary deviance, secondary deviance**. Write these terms on the chalkboard. Then have students develop a definition for each term, based on what they think it means. Write the definitions on the chalkboard and ask a volunteer to record them on a piece of paper. After students have read Section 1, ask them to revise the definitions based on the material presented in the section.

Introducing the Section

Begin by asking a volunteer to define the term *deviance*. Then have the class consider the following question: "Since people are socialized to accept the norms of society, why does deviance exist?" Write the students' answers on the chalkboard and group them under the headings Cultural-Transmission, Structural-Strain, Control, Conflict, Labeling (guide students toward sociological rather than psychological explanations of deviance and continue until each of the five headings is on the chalkboard). Then tell students that these five headings reflect the most important sociological theories concerning the existence of deviance, the focus of Section 1.

Suggested Teaching Strategies

1. **Summarizing Information (I)** After reviewing the five theories of deviance outlined in the section, ask students to close their notebooks and summarize the main points of each theory. The summaries can be used as a quiz.
2. **Learning from Charts (I)** Place Transparency 6, which focuses on Merton's structural-strain theory of deviance, on an overhead projector and ask the questions contained in the accompanying teacher's notes. Transparencies and accompanying teacher's notes are found in the *Teacher's Resource Binder.*
3. **Debating Idea (I, II)** To help students understand the significance of stigma, have selected volunteers debate the following statement: "All cars belonging to people convicted of driving under the influence of alcohol should carry a decal that reads 'Warning: Drunk Driver.'"

Suggested Enrichment Activities

1. **Exploring Cross-Cultural Perspectives (I)** Have students complete the appropriate Cross-Cultural Perspectives Worksheet, found in the *Teacher's Resource Binder.*
2. **Observing Social Norms (II, III)** Ask the class to read the Applying Sociology feature on textbook pages 180–181. Then organize the class into two-member groups. Instruct one member of each group to conduct the experiments outlined in the feature.

Instruct the other member of each group to act as a detached observer, taking notes on each encounter. Have interested students develop additional experiments to test the effects of norm violations. Discuss the research findings in class.

Suggested Assignments

1. **Organizing Information (I)** As homework, have students complete the appropriate Critical Skills Mastery Worksheet, found in the *Teacher's Resource Binder.*
2. **Writing Creatively (I)** To reinforce the point that low levels of deviance have positive social functions, have students write an imaginative short story about a society in which norm violations never occur. Ask volunteers to read their stories aloud to the class for class discussion.
3. **Exploring Multicultural Perspectives (III)** Have interested students conduct library research to find examples of subcultural or cross-cultural practices that are considered normal within that subculture or culture, but that might be seen as deviant by the majority of Americans. Help students to view these practices within the context of cultural relativism.

Closing the Section

Close the section by having students write position papers stating which of the five theories of deviance they believe offers the best explanation for the existence of deviance. Caution students to provide sound reasons for their positions. Have volunteers read their papers to the class for class discussion.

Assessing the Section

Have students complete the Section 1 Review.

Answers to Applying Sociology *(pages 180–181)*

Answers will vary, but students should observe norms in sufficient number to be able to discuss their findings in class.

Answers to Section 1 Review *(page 186)*

Define *deviance:* behavior that violates significant social norms; ***differential association:*** proportion of associations a person has with deviant versus nondeviant individuals; ***primary deviance:*** nonconformity that goes undetected by those in authority; ***secondary deviance:*** nonconformity that results in the individual being labeled as deviant and accepting the label as true

1. Each society determines which norm violations are considered deviant. Some norm violations are unavoidable. Other norm violations are considered deviant in one situation but not in others.
2. **(a)** A stigma is a mark of social disgrace that sets the deviant apart from the rest of society. **(b)** Various types of stigma have been used throughout history to distinguish deviants from nondeviants. The ancient Greeks, for example, cut or burned signs onto the bodies of criminals as warnings that these people were to be avoided. Other signs of stigma used his-

torically include chain gangs, public punishments, and public executions. In the United States today, prisoners wear uniforms and are assigned numbers as visible signs of disgrace.

3. The five functions of deviance are to unify the group by drawing clear boundaries between conformers and nonconformers; to clarify norms by showing societal members which behaviors are acceptable and which behaviors are unacceptable; to diffuse tension by allowing people to vent anger and frustration through minor norm violations; to identify social problems, in that a large number of norm violations indicate that something in the social system needs to be changed; and to provide jobs for many people, such as judges, lawyers, police officers, prison guards, and crime reporters.
4. Cultural-transmission theory holds that deviant behavior is learned through social interaction with persons who are engaging in deviant acts. Structural-strain theory explains deviance as attempts to attain certain goals by individuals who do not have access to legitimate means. Control theory sees deviance as a natural occurrence and conformity as the result of effective social control. Conflict theory holds that competition and social inequality lead to deviance. In essence, those people with power commit deviant acts in order to maintain their power, whereas those people without power commit deviant acts either to obtain economic rewards or because they have low self-esteem and feelings of powerlessness. Labeling theory focuses on how people come to be regarded as deviant, given that all people commit some type of deviant acts at some point or another. Labeling theory holds that some norm violations are considered insignificant and those who commit them are not labeled as deviant. Only people who violate important norms are regarded as deviant.

SECTION 2 *(pages 187–195)*

CRIME

Section Overview

Sociologists recognize five categories of crime: violent crime, crime against property, victimless crime, white-collar crime, and organized crime. Once a crime has been committed and reported, it falls under the jurisdiction of the criminal justice system. The criminal justice system is made up of the police, the courts, and corrections. A special category of the criminal justice system in the United States is the juvenile justice system. The juvenile justice system is designed to serve offenders who are under the age of 18.

Previewing Key Terms

Section 2 contains the following key terms: **crime, white-collar crime, crime syndicate, plea bargaining, corrections, recidivism**. Have students look up each of these terms in the Glossary. Ask students to prepare a fill-in-the-blank quiz using these terms. Have students write their quiz items on one side of the page and their answers on the other side. Then have students exchange papers and complete the quizzes.

Introducing the Section

Have students list ways in which they try to prevent crime. Possible answers include: locking all doors and windows at home, chaining bicycles, walking in groups late at night, and so on. Then ask: "Is crime a more significant social problem now than when your parents were teenagers? Why or why not?" Then request five volunteers to prepare a panel discussion in which students speak for the following characters: a police officer, a judge, a parole officer, a prison warden, and a concerned citizen. Encourage students to suggest ways in which each of these individuals might help to control crime.

Suggested Teaching Strategies

1. **Analyzing Newspaper Articles (I)** Review with the class the definition of crime and the characteristics of each of the five categories of crime discussed in the section. Then instruct students to collect newspaper articles about the commission of various crimes. Have students bring the articles to class to use as the basis of a discussion of crime in the United States.
2. **Learning from Graphs (I)** Place Transparency 7, which focuses on arrests by type of crime, on an overhead projector and ask the questions contained in the accompanying teacher's notes. Transparencies and accompanying teacher's notes are found in the *Teacher's Resource Binder*.
3. **Writing Creatively (I, II)** Have each student choose a type of crime and write a short story that involves a crime being committed. When students have finished, ask volunteers to read their stories aloud. Then have the class use what it has learned in the section to identify the kind of crime being committed in each story.
4. **Debating Ideas (I, II)** Have selected students debate the following statement: "Juvenile offenders who commit serious crimes should be tried according to adult laws."

Suggested Enrichment Activities

1. **Interpreting Tables (I)** Have students complete the appropriate Developing Research Skills Worksheet, found in the *Teacher's Resource Binder*.
2. **Conducting Field Research (II, III)** Plan a trip to a local jail or prison. Before going on the field trip, have selected students prepare research papers on prison life. After the field trip, have the selected students present their papers to the class. Follow the presentations with a discussion of how the information contained in the reports was supported by or contradicted by first-hand observation.

Suggested Assignments

1. **Organizing Ideas (I)** As homework, have students complete the appropriate Graphic Organizer Worksheet, found in the *Teacher's Resource Binder*.

2. **★Thinking about Sociology: Interpreting Statistics (I)** After discussing the material covered in the Developing Sociological Imagination feature on textbook pages 196–197, have students complete the Practicing the Skill section on page 197.
3. **Conducting a Poll (I, II)** Have students ask five people (friends, family members, neighbors) the following question: "What do you think is the primary cause of teenage crime?" Have students report their findings in class and tally the results. Is there one cause that appears most often? Have students speculate why this may be so.

Closing the Section

Close the section by having students complete the appropriate Understanding Sociological Ideas Worksheet, found in the *Teacher's Resource Binder*.

Assessing the Section

Have students complete the Section 2 Review.

Answers to Section 2 Review *(page 195)*

Identify *crime*: any act that is labeled as such by those in authority, is prohibited by law, and is punishable by the government; ***crime syndicate:*** large-scale organization of professional criminals that controls some vice or business through violence or the threat of violence; ***recidivism:*** repeated criminal behavior

1. There are several problems with official crime statistics. First, not all complaints handled by the police are officially reported. Offenses considered less serious by the police tend not to be reported. Second, individuals are less likely to report a crime if friends or family members are involved. Third, police are more likely to report serious crimes if the victims are from a higher social class. Fourth, police are more likely to file a report if the victims are polite and respectful. Finally, victims of sexual assault are less likely to report these crimes to the police.
2. The five types of crime are violent crime, crime against property, victimless crime, white-collar crime, and organized crime. Violent crime, which includes murder, forcible rape, robbery, and aggravated assault, makes up a very small percentage of all crimes, but only because the rate of other types of crime is so high. Crime against property involves either stealing someone else's property or intentionally causing damage to it. Included in this category are burglary, larceny, motor vehicle theft, and arson. These crimes are much more common than violent crimes. Victimless crime, such as prostitution, gambling, illegal drug use, and vagrancy, are labeled as such because it is the person who is committing the crime who is most directly affected by the crime. White-collar crime involves high-status individuals who commit illegal acts in the course of their professional lives. Examples of white-collar crime include fraud, tax evasion, and embezzlement. Organized crime involves illegal acts committed by large-scale organizations of professional criminals. Such activities

include drug trafficking, illegal gambling, unfair labor practices, and cheating on income tax returns.

3. **(a)** Sociologists generally attribute changes in the crime rate to changes in the composition of the population. The age composition of a population is of particular importance, since the majority of crimes are committed by people under the age of 25. As the size of the under-25 population increases or decreases, crime rates typically change in the same direction. **(b)** In the 1980s and 1990s, an additional factor—illegal drug use—became involved in an increase in the crime rate.

4. **(a)** The three main components of the criminal justice system are the police, the courts, and corrections. The police have the most immediate control over who is arrested. Not everyone who is involved in criminal behavior is arrested. The police consider the severity of the crime, the wishes of the victim, the attitude of the suspect, the presence of bystanders, and the race of the offender. The courts take control of the process after the arrest. Ninety percent of all criminal cases never reach the courts because of plea bargaining. Individuals who are found guilty of a criminal offense are subject to corrections, or punishment. Corrections serve four basic functions: retribution, deterrence, rehabilitation, and social protection. **(b)** The existence of a separate justice system for juveniles is justified by the belief that people under the age of 18 cannot be expected to be as responsible as adults. It has been thought that juvenile offenders need a special, more considerate kind of treatment. In actuality, however, the separate justice system meant that juveniles were denied equal protection under the law. To protect juveniles from these abuses, the courts now guarantee that juvenile defendants receive the same rights and privileges as adult defendants.

Answers to Developing Sociological Imagination *(pages 196–197)*

1. The title of the graph is "Violent Crime Rates (per 100,000 population) by Type of Area." The source of the graph is the *Statistical Abstract of the United States.*
2. The data provide the number of crimes per 100,000 persons in the population for metropolitan statistical areas, other cities, and rural areas.
3. Metropolitan statistical areas experienced the highest rate of crime.
4. The rates for aggravated assault were the highest in all geographic areas. Robbery was the second most common type of violent crime in metropolitan statistical areas and other cities. Murder/manslaughter was the least common violent crime in all areas. In rural areas, forcible rape was more common than robbery.
5. The data show that all types of violent crime are more common in large metropolitan areas than in smaller cities and rural areas.

Closing the Chapter

Have students complete the Chapter 8 Review Worksheet, found in the *Teacher's Resource Binder.*

Assessing the Chapter

Have students complete the Chapter 8 Review, found on page 198 of the *Pupil's Edition.*

Give students the Chapter 8 Form A Test and, if desired, the Chapter 8 Reteaching Worksheet and Form B Test, found in the *Teacher's Resource Binder.*

Answers to Chapter 8 Review *(page 198)*

Reviewing Sociological Terms

1. Recidivism
2. crime syndicate
3. plea bargaining
4. crime
5. deviance

Thinking Critically about Sociology

1. **(a)** Structural-strain theory and control theory are similar in that they both look to the social structure for explanations of deviant behavior. **(b)** Structural-strain theory holds that deviance is an inevitable development of values, norms, and social structure. While everyone in a society learns the basic values, not everyone has equal access to the legitimate means for obtaining the valued goals. The stress associated with this situation leads some people to use illegitimate means to obtain these goals. Control theory, on the other hand, sees conformity as an outcome of effective social control. Individuals who are integrated into the community are not likely to commit deviant acts. They have too much to lose. Individuals who are only weakly integrated into the community are more likely to commit deviant acts.
2. **(a)** The following factors appear to determine whether a police officer will file a formal crime report: whether friends or family members of the victim are involved; the social class of the victim; and the attitude of the person making a complaint. **(b)** The following factors appear to determine whether a police officer will arrest a suspected criminal: the seriousness of the crime; the wishes of the victim; the attitude of the suspect; the presence of bystanders; and the race of the suspect.
3. **(a)** According to conflict theory, people in power commit deviant acts in order to preserve their privileged positions. **(b)** According to conflict theory, people without power commit deviant acts in order to obtain economic rewards or because they have low self-esteem.
4. **(a)** Deviance serves to unify the group by drawing a sharp line between those people who conform and those people who do not conform. Deviance serves to clarify norms by drawing a sharp line between behavior that is acceptable and behavior that is unacceptable. **(b)** Minor acts of deviance are considered a safety valve for society because they allow individuals to act out their frustrations and anger without seriously disrupting the social order.
5. **(a)** Labeling theory differs from other theories of deviance in that it focuses on how individuals come to be labeled as deviant rather than on why they

commit deviant acts. **(b)** Primary deviance is deviance that goes undetected by those in authority. Secondary deviance, on the other hand, is deviance that results in the individual being labeled as deviant and accepting the label as true.

6. **(a)** Anomie is the situation that arises when the norms of society are unclear or are no longer applicable. **(b)** When people experience anomie, they can respond in any of four ways: innovation—devising new ways to achieve valued goals; ritualism—giving up valued goals but continuing to follow rules for behavior; retreatism—rejecting both the goals and the acceptable means to achieve them; rebellion—attempting to substitute a new set of goals and a new set of means for attaining those goals.

7. The four basic functions of corrections are retribution, deterrence, rehabilitation, and social protection. Retribution serves as revenge for the victim and for society. Deterrence serves to discourage offenders and nonoffenders from committing crimes in the future. The rehabilitation function serves to reform criminals so that they can be returned to society as law-abiding citizens. The social protection function serves to limit the freedom of criminals so that they cannot commit additional crimes.

8. Differential association refers to the proportion of an individual's contacts that are with deviant rather than nondeviant individuals. According to cultural-transmission theory, if the majority of a person's associations are with deviant individuals, then he or she likely will be socialized into deviant behavior. If, on the other hand, the great proportion of a person's associations are with nondeviant individuals, then he or she likely will be socialized to conform.

Exercising Sociological Skills

1. There are four basic sets of norms that govern behavior in conversations—those regarding social distance, hand gestures, eye contact, and facial expressions. In terms of social distance, various distances are considered appropriate for different types of conversations. Generally, the more intimate the relationship, the closer people are allowed to stand. Formal relationships require greater personal distance. If one stands too close to another person, that person may believe the other is being rude or threatening. On the other hand, standing too far away may convey fear or lack of interest. The norms guiding eye contact say that one should look, but not stare, at the person who is speaking. Staring may seem threatening, but avoiding the other person's face may indicate guilt or lack of interest.

2. Some young people join gangs because they see them as the only escape from poverty, broken families, and limited economic opportunities. Others are attracted by the sense of rebellion that gangs represent or the companionship and protection offered by the gangs. Some young people join gangs because they or their families have been threatened with violence or death if they do not join.

3. The table on page 187 and the graphs on pages 188, 190, and 191 indicate that persons arrested for criminal behavior are most likely to be male, white,

and between the ages of 18 and 34. Driving under the influence and larceny are the crimes most commonly committed. Between 1982 and 1991, the rates of aggravated assault and robbery varied widely. The rates for larceny and burglary also varied during this period, but to a lesser extent than aggravated assault and larceny. The rates for murder and forcible rape remained fairly constant during this time period.

Extending Sociological Imagination

1. Answers will vary. For example, other jobs that are affected by the existence of deviance include pawnbrokers, who may handle stolen goods as well as goods left as collateral for loans, guard dog trainers, manufacturers of gun paraphernalia, gun shop owners, and self-defense instructors.

2. Answers will vary.

3. Answers will vary.

Answers to Interpreting Primary Sources *(page 199)*

1. Business pays for the high cost of crime against American companies by passing this cost on to consumers in the form of higher prices.

2. It is impossible to know how much employee crime costs business each year because most companies are too embarrassed to report employee crime or simply never see it.

Closing the Unit

Have students complete the Unit 2 Review Worksheet, found in the *Teacher's Resource Binder.*

Assessing the Unit

Have students complete the Unit 2 Review, found on page 201 of the *Pupil's Edition.*

Give students the Unit 2 Form A Test and, if desired, the Unit 2 Reteaching Worksheet and Form B Test, found in the *Teacher's Resource Binder.*

Answers to Unit 2 Review *(page 201)*

Reviewing Sociological Ideas

1. **(a)** Personality is the sum total of behaviors, attitudes, beliefs, and values that are characteristic of an individual. The self is our conscious awareness of possessing a distinct identity that separates us from other members of society. **(b)** According to Locke, every newborn baby is a *tabula rasa,* or clean slate, on which anything can be written. In other words, personality development and the sense of self are totally dependent on one's social experiences. Cooley believed that personality development is influenced by the development of the looking-glass self, an interactive process by which we develop an image of ourselves based on how we imagine we appear to others. Mead extended Cooley's theory to include taking the role of the other. This role-taking is at the base of the socialization process because it allows us to anticipate what others expect of us and to see ourselves through the eyes of others.

2. **(a)** An instinct is an unchanging, biologically inherited behavior pattern. **(b)** Sociobiologists believe that

most human behaviors are rooted in genetics. **(c)** Contemporary sociologists believe that human behavior is a function of the social environment and social learning.

3. **(a)** Puberty is the physical maturing that makes an individual capable of sexual reproduction. Adolescence is the period between the normal onset of puberty and the beginning of adulthood. **(b)** Puberty is a universal phenomenon because it is biologically based. **(c)** The characteristics of adolescence include biological growth and development; undefined status that includes vague behavioral expectations; increased decision making; increased pressure from parents and peers; and the search for self.

4. **(a)** Dating is an informal, flexible pattern of interaction that is controlled by the dating partners rather than by their parents. It may end in marriage but it has other functions as well. Courtship is a formal, ritualized pattern of mate selection. It tends to be male dominated and under the control of parents or other adults. **(b)** Dating developed in the United States as a result of several social changes associated with industrialization. As Americans moved from farms to cities, young people had more leisure time and less parental supervision. Additionally, the rise of coeducation meant that young people had more opportunities to interact with the opposite sex. Cars and telephones also made dating more common. These inventions gave young people the freedom to arrange dates without parental intervention. Finally, changes in women's social and political status in the 1920s made it more acceptable for unmarried women and men to spend time alone together.

5. **(a)** Unemployment is the situation that occurs when people do not have jobs but are actively seeking employment. **(b)** The United States economy is considered to have full employment when 95 percent of the labor force is employed. Thus, 5 percent unemployment is considered acceptable.

6. **(a)** Alzheimer's disease is an organic condition that results in the progressive destruction of brain cells. Only about 5 to 10 percent of the elderly population suffers from mental impairment. **(b)** One of the earliest symptoms of Alzheimer's disease is the inability to remember current events, even though the far past can be clearly remembered. Then the individual begins to forget how to do simple tasks. As memory loss continues, the person may be hostile and disoriented. Eventually, eyesight, speech, and muscle coordination begin to fail. In the final stages of the disease, the person may regress to a childlike stage and no longer be able to control bodily functions.

7. **(a)** Primary deviance is deviance that goes undetected by the authorities, whereas secondary deviance is deviance that results in the person being labeled as deviant and accepting the label as true. **(b)** Once labeled as deviant, people are not expected to act in nondeviant ways. All their subsequent behavior is interpreted as a reflection of underlying deviance.

Synthesizing Sociological Ideas

1. **(a)** A total institution is a setting in which people are isolated from the rest of society for a set period of time and are subject to the control of officials of varied ranks. **(b)** Total institutions resocialize individuals by changing dress, hairstyle, speech, and freedom of movement. By breaking down the person's self-concept, the total institution can more easily convince the individual to conform to new norms and roles.

2. **(a)** Individuals born first or last have a different perspective than those born in the middle. First-born children are more likely to be achievement-oriented, cooperative, and cautious than later-born children. Later-born children tend to be better in social relationships and more affectionate, friendly, and creative. **(b)** The characteristics we think of as human depend on social interaction, particularly on communication through language or nonverbal communication.

3. **(a)** The primary agents of socialization are the family, the peer group, the school, and the mass media. The family is the most important agent of socialization in almost every society. It is within the family that children learn to behave in acceptable ways, to develop close emotional ties, and to internalize the norms and values of society. Peer groups are composed of individuals of roughly equal age and social characteristics. The socialization that occurs within the peer group is informal and unstructured. The school is another important agent of socialization. In addition to teaching academic subjects, schools transmit cultural values such as patriotism, responsibility, and good citizenship. Finally, the mass media, which includes newspapers, magazines, books, television, radio, and films, is an influential agent of socialization. Of the various forms of mass media, television probably has the most influence on socialization. **(b)** The family is the most important agent of socialization because it is within the family that children learn to behave in acceptable ways, to develop close emotional ties, and to internalize the norms and values of society.

4. **(a)** The use of drugs, other than inhalants, generally has declined in recent years. **(b)** Among the consequences of teenage sexuality are unplanned pregnancy (and the resulting socioeconomic difficulties) and increased risk of sexually transmitted diseases. Teenage mothers are more likely to have low-birth-weight babies, to die during childbirth, to drop out of school, and to have lower lifetime earnings. **(c)** The predictors of teenage suicide are alcohol or drug use; triggering events; age; sex; population density; family relations; and the cluster effect.

5. **(a)** The first stage of men's development is the early adult transition. The most important tasks facing men in this period are leaving home and emotionally separating from parents. The second stage is entering the adult world. During this stage, young men are expected to explore a variety of relationships and career opportunities and to become responsible members of society. The third stage is the age-30 transition, when men examine the choices they have made, reevaluate their commitments, and often make changes in what directions their lives will take. The fourth stage is the settling down period, when men try to establish themselves in society, usually in the work world, form true commitments to family, friends, and other valued roles and relationships, and

establish their identities apart from mentors. The fifth stage is the mid-life transition, which is characterized by self-examination. **(b)** The three phases of adult female development are leaving the family, entering the adult world, and reentering the adult world. The first period for women begins with leaving the family home, becoming emotionally independent from parents, and making a life plan. In many cases, the life plan is largely determined by marriage. The second phase of women's development involves entering the adult world. In the U.S. today, many women work before marriage and continue to do so after marriage. Among about half of these women, however, work stops temporarily with the birth of children. The final stage begins when women reenter the work world or reevaluate their life roles once children reach school age.

6. The first personality type identified by the Kansas City study is the integrated personality. Three adapting patterns associated with this are the reorganizers, the focused, and the disengaged. The second type is the armored personality, which includes the holders and the constructors. The third personality type is the passive-dependent personality. The typical adapting patterns for this type are succorance-seeking and apathy. The final personality type is the unintegrated personality. The primary adapting pattern for this personality type is disorganized.

7. **(a)** White-collar crime is a crime that is committed by an individual or individuals of high social status in the course of their professional lives. **(b)** White-collar crime costs society billions of dollars each year. **(c)** A crime syndicate is a large-scale organization of professional criminals that controls some vice or business through violence or the threat of violence. **(d)** Crime syndicates make money through activities such as loansharking, drug trafficking, illegal gambling, and hijacking.

8. **(a)** The five positive functions of deviance are to unify the group by drawing clear boundaries between conformers and nonconformers; to clarify norms by showing societal members which behaviors are acceptable and which are unacceptable; to diffuse tension by allowing people to vent anger and frustration through minor norm violations; to identify social problems, in that a large number of norm violations indicate something in the social system needs to be changed; and to provide jobs for many people. **(b)** The functions served by corrections in society are retribution, deterrence, rehabilitation, and social protection.

Applying Sociological Imagination

1. Answers will vary.
2. Answers will vary.
3. Answers will vary.

UNIT 3 *(pages 202–289)*

SOCIAL INEQUALITY

CHAPTER 9
SOCIAL STRATIFICATION

CHAPTER 10
RACIAL AND ETHNIC RELATIONS

CHAPTER 11
GENDER, AGE, AND HEALTH

Unit Overview

Unit 3 focuses on social inequality—the unequal distribution of social rewards and scarce resources. The unit begins with an examination of social stratification, including types of stratification systems, theories of stratification, and an analysis of social class and poverty in the United States. In the remaining two chapters of the unit, access to social rewards and scarce resources is examined in the contexts of race, ethnicity, gender, age, and health.

Unit Goals

At the end of the unit, students should be able to

1. Identify two types of stratification systems, and recognize the social rewards upon which stratification is based.
2. Compare and contrast two major theories of social stratification.
3. Outline the characteristics of the American class system, and discuss poverty in the United States.
4. Describe the characteristics of minority groups, and identify types of minority group treatment.
5. Discuss the experiences of various minority groups in the United States.
6. Understand the nature of prejudice and discrimination.
7. Determine the characteristics of social inequality based on gender, age, and health.

Unit Skills

Three skills are developed in Unit 3.

* THINKING ABOUT SOCIOLOGY: *Determining Cause and Effect* (Chapter 9; PE pages 226–227; TM page 65)
* THINKING ABOUT SOCIOLOGY: *Identifying Assumptions* (Chapter 10; PE pages 254–255; TM page 71)
* THINKING ABOUT SOCIOLOGY: *Analyzing Sociological Viewpoints* (Chapter 11; PE pages 284–285; TM page 76)

Suggestions for teaching the skills appear on the TM pages just mentioned. The suggestions are clearly identified by the ★ symbol. Each skill is reinforced in the Chapter Review under Exercising Sociological Skills. Answers to the questions in the textbook's skill features appear in the Answers to Developing Sociological Imagination sections of this *Teacher's Manual.*

Introducing the Unit

Inform the class that the administrators of your school have sent a notice to all teachers stating that students now must be graded according to the following scale:

Males over six feet tall: 90–100 = A; 80–89 = B; 70–79 = C; 60–69 = D; 59 and below = F

All other males: 94–100 = A; 86–93 = B; 78–85 = C; 69–77 = D; 68 and below = F

Females under five feet tall: 96–100 = A; 88–95 = B; 80–87 = C; 71–79 = D; 70 and below = F

All other females: 98–100 = A; 90–97 = B; 82–89 = C; 73–81 = D; 72 and below = F

When students complain about the new grading scale, ask them why they think it is unfair. Write their reasons on the chalkboard. Once they have voiced all of their complaints, tell them that all societies have methods by which to control access to scarce resources and social rewards. If access is determined on the basis of ascribed characteristics, as it is in this grading scale, individuals have little opportunity to change their standing in society. If, on the other hand, access is determined on the basis of achieved characteristics, people have increased control over their lives. How access is controlled determines the degree of social inequality in a society.

After assuring students that the old grading system still is in effect, close the discussion by telling the class that Unit 3 will explore the social consequences of the ways in which societies control access to scarce resources and social rewards. Among the topics covered will be social stratification, including an analysis of social class and poverty in the United States, and the effects of race, ethnicity, gender, age, and health on access to social rewards.

References for Teachers

Andersen, M.L. *Thinking about Women: Sociological Perspectives on Sex and Gender.* New York: Macmillan, 1988. Theoretically grounded sociological analysis of women in contemporary American society.

Asante, Molefi K., and Mattson, Mark T. *Historical and Cultural Atlas of African Americans.* New York: Macmillan, 1992. Resource book that combines demographic maps and graphics with text to chronicle African American history.

Bartlett, Donald L., and Steele, James B. *America: What Went Wrong?* Kansas City, MO: Andrews and McMeel, 1992. Examines the social and economic forces that are pushing the United States toward a two-class society—the wealthy and the poor.

Chalk, Frank, and Jonassohn, Kurt. *The History and Sociology of Genocide: Analyses and Case Studies.* New

Haven, CT: Yale University Press, 1990. Analyzes case studies of genocide from ancient times to the present.

Duckitt, John. *The Social Psychology of Prejudice*. Westport, CT: Greenwood Press, 1992. Good introductory text on the social and psychological causes and consequences of prejudice.

Fanning, Beverly J. *Workfare* vs. *Welfare*. Hudson, WI: GEM Publications, 1989. Anthology of 21 readings that discuss a variety of issues concerning welfare and poverty.

Jones, Maldwyn Allen. *American Immigration*. Chicago: University of Chicago Press, 1992. Traces how immigration to the United States has influenced the ethnic mosaic of the nation.

Kurtz, Richard A., and Chalfant, Paul. *Sociology of Medicine and Illness*. Needham Heights, MA: Allyn & Bacon, 1991. Examines the issues of health and illness from a sociological perspective.

Race and Ethnic Relations 92/93. Guilford, CT: Dushkin Press, 1992. Collection of 49 articles that focus on ethnic and racial pluralism in the United States.

Rose, Stephen. *Social Stratification in the United States: The American Profile Poster Revised and Expanded*. New York: W.W. Norton, 1992. Poster and 41-page booklet that contain data on such variables as income, wealth, race, and occupational status in the United States.

Schlesinger, Arthur M. *The Disuniting of America: Reflections on a Multicultural Society*. New York: W.W. Norton, 1992. Presents the controversial view that bilingualism and multiculturalism are divisive forces in modern American society.

The Young and the Old: A Sourcebook on Aging. Portland, ME: J. Weston Walch, 1988. Collection of lessons with reproducible activities that focus on various aspects of aging and the elderly.

Readings for Student Enrichment

Bode, Janet. *New Kids on the Block: Oral Histories of Immigrant Teens*. New York: Franklin Watts, 1989. Presents the stories of 11 teenagers who came to the United States because of persecution or lack of opportunities in their own countries; helps students understand how prejudice and discrimination can affect the quality of life.

Bowe, Frank. *Equal Rights for Americans with Disabilities*. New York: Franklin Watts, 1992. Describes what it is like to grow up as a person with a disability, and discusses the civil rights issues that inspired the disability rights movement; helps students explore the social and psychological consequences of having a disability.

Brown, Dee. *Bury My Heart at Wounded Knee: An Indian History of the American West*. New York: Henry Holt, 1991. Detailed account of the experiences of Native Americans during the second half of the nineteenth century; enables students to examine the experiences of Native Americans from the point of view of the Native Americans themselves.

Chute, Carolyn. *The Beans of Egypt*. New York: Ticknor & Fields, 1985. Tale of a poverty-stricken extended family in rural Maine; provides students with insights into the consequences of poverty.

Fernandez-Shaw, Carlos. *The Hispanic Presence in North America: From 1492 to Today*. New York: Facts on File, 1991. Explores the richness of Hispanic history and the importance of Hispanic cultural influence in the United States; helps students develop a multicultural perspective.

Haley, Alex. *The Autobiography of Malcolm X*. New York: Ballantine Books, 1992. Personal story of a man who came up from the streets to become one of the most influential and controversial African American leaders of the twentieth century; helps students analyze race relations in the United States.

Heinlein, Robert. *The Moon Is a Harsh Mistress*. New York, Ace Books, 1987. Tells the tale of the descendants of prisoners sent to the moon when it was a penal colony for Earth; allows students to examine how the roles of men and women change when females are greatly outnumbered by males.

Kranz, Rachel. *Straight Talk about Prejudice*. New York: Facts on File, 1992. Discusses prejudice and stereotypes as they apply to a number of American minority groups; helps students learn how they can combat prejudice in their own schools.

Lee, Harper. *To Kill a Mockingbird*. New York: Warner Books, 1982. Novel set in the South during the 1930s; allows students to explore the effects of social stratification and prejudice.

Orwell, George. *1984*. New York: New American Library, 1983. Pessimistic prediction about the future of society; enables students to examine the consequences of enforced stratification.

Rowan, Carl T. *Dream Makers, Dream Breakers: The World of Thurgood Marshall*. Boston, MA: Little, Brown, 1992. Chronicles the life and times of Supreme Court Justice Thurgood Marshall; provides students with insights into the life of one of the twentieth century's most influential fighters for equal rights and equal justice under the law.

Stefoff, Rebecca. *Women of the World: Women Travelers and Explorers*. New York: Oxford University Press, 1992. Traces the adventures of nine courageous women from history; helps students develop an appreciation for the accomplishments of women.

Steinbeck, John. *Of Mice and Men*. New York: Penguin Books, 1978. Short novel about two men, one of whom is retarded; enables students to examine prejudiced reactions to people with disabilities.

Takaki, Ronald. *Strangers from a Different Shore: A History of Asian Americans*. New York: Penguin Books, 1989. Details 150 years of Asian immigration to the United States; helps students develop a multicultural perspective.

Walker, Alice. *The Color Purple*. New York: Washington Square Press, 1983. Novel about a young African American woman in the South; enables students to examine the issue of women's rights (this book may not be suitable for all students).

Multimedia Materials

The selected materials listed below may be useful during the study of Unit 3. The following abbreviations are used in the list:

c = color
b&w = black & white
f = film
fs = filmstrip
vhs = videocassette

lvd = laser videodisc
sim = simulation
sw = software
g = game

Chapter 9

Down and Out in America (vhs, c; 57 min.) SSSS. Director Lee Grant presents interviews with some of Minnesota's poverty-stricken and homeless citizens.

Home Street Home (vhs; 47 min.) FIV. NBC News documentary that examines the plight of America's homeless people.

I'm a Fool (vhs; 38 min.) ZM. Dramatization of a short story by Sherwood Anderson, in which a poor boy pretends to be wealthy in order to impress a girl and finds that his lies only complicate the relationship.

India Unveiled: Modern India (vhs; 28 min.) EBEC. Examines the effects that industrialization and modern technology have had on Indian society.

Our Nation's Homeless: Who, Where, and Why? (fs on vhs, c; 22 min.) SSSS. Explores the nature of homelessness in the United States and why so many people are losing their homes.

South Africa: After Apartheid (f, vhs, c; 25 min.) NGS. Examines the policy of apartheid in South Africa, including its origins, enforcement, and effects on South Africa's people and economy.

South Africa Belongs to Us (vhs; 35 min.) CSS. Documentary that presents interviews with five black South African women to show how the policy of apartheid affected their lives.

Young, Rich, and Black in the U.S.A. (vhs, c; 28 min.) FHS. Specially adapted Phil Donahue program that focuses on the lives of young, affluent African Americans in the United States.

Chapter 10

America: The New Immigrants (vhs, c; 60 min.) ZM. Explores the challenges facing immigrants to the United States, including the perceptions of people already living in their communities and the responses of the immigrants themselves.

Eye of the Storm: A Look at Racial Prejudice (vhs, c; 25 min.) FM. ABC News documentary of a startling classroom experiment on prejudice conducted by a third-grade teacher.

From Dreams to Reality: A Tribute to Minority Inventors (vhs, c; 28 min.) SSSS. Narrator Ossie Davis discusses the contributions made to American science, technology, and medicine by inventors such as George Washington Carver, Phillip Stevens, and Ysidore Martinez Martinez.

Heritage in Black (vhs; 27 min.) EBEC. Focuses on the 200-year-old struggle of African Americans to achieve freedom, and examines their contributions to science, industry, education, music, labor, and sports.

Immigration: Maintaining the Open Door (sim, sw; 30 student booklets) ZM. Simulation that puts students in the role of president of the United States, faced with the decision of what to do with a group of refugees seeking asylum.

Impressions of Prejudice (vhs; 18 min.) GA. Presents the works of Sandburg, Shakespeare, Hughes, Malcolm X, and others to explore literary responses to racism, sexism, and religious bigotry.

Journey to Freedom: The Immigrant Experience (lvd; 13 min.) AM. Uses newsreel footage, vintage photographs, and artwork to explore the history of American immigration over the past century.

My Brother's Keeper: The Holocaust Through the Eyes of an Artist (fs, vhs; 16 min.) SVE. Artist Israel Bernbaum's paintings document the horrors of the Warsaw Ghetto and its destruction by the Nazis during World War II.

Prejudice: Decisions, Decisions (sim, sw; 28 student booklets) ZM. Simulation in which students play the role of a town mayor faced with a controversy involving racial prejudice.

Trail of Death (vhs; 27 min.) CSS. Documentary that discusses the forced nineteenth-century relocation of the Menominee band of Potawatomi Indians.

Under Our Skin: Exploring Racial and Cultural Differences (vhs, c; 32 min.) SSSS. Student-created, student-staged play in which young people explore their experiences in confronting prejudice and stereotypes.

The Wave (vhs; 48 min.) FIV. Recreates the classroom experiment in which a high school teacher formed his own "Reich" to demonstrate why the German people could so willingly accept Nazism.

Who Is an American? (vhs, c; 26 min.) SSSS. Explores why, how, and from where immigrants came to the United States, and why the United States is a "salad bowl" rather than a "melting pot."

Who Is Peter Iswolsky? (vhs; 26 min.) BF. Presents an anti-racism workshop in which various people discuss how they feel about the issues of race and racism.

Chapter 11

The Aging of America (vhs; 21 min.) GA. Explores the stereotypes, problems, and solutions of an aging population that is staying younger longer.

The Aging of America: CNN Special Report (vhs, c; 30 min.) SSSS. Focuses on some of the problems faced by today's elderly population, such as Alzheimer's disease, the inadequacy of Social Security income, and physical and emotional stresses.

AIDS: Changing Lifestyles (vhs; 15 min.) GA. Presents a forum of AIDS experts, teenagers, and AIDS victims who discuss what people can do to protect themselves from this deadly disease.

AIDS, Updated Version (lvd) CMFV. Former United States Surgeon General C. Everett Koop provides basic information about AIDS, including how human immunodeficiency virus is and is not transmitted.

Main Street: He's My Brother (vhs; 8 min.) FIV. Explores the challenges and rewards of having a sibling who is disabled in this story of a teenage girl whose younger brother is autistic.

Medical Technology (f, vhs, c; 25 min.) NGS. Fascinating presentation of modern medical advances, such as imaging systems that look inside the body, computers that design prosthetics, and lasers that allow noninvasive methods of surgery.

Suzi's Story (vhs; 58 min.) FIV. Documentary of the last months of life of Suzi Lovegrove as she battles AIDS and the prejudice and discrimination that surrounds this fatal disease.

Who You Are and What You Are: Understanding Sex Roles (fs on vhs; 40 min.) GA. Explores sex-role related issues involving careers, marriage, sexuality, romance, and relationships between men and women.

Women at Work: Change, Choice, Challenge (vhs; 19 min.) EBEC. Seven women discuss their attitudes toward work, their reasons for their career choices, and their views of their work-family relationships.

Women: Our Changing Role (vhs; 15 min.) BF. Explores the current situation of African women, caught between traditional role expectations and evolving opportunities in education and business.

Women's Rights (vhs; 23 min.) EBEC. Focuses on a situation in which a teenage girl wants to swim on the boy's team in a state that prohibits her from doing so, and shows her lawyer arguing the constitutionality of the case in court.

CHAPTER 9 *(pages 204–229)*

SOCIAL STRATIFICATION

SECTION 1
SYSTEMS OF STRATIFICATION

SECTION 2
THE AMERICAN CLASS SYSTEM

SECTION 3
POVERTY

Chapter Overview

Social stratification is the ranking of individuals or categories of individuals on the basis of unequal access to scarce resources and social rewards. Stratification by definition implies social inequality. There are two basic types of stratification systems—caste systems and class systems. In caste systems, resources and rewards are distributed on the basis of ascribed statuses. In class systems, on the other hand, the distribution of resources and rewards is determined on the basis of achieved statuses. The three most common rewards on which social stratification is determined are wealth, power, and prestige.

Two major theoretical approaches have been used to explain stratification: functionalist theory and conflict theory. Functionalists view stratification as a necessary feature of the social structure. Conflict theorists, on the other hand, see competition over scarce resources as the cause of social inequality.

The United States has a class system. Sociologists do not agree on the number of class divisions there are in the United States. Many sociologists, however, adopt a five-category classification system: upper class, upper-middle class, lower-middle class, working class, and lower class. Although the United States is one of the richest nations in the world, daily life is a constant struggle for some people. More than 35 million Americans—approximately 14 percent of the population—live in poverty.

Chapter Objectives

At the conclusion of the chapter, students will be able to

1. Define social stratification and social inequality.
2. Identify the characteristics of caste systems and class systems.
3. Determine which social rewards serve as the most common basis of social stratification.
4. Compare and contrast the two major theories of social stratification.
5. Identify the characteristics of the American class system.
6. Discuss the situation of the poor in America, and describe what steps have been taken by the federal government to lessen the effects of poverty.

Introducing the Chapter

To introduce Chapter 9, have students read the section titles and the subheads contained within each section of the chapter. Then ask: "Based on the information you have just read, what questions do you expect to be answered by this chapter?" Have a volunteer record the responses on the chalkboard. When the list of questions is completed, have students copy the questions and place their lists in their study notebooks for use later in this chapter.

Chapter 9 Suggested Lesson Plans

Day 1	**Suggested Procedures:** Introducing the Unit; Introducing the Chapter; Section 1 Previewing Key Terms; Introducing the Section **Materials:** PE: pp. 202–213; TM: pp. 57–61
Day 2	**Suggested Procedures:** Section 1 Strategies and Assignments **Materials:** PE: pp. 206–213; TM: pp. 61–62; TRB: Transparency 8, Worksheet
Day 3	**Suggested Procedures:** Section 2 Previewing Key Terms; Introducing the Section; Strategies and Assignments **Materials:** PE: pp. 214–218; TM: pp. 62–64; TRB: Assorted Worksheets
Day 4	**Suggested Procedures:** Section 3 Previewing Key Terms; Introducing the Section; Strategies and Assignments **Materials:** PE: pp. 219–227; TM: pp. 64–65; TRB: Assorted Worksheets

SECTION 1 *(pages 206–213)*

SYSTEMS OF STRATIFICATION

Section Overview

There are two basic types of stratification systems—caste systems and class systems. Caste systems distribute scarce resources and rewards on the basis of ascribed characteristics, whereas class systems base distribution on achieved characteristics.

The three most common rewards on which social stratification is determined are wealth, power, and prestige. An individual's wealth is made up of his or her assets and income. Power is the ability of an individual or group to get others to act in a certain way regardless of personal wishes. Prestige is the respect, honor, recognition, or courtesy an individual receives from other members of society.

Functionalists hold that stratification exists because certain roles in society must be performed if the system is to be maintained. Society ensures that these roles will be fulfilled by providing higher rewards for their performance. Conflict theorists, on the other hand, argue that stratification exists because various groups within society compete with one another for scarce resources. Once a group gains power, it is able to shape public policy and public opinion to its own advantage, thereby maintaining its position of power.

Previewing Key Terms

Section 1 contains the following key terms: **social stratification, social inequality, caste system, exogamy, endogamy, class system, means of production, bourgeoisie, proletariat, social class, socioeconomic status (SES), wealth, power, prestige**. Have students prepare riddles, using the key terms as answers. For example: "I am the ability to control the behavior of others, with or without their consent. What am I?" *(power)* Tell students to write their riddles on one side of the paper and the answers on the other side. Completed sets of riddles can be exchanged among students and answered. Then have students put their papers in their study notebooks for later review.

Introducing the Section

Define for the class the terms *social stratification* and *social inequality*. After defining the terms, tell the class that all societies are stratified in some way—only the methods of stratification differ. Next ask students to list possible reasons why large unstratified societies have never existed. Finally, ask students to indicate the criteria they would use to stratify a society if it were up to them to decide how best to distribute scarce resources and social rewards. Use the discussion as a lead-in to a lecture on caste systems and class systems.

Suggested Teaching Strategies

1. **Analyzing Ideas (I)** Ask the class to consider the following question: "Why has it been so difficult to change the caste system in India." Write the responses on the chalkboard under the headings Functionalist Theory and Conflict Theory. Then have students evaluate which of the two theories is most convincing in explaining the system of stratification in India.
2. **Contrasting Ideas (I)** Have students contrast the Marxian definition of social class with the definition most often used by sociologists today. Then ask: "Why do most contemporary sociologists reject the Marxian definition of social class?"
3. **Interpreting Graphs (I)** Place Transparency 8, which focuses on the distribution of income and assets in the United States, on an overhead projector and ask the questions contained in the accompanying teacher's notes. Transparencies and accompanying teacher's notes are found in the *Teacher's Resource Binder*.
4. **Debating Ideas (I, II)** Have interested students debate the following statement: "There should be a limit on the amount of money that corporate executives can earn."
5. **Working in Groups (II, III)** Organize the class into four groups. Have each group conduct research and prepare oral presentations on current patterns of stratification in one of the following nations: India, the United States, Great Britain, South Africa.

Suggested Enrichment Activities

1. **Exploring Cross-Cultural Perspectives (I)** Have students complete the appropriate Cross-Cultural Perspectives Worksheet, found in the *Teacher's Resource Binder*.
2. **Researching Ideas (III)** Have interested students locate and summarize the views of stratification presented by functionalist theorists Kingsley Davis and Wilbert Moore or by conflict theorist Ralf Dahrendorf. Ask the students to share their information with the class.

Suggested Assignments

1. **Using Sociological Imagination (I)** As homework, have students write a short essay in response to the following question: "How would your life be different from what it is today if you had been born in India as a member of the untouchables caste?" Have volunteers share their essays with the class.
2. **Interpreting Tables (I)** Have students read the Applying Sociology feature on textbook pages 212–213 and then answer the questions found at the end of the feature.
3. **Comparing Ideas (I)** Have students compare and contrast the functionalist and conflict views of social inequality.

Closing the Section

Close the section by having students ask five people the following question: "Which would you rather have: wealth, power, or prestige?" Instruct students to take notes on the reasons why the respondents have answered a certain way. Then, in class, tally the responses and use the results as the basis of a discussion on the dimensions of social stratification.

Assessing the Section

Have students complete the Section 1 Review.

Answers to Section 1 Review *(page 211)*

Define *social stratification:* ranking of individuals or categories of people on the basis of unequal access to scarce resources and social rewards; ***social inequality:*** unequal sharing of social rewards and resources; ***endogamy:*** marriage within one's own social category; ***means of production:*** tools, buildings, and materials needed to produce goods and services; ***bourgeoisie:*** owners of the means of production; ***proletariat:*** people who sell their labor in exchange for wages; ***socioeconomic status (SES)***: rating of social class that combines social factors such as educational level, occupational prestige, and place of residence with the economic factor of income

1. **(a)** Karl Marx defined social class in terms of ownership of the means of production. Following this definition, society is divided into two classes—the owners of the means of production and the workers who sell their labor in exchange for wages. According to Marx, there is inequality in capitalist societies because the owners of the means of production get all of the profits but the workers do all of the actual work. **(b)** The definition of social class used in the textbook builds on the work of Max Weber. Weber focused on three bases of social class—wealth, power, and prestige. Thus, this definition of social class is broader than Marx's definition, which rests on a relationship to the means of production.
2. **(a)** In a caste system, scarce resources and social rewards are distributed on the basis of ascribed statuses. A newborn's caste is determined by the status of the parents. Effort and talent cannot help the individual move to a higher caste. Caste systems have rigid rules prohibiting marriage outside of one's own caste. **(b)** In a class system, social rewards and scarce resources are distributed on the basis of achieved statuses. Thus, individuals in a class system may have some control over their positions in the stratification system.
3. The three dimensions of social stratification are wealth, power, and prestige. Wealth consists of the value of everything a person owns and the money the person earns through wages and salaries. Power can be based on physical force, special skill or knowledge, social status, personal characteristics, or custom and tradition. Prestige is the respect, honor, recognition, or courtesy an individual receives from other members of society. In American society, occu-pation tends to be the most important determinant of prestige.
4. **(a)** Functionalists view stratification as a necessary feature of society. There are certain roles in every society that must be performed. To ensure that these roles are performed, society provides differential rewards. The more important the role, the higher the rewards. **(b)** Conflict theorists believe that the cause of social inequality is competition over scarce resources. Once a group gains power, it shapes public policy and public opinion so that it can maintain its position of power.

Answers to Applying Sociology *(pages 212–213)*

1. There appears to be no systematic relationship between occupational prestige and annual salary.
2. Some skilled craft jobs, such as longshoreman, brick-layer, and meat cutter, have relatively low prestige but fairly high wages.
3. Some occupations, such as college professor and min-ister, have relatively low salaries but high prestige.
4. Two education-oriented occupations, college pro-fessor and high school teacher, have a large gap between prestige and salary. The occupation of min-ister may have the largest gap.

SECTION 2 *(pages 214–218)*

THE AMERICAN CLASS SYSTEM

Section Overview

Sociologists use three basic techniques to rank individ-uals according to social class—the reputational method, the subjective method, and the objective method. Using these three methods, the population can be organized into the upper class, upper-middle class, lower-middle class, working class, and lower class.

Because the United States has an open class system, social mobility is possible. Social mobility is the move-ment between or within social classes or strata. Among the types of social mobility studied by sociologists are vertical mobility, horizontal mobility, and intergenera-tional mobility.

Previewing Key Terms

Section 2 contains the following key terms: **reputational method, subjective method, objective method, social mobility, vertical mobility, horizontal mobil-ity, intergenerational mobility**. Have students look up each one of these terms in the Glossary. Then ask the following questions: "What do the terms 'reputational method,' 'subjective method,' and 'objective method' have in common?" *(They all refer to techniques used by sociologists to rank individuals on the basis of social class.)* "What do the terms 'social mobility,' 'vertical mobility,' 'horizontal mobility,' and 'intergenerational mobility' have in common?" *(They all refer to movement within or between social classes.)*

Introducing the Section

Select five volunteers from the class and tell them that they are to use their sociological imaginations to portray members of various social classes in the United States. Then assign each of the five students one of the following social-class groups: upper-class, upper-middle class, lower-middle class, working class, and lower class. Have the five students sit in front of the class as a panel, and tell the class that they are to "interview" these people concerning their perceptions of life in the United States. The five students should answer as though they were members of the social classes they represent. Possible questions might include: "How do you spend your leisure time?" "What kind of job do you have?" "How did the recent economic recession affect your family?" and so on. After the panelists have answered the class's questions, have the class critique the answers in terms of how accurately they reflected the various social classes. Then tell the class that Section 2 will introduce them to the American class system and the characteristics of the various social classes.

Suggested Teaching Strategies

1. **Analyzing Sociological Methods (I)** After reviewing the three methods commonly used to rank individuals according to social class, ask students to identify the possible strengths and weaknesses of each method.
2. **Understanding Ideas (I)** Write the following five social-class categories on the chalkboard: upper class, upper-middle class, lower-middle class, working class, lower class. Then have students list the characteristics they associate with each social class. Next write on the chalkboard a list of occupations such as nurse, office manager, factory worker, bank president, sales clerk, and police officer. Ask students to indicate into which social class they would place each occupation and to give reasons for the choices they have made.
3. **Writing an Essay (I)** Have students answer the following essay questions: (a) What do sociologists mean by social mobility, vertical mobility, horizontal mobility, and intergenerational mobility? (b) What are some of the structural causes of upward and downward mobility?

Suggested Enrichment Activities

1. **Understanding Ethics (I)** Have students complete the appropriate Developing Research Skills Worksheet, found in the *Teacher's Resource Binder*.
2. **Seeing Relationships (II)** Ask interested students or groups of students to collect product advertisements from a wide variety of magazines. Then have students analyze the advertisements to determine whether the types of products and the styles of advertisements differ depending on which social class is the intended market. Have the students share their analyses with the class.

Suggested Assignments

1. **Organizing Ideas (I)** As homework, have students complete the appropriate Graphic Organizer Worksheet, found in the *Teacher's Resource Binder*.

2. **Working in Groups (I, II)** Organize the class into small groups and have each group select one of the five social classes discussed in the section. (Instruct group members not to tell the other groups which social class they have chosen.) Have the members of each group collect magazine photographs that reflect the social class they have chosen and create a collage of those photographs. Then, one at a time, have the groups present their collages to the class and have the class guess which social class is being portrayed. As a follow-up, have the class discuss the degree to which Americans are aware of social class variations, and the differential treatment afforded to members of the various social classes.
3. **Linking the Past to the Present (II, III)** Have interested students use library sources to locate historical quotations that focus on social class variations in the United States. Conduct a class discussion in which students evaluate how valid these quotations are in today's society.

Closing the Section

Close the section by having students summarize what they have learned about social class ranking techniques, social class variations, and types of social mobility.

Assessing the Section

Have students complete the Section 2 Review.

Answers to Section 2 Review *(page 218)*

Define *social mobility:* movement between or within social classes or strata

1. The three techniques used by sociologists to rank individuals on the basis of social class are the reputational method, the subjective method, and the objective method. In the reputational method, individuals in the community are asked to rank other community members based on what they know of their characters and life-styles. In the subjective method, individuals are asked to determine their own social rank. In the objective method, sociologists use factors such as education, income, and occupation to assign persons to social classes.
2. **(a)** Between 1 and 3 percent of Americans fall into the upper class. Another 10 to 15 percent belong to the upper-middle class. Thirty to 35 percent are members of the lower-middle class. The largest social class is the working class, with roughly 40 to 45 percent of all Americans. Finally, the lower class includes about 20 to 25 percent of all Americans. **(b)** People in the upper-upper class typically have been wealthy for generations. Most of their money comes from inheritance. They live a life of privilege and power. The lower-upper class has the same privileges as the upper-upper class, even though they typically have earned their money rather than inherited it. People in the upper-middle class are high-income business and professional people and their families. Their class membership is based on earned income rather than on inherited wealth. They tend to be very well-educated,

career-oriented people. Those in the lower-middle class have white-collar jobs that require less education and provide lower incomes than those in the upper-middle class. People in the lower-middle class must work hard to hold onto what they have. Many of the people in the working class perform manual labor. While their blue-collar jobs may provide more money than some lower-level white-collar jobs, blue-collar jobs are less prestigious. Because working-class people tend not to have any substantial savings, they are especially vulnerable to economic setbacks. The lower class consists of poor people—those who are unemployed, elderly, homeless, unskilled, and underemployed. Because they typically have low levels of education, people in the lower class have limited prospects for escaping poverty.

3. Vertical mobility refers to movement between social classes or strata. Horizontal mobility refers to movement within a social class or stratum. Intergenerational mobility, a special form of vertical mobility, refers to status differences between generations in the same family.

4. (a) Such things as advances in technology, changes in merchandising patterns, and increases in the general level of education in the population can lead to upward mobility. When technology changes, the available jobs change also. While workers are displaced from their jobs in the short-run, long-run opportunities involve upgraded skills. Changes in the service sector of the economy have increased the number of workers in high-status jobs in insurance, real estate, and the credit industry. Finally, as the overall level of education of the population increases, upward mobility increases as well. (b) Changes in the economy can be a major cause of downward mobility. Changes in the demand for certain types of labor, due to shifts in consumer tastes, for example, can put people out of work.

SECTION 3 (pages 219–225)

POVERTY

Section Overview

Poverty is a serious problem in the United States. Not everyone, however, runs an equal risk of being poor. Poverty varies by characteristics such as age, race, and ethnicity. Children, women, African Americans, and Hispanic Americans, for instance, are at a higher risk of being poor than are white adult males. Two major ways in which poverty affects people are in terms of life chances and patterns of behavior.

In the 1960s, President Lyndon B. Johnson instituted a program called the War on Poverty. Since then, the United States has taken an active role in attempting to reduce social inequality in America. The two principal ways in which the government attempts to reduce social inequality are through transfer payments and government subsidies.

Previewing Key Terms

Section 3 contains the following key terms: **poverty, poverty level, life chances, life expectancy, transfer payments.** Have students look up each of these terms in the Glossary. Then instruct them to write a paragraph about poverty in the United States, using all of the key terms in the list. Completed paragraphs may be placed in the students' study notebooks for later review.

Introducing the Section

Introduce the section by showing the film *Our Nation's Homeless: Who, Where, and Why?* (rental information can be found in the introductory section of this *Teacher's Manual*). After discussing the film, ask: "In addition to the possibility of becoming homeless, what are the other consequences of poverty?" When no new ideas are forthcoming, tell the class that Section 3 will introduce them to the sociological perspective on poverty in the United States and the ways in which the government is attempting to help the situation.

Suggested Teaching Strategies

1. **Learning from Photographs (I)** Have students turn to textbook page 220 and examine the three photographs on the page. Then instruct students to write a short essay in response to the following question: "Based on these photographs, what are some of the consequences of poverty for children?"

2. **Working in Groups (I, II)** Contact the local welfare department to find out how much money a welfare family of four is allotted for food per week. Then organize the class into small groups. Tell half the groups that they are to create a week's worth of menus for a middle-class family of four that can be prepared for $100. Tell the other half of the groups that they are to create menus for a poor family of four that can be prepared for the amount of money allotted by the local welfare department. Have the groups price food before preparing the menus. Compare the nutritional value and variety of the menus in class.

3. **Drawing a Bar Graph (II, III)** Have students conduct library research to find out what percentage of the population lived below the poverty level for each decade from 1930 to 1990. Have the students display this information in a bar graph. Then ask: "Why has it been so difficult to eliminate poverty in the United States? What can be done to solve this serious social problem?"

4. **Summarizing Information (III)** Ask selected students to locate and summarize articles on the poor in America from current news magazines. Have the students share their summaries with the class. Use the summaries as the basis of a discussion concerning the characteristics of the poor and the effects of poverty.

Suggested Enrichment Activities

1. **Extending Ideas (III)** Ask interested students to expand on the information presented in the Case Study feature on textbook page 221 by researching the problems of the rural poor.

2. **Writing a Research Report (III)** Have interested students write research reports on one of the following transfer payment programs: Social Security, Supplemental Security Income, unemployment insurance, or Aid to Families with Dependent Children.

Suggested Assignments

1. **Understanding Ideas (I)** As homework, have students complete the appropriate Understanding Sociological Ideas Worksheet, found in the *Teacher's Resource Binder.*
2. **Forming Generalizations (I)** Have students complete the appropriate Critical Skills Mastery Worksheet, found in the *Teacher's Resource Binder.*
3. ★**Thinking about Sociology: Determining Cause and Effect (I)** Have students read the Developing Sociological Imagination feature on textbook pages 226–227 and then complete the assignment under Practicing the Skill.
4. **Conducting Interviews (III)** Ask interested students to interview members of your local government to find out what programs are available to help the poor and homeless in your community. Have students report their findings to the class.

Closing the Section

Close the section by having students retrieve the lists of questions they compiled during the Introducing the Chapter activity. Ask selected students to read the questions aloud to the class, one at a time, and have volunteers supply answers to the questions. If students have difficulty supplying the correct information, offer clarifications at this time.

Assessing the Section

Have students complete the Section 3 Review.

Answers to Section 3 Review *(page 225)*

Define *poverty:* standard of living that is below the minimum level considered decent and reasonable by society; *poverty level:* minimum annual income needed by a family to survive; *life chances:* likelihood individuals have of sharing in the opportunities and benefits of society; *life expectancy:* average number of years a person born in a particular year can expect to live; *transfer payments:* principal way in which the government attempts to reduce social inequality by redistributing money among various segments of society

1. The poverty level is the minimum annual income needed by a family to survive. The poverty level is determined by calculating the cost of providing an adequate diet (based on the Department of Agriculture's minimum nutritional standards) and multiplying it by three, since the poor tend to spend a third of their income on food.
2. In terms of age, the largest percentage of Americans living in poverty are children. Over 40 percent of America's poor are under the age of 18. In regard to gender differences in the likelihood of living in poverty, more than 60 percent of the poor adults in this country are women. Poverty rates also vary by race and ethnic background. African Americans and Hispanic Americans are more likely than whites to be poor in America.
3. The poor differ from the wealthier segments of society in many important respects. One of the most important differences relates to health and length of life. The poor have the highest rates of heart disease, tuberculosis, diabetes, cancer, arthritis, anemia, pneumonia, and influenza. Infant mortality is twice as high among the poor as it is among the general population. Thus, life expectancy is reduced for the poor. The poor also are at a disadvantage in regard to housing. They must spend a higher percentage of their income on housing costs. Often, their housing is inadequate and dangerous. Children of the poor are more likely to experience environmental hazards such as lead-paint poisoning and fires. Educational opportunities for the poor also are limited. Schools in low-income neighborhoods are not adequately funded. Drop-out rates are higher in poor communities and college is financially impossible for many.
4. The two principal ways in which the government attempts to reduce social inequality are transfer payments and subsidies. Transfer payments are attempts to redistribute the society's wealth. A proportion of money collected through taxes is given to people who are in need of assistance—the poor, the elderly, people with disabilities, and the unemployed. Subsidies, on the other hand, involve transfers of goods and services rather than cash to the needy. Examples of subsidies include food stamps, housing subsidies, and school lunches.

Answers to Developing Sociological Imagination *(pages 226–227)*

Conversion of low-cost and abandoned housing units to condominiums, conversion of low-cost rooming houses to expensive apartments, and the replacement of businesses catering to low-income people by those catering to wealthier people have reduced the number of homes available to people with low incomes. Complicating the situation is the fact that the government did away with the subsidies and tax shelters that once were used to entice builders to provide low-rent housing. These factors have resulted in an enormous increase in the number of homeless people in the United States. Concern over this situation has led many communities to take steps to help the homeless.

Closing the Chapter

Have students complete the Chapter 9 Review Worksheet, found in the *Teacher's Resource Binder.*

Assessing the Chapter

Have students complete the Chapter 9 Review, found on page 228 of the *Pupil's Edition.*

Give students the Chapter 9 Form A Test and, if desired, the Chapter 9 Reteaching Worksheet and Form B Test, found in the *Teacher's Resource Binder.*

Reviewing Sociological Terms

1. Social inequality
2. social class
3. endogamy
4. Social stratification
5. poverty

Thinking Critically about Sociology

1. **(a)** Socioeconomic status is a rating that combines social factors such as educational level, occupational prestige, and place of residence with the economic factor of income. **(b)** Socioeconomic status determines an individual's relative position in the stratification system.
2. **(a)** Life chances refer to the likelihood individuals have of sharing in the opportunities and benefits of society. **(b)** The poor have poorer health, a shorter life expectancy, and higher infant mortality primarily because they have less money to spend on food and medical care.
3. The reputational method is suitable only in the study of small communities. Findings from these studies cannot be generalized to other communities. The subjective method is problematic because people usually do not place themselves in the upper or lower social classes. The objective method produces different rankings depending on which specific social and economic factors are used.
4. **(a)** In 1950, India's caste system was abolished as the legal basis for determining access to public facilities, legal protection, and economic resources. Endogamy also was eliminated as a precondition for marriage. In rural areas, however, the caste system still plays an important role in organizing daily life. **(b)** The forces of industrialization are moving India away from the caste system.
5. According to the table on page 219, poverty levels are as follows: 1 person: $6,932; 2 persons: $8,865; 3 persons: $10,860; 4 persons: $13,924; 5 persons: $16,456; 6 persons: $18,587; 7 persons: $21,058; 8 persons: $23,605; 9 persons or more: $27,942.
6. More than one-fourth of America's poor do not receive any form of governmental assistance. There are several reasons for this. Some of the poor cannot qualify because they have assets such as a car. In the case of AFDC, two-parent families can qualify only when the primary breadwinner is unemployed. Another reason is the unavailability of resources and insufficient personnel to process requests for assistance. Finally, many poor people simply do not request help from the government.
7. Answers will vary, but students should supply one example of each of the three types of social mobility discussed in the chapter.
8. Students' charts should include information from the discussion of social classes found on textbook pages 215–217.

Exercising Sociological Skills

1. Generally, skilled crafts such as electrician, machinist, and bricklayer are most likely to be unionized.

These jobs, which tend to be male-dominated, have higher salaries than female-dominated jobs with similar skill levels, such as typist, cashier, and bank teller. College professors and high school teachers also may be unionized, as are mail carriers. The American Medical Association also functions like a union in many respects, lobbying for special privileges that keep physicians' salaries high.
2. The rural poor face special problems. For example, they seldom have easy access to government services and health-care facilities. In addition, the loss of many jobs that traditionally supported rural areas, such as mining, timber, and manufacturing, contributes to an already difficult situation.
3. Answers will vary, but students should discuss the basic and complex causal relationships contained in the articles they have chosen.

Extending Sociological Imagination

1. Answers will vary. Consider having students use the information from their reports to write an editorial for the school newspaper.
2. Answers will vary.

Answers to Interpreting Primary Sources *(page 229)*

1. The loss of subsidies and tax shelters discouraged private investors from providing low-cost housing for the poor.
2. The following are some of the ways that communities are battling homelessness: fixing up abandoned buildings and constructing new homes for the poor; applying pressure on local governments to protect tenants from unfair evictions; lobbying for stricter enforcement of health and safety codes; persuading banks to open up branches in minority neighborhoods and increase available mortgage loans for low-income consumers; publishing reports on the plight of the homeless.

CHAPTER 10 *(pages 230–257)*

RACIAL AND ETHNIC RELATIONS

SECTION 1
RACE, ETHNICITY, AND THE SOCIAL STRUCTURE

SECTION 2
PATTERNS OF INTERGROUP RELATIONS

SECTION 3
MINORITY GROUPS IN THE UNITED STATES

Chapter Overview

Race and ethnicity refer to two separate sets of characteristics. In sociological terms, a race is a category of people who share inherited physical characteristics and who are perceived as being a distinct group. Ethnicity is the set of cultural characteristics that distinguishes one group from another group.

No particular skin color, physical feature, or ethnic background is by nature superior or inferior. The value placed on specific characteristics is determined by those who hold power in society—in other words, the dominant group. By establishing the values and norms of society, members of the dominant group consciously and unconsciously create a social structure that operates in their favor. Their positions of power allow them to enjoy certain privileges, such as better housing, better schools, and higher incomes.

The resources and rewards found in society are limited. Consequently, the privileged position of the dominant group often is gained at the expense of the life chances of minority groups within society. A minority group is a category of people who share physical characteristics or cultural practices that result in group members being denied equal treatment.

Minority group members face the related problems of discrimination and prejudice. Discrimination is the denial of equal treatment to individuals based on their group membership. Prejudice, on the other hand, is an unsupported generalization about a category of people. The most common sources of discrimination and prejudice are stereotyping, scapegoating, and the social environment.

Treatment of minority groups can range from total acceptance to total rejection. The most common patterns of acceptance include assimilation, cultural pluralism, and legal protection. Population transfer, subjugation, and extermination are the most common patterns of rejection.

Not all groups in the United States have been equally successful in carving out a secure place in society. Among the racial and ethnic groups that have faced the most difficulty in gaining acceptance are African Americans, Hispanic Americans, Asian Americans, Native Americans, and white ethnics.

Chapter Objectives

At the conclusion of the chapter, students will be able to

1. Define race, ethnicity, ethnic group, and minority group.
2. Identify the five characteristics that distinguish minority groups from other groups in society.
3. Define discrimination and prejudice, and determine their three main sources.
4. Describe the five most common patterns of minority group treatment.
5. Explain the conditions under which minority groups live in the United States.

Introducing the Chapter

Show the class the film *Under Our Skin: Exploring Racial and Cultural Differences* (rental information can be found in the introductory section of this *Teacher's Manual*). In this film, young people use music, dance, and drama to chronicle their experiences with prejudice and stereotypes. Following the film, ask students to discuss their reactions to the views presented by the young actors. Then ask students to share with the class any of their own or their friends' experiences with discrimination and prejudice. Close by telling students that Chapter 10 will explore the issues of discrimination and prejudice in the context of racial and ethnic relations.

Chapter 10 Suggested Lesson Plans

Day 1	**Suggested Procedures:** Introducing the Chapter; Section 1 Previewing Key Terms; Introducing the Section **Materials:** PE: pp. 230–235; TM: pp. 66–68
Day 2	**Suggested Procedures:** Section 1 Strategies and Assignments **Materials:** PE: pp. 232–235; TM: pp. 68; TRB: Assorted Worksheets
Day 3	**Suggested Procedures:** Section 2 Previewing Key Terms; Introducing the Section; Strategies and Assignments **Materials:** PE: pp. 236–244; TM: pp. 69–70; TRB: Transparency 9, Assorted Worksheets
Day 4	**Suggested Procedures:** Section 3 Previewing Key Terms; Introducing the Section; Strategies and Assignments **Materials:** PE: pp. 245–255; TM: pp. 70–72; TRB: Worksheet
Day 5	**Suggested Procedures:** Closing the Chapter; Assessing the Chapter **Materials:** PE: pp. 256–257; TM: pp. 72–73; TRB: Review Worksheet, Tests, Reteaching Worksheet

SECTION 1 *(pages 232–235)*

RACE, ETHNICITY, AND THE SOCIAL STRUCTURE

Section Overview

A race is a category of people who share inherited physical characteristics and who are perceived by others as being a distinct group. Ethnicity, on the other hand, refers to the cultural characteristics that distinguish one group from another group. The people who share a common cultural background and a common sense of identity are called an ethnic group. When a racial or ethnic group possesses physical characteristics or cultural practices that result in the group being denied equal treatment in society, the group is classified as a minority group.

Previewing Key Terms

Section 1 contains the following key terms: **race, ethnicity, ethnic group, minority group**. Write the following four questions on the chalkboard and have students copy them into their study notebooks. (1) What is the sociological definition of race? (2) What is the sociological definition of ethnicity? (3) What is an ethnic group? (4) What is a minority group? Then have students turn to the Glossary and use the definitions there to answer the four questions. Instruct students to keep this material in their study notebooks for later review.

Introducing the Section

Begin by having students write short position papers that either support or refute the following statement: "Everyone in the United States is a member of some minority group." Then instruct students to turn to textbook page 235 and read the list of five characteristics used by sociologists to distinguish minority groups from other groups in society. Ask students to revise their position papers based on what they have just read. Then have volunteers read their papers to the class for class discussion.

Suggested Teaching Strategies

1. **Classifying Ideas (I)** Ask students to identify various racial and ethnic groups that exist in the United States. Write the names of these groups on the chalkboard. When no new ideas are forthcoming, ask students to indicate which groups are racial groups and which groups are ethnic groups. Discuss with the class whether any of the groups are difficult to classify, and, if so, why.
2. **Working in Groups (I, II)** Organize the class into several small groups. Ask each group to use discarded magazines to create a collage showing the lifestyles and characteristics of a specific racial or ethnic group. Have the groups share their collages with the class.
3. **Exploring Multicultural Perspectives (III)** Have students conduct library research and prepare brief reports on holidays and festivals celebrated by various racial, ethnic, and religious groups (examples might include Kwanzaa, Rosh Hashanah, St. Patrick's Day, Cinco de Mayo, and so on). Ask volunteers to read their reports to the class. Then have the class discuss how such festivals and celebrations help people to develop pride in their cultural heritages.

Suggested Enrichment Activities

1. **Exploring Cross-Cultural Perspectives (I)** Have students complete the appropriate Cross-Cultural Perspectives Worksheet, found in the *Teacher's Resource Binder.*
2. **Conducting Library Research (III)** Have interested students conduct library research on some of the racial classification systems that have been popular

at various times in history. Ask the students to report their findings to the class.
3. **Using Sociological Imagination (III)** Have interested students or groups of students write one-act plays about a group of extraterrestrials who come to Earth for the first time. The scripts should concentrate on the reactions of Earth's people to the group of aliens and the characteristics that distinguish the aliens from the people of Earth. Have selected students act out some of the plays in class, then use the plays as the basis of a discussion concerning minority groups in society.

Suggested Assignments

1. **Seeing Relationships (I)** As homework, have students list the names of four minority groups in the United States and explain how each group meets the five characteristics of a minority group.
2. **Identifying Ideas (I)** Have students complete the appropriate Developing Research Skills Worksheet, found in the *Teacher's Resource Binder.*

Closing the Section

Close the section by asking students to distinguish in writing between (a) race and ethnicity and (b) dominant groups and minority groups. If students appear to have difficulty with any of this information, offer clarifications at this time.

Assessing the Section

Have students complete the Section 1 Review.

Answers to Section 1 Review *(page 235)*

Define *race:* category of people who share inherited physical characteristics and who are perceived by others as being a distinct group; ***ethnic group:*** individuals who share a common cultural background and a common sense of identity

1. **(a)** The three racial categories into which people are classified are Caucasoids, Mongoloids, and Negroids. **(b)** Caucasoids typically have fair skin and straight or wavy hair. Mongoloids generally have yellowish or brownish skin and distinctive folds on their eyelids. Negroids typically have dark skin and woolly hair.
2. **(a)** Ethnicity is the set of cultural characteristics that distinguishes one group from another group. **(b)** Ethnicity generally is based on characteristics such as national origin, religion, language, customs, and values.
3. **(a)** A minority group is a category of people who share physical characteristics or cultural practices that result in the group being denied equal treatment. **(b)** Five characteristics that distinguish minority groups from other groups in society are identifiable physical or cultural characteristics that differ from those of the dominant group; unequal treatment by members of the dominant group; group membership based on ascribed statuses; strong bonds among members and a shared sense of loyalty to the group; and the tendency to marry within the group.

SECTION 2 *(pages 236–244)*

PATTERNS OF INTERGROUP RELATIONS

Section Overview

Discrimination and prejudice are common features of the minority group experience. Societal discrimination can appear in one of two forms: legal discrimination and institutionalized discrimination. Discrimination, in either of its two forms, involves behaviors. In contrast, prejudice refers to attitudes. Prejudiced beliefs that serve as justifications for open discrimination often take the form of racism.

Discrimination and prejudice arise from a number of sources. Among the sources recognized by sociologists are stereotyping, scapegoating, and the social environment.

Societies react to minority groups in a number of ways. The most common patterns of minority group treatment noted by sociologists are assimilation, cultural pluralism, legal protection, population transfer, subjugation (including slavery, de jure segregation, and de facto segregation), and extermination (genocide).

Previewing Key Terms

Section 2 contains the following key terms: **discrimination, prejudice, legal discrimination, institutionalized discrimination, self-fulfilling prophecy, racism, stereotype, scapegoating, assimilation, cultural pluralism, subjugation, slavery, segregation, de jure segregation, de facto segregation, genocide**. Ask students to create a Word Search puzzle using these terms. Then have them exchange papers and complete the puzzles. Students may place their puzzles in their study notebooks for later review.

Introducing the Section

Introduce the section by showing the film *The Wave* (rental information can be found in the introductory section of this *Teacher's Manual*). In this film, a high school teacher conducts an experiment that ultimately shows how easily people can be manipulated into embracing discriminatory behavior and prejudiced attitudes. After showing the film, ask the class if students in their school would react the way that the students in the film reacted. Make sure that students give reasons for their responses. Then tell them that discrimination and prejudice, the focus of Section 2, are common features of the minority group experience.

Suggested Teaching Strategies

1. **Understanding Ideas (I)** After defining discrimination and prejudice for the class, ask students to provide examples of legal discrimination, institutionalized discrimination, and prejudice as a self-fulfilling prophecy. Use the examples as the basis of a class discussion.

2. **Interpreting Graphs (I)** Place Transparency 9, which focuses on patterns of prejudice and discrimination, on an overhead projector and ask the questions contained in the accompanying teacher's notes. Transparencies and accompanying teacher's notes are found in the *Teacher's Resource Binder*.

3. **Working in Groups (II, III)** Organize the class into six small groups and assign each group one of the six patterns of minority group treatment discussed in the section. Instruct the members of each group to examine newspaper, magazine, and reference materials for a contemporary or historical example of the pattern they have been assigned. Group members should use the information they have located to prepare a short report for the class.

Suggested Enrichment Activities

1. **Composing a Paragraph (I)** Have students complete the appropriate Critical Skills Mastery Worksheet, found in the *Teacher's Resource Binder*.

2. **Making Oral Presentations (III)** Have interested students research and prepare oral presentations on one of the following topics: the 1896 Supreme Court case of *Plessy* v. *Ferguson* and the 1954 case of *Brown* v. *Board of Education of Topeka,* the origin of the term "ghetto," or the efforts of American women to gain the right to vote.

Suggested Assignments

1. **Organizing Ideas (I)** As homework, have students complete the appropriate Graphic Organizer Worksheet, found in the *Teacher's Resource Binder*.

2. **Analyzing Sociological Research (I)** Have students read the Applying Sociology feature on textbook pages 240–241 and then answer the questions at the end of the feature.

Closing the Section

Close the section by having students identify in writing the three sources of discrimination and prejudice and the six patterns of minority group treatment. If students appear to have difficulty with any of this material, offer clarifications at this time.

Assessing the Section

Have students complete the Section 2 Review.

Answers to Applying Sociology *(pages 240–241)*

1. Facing discrimination on a daily basis would result in a negative self-image among the children experiencing the discrimination. They might come to expect failure and might believe that success in school is an impossible goal. This belief might even lead them to drop out of school.

2. The discrimination practiced in the experiment led the children to believe that brown-eyed people are cleaner, more civilized, and smarter than blue-eyed people. The children also came to believe that blue-eyed people have poor memories and are careless. The type of indoctrination the children in the experiment

received could just as easily lead to discrimination based on skin color—racism—had race rather than eye color been the focus of concern.

3. The dominant group believed it actually was superior because it received frequent and consistent reinforcement from the teacher for this belief. Real-life examples of this type of situation include the Nazi belief system and the South African system of apartheid.

Answers to Section 2 Review *(page 244)*

Define *discrimination:* denial of equal treatment to individuals based on their group membership; *prejudice:* unsupported generalization about a category of people; *racism:* belief that one's own race or ethnic group is naturally superior to other races or ethnic groups; *slavery:* ownership of one group of people by another group; *de jure segregation:* segregation based on laws; *de facto segregation:* segregation based on informal norms

Identify *active bigot:* person who is prejudiced and who openly discriminates against others; *timid bigot:* person who is prejudiced but who is afraid to discriminate because of societal pressure; *fair-weather liberal:* person who is not prejudiced but who discriminates anyway because of societal pressure; *all-weather liberal:* person who is not prejudiced and who does not discriminate

1. **(a)** Legal discrimination is based on laws and can be eliminated by a simple change in the laws. Institutionalized discrimination, on the other hand, results from the way a society is structured. This type of discrimination is an outgrowth of former discrimination and is much more difficult to change. **(b)** Some examples of legal discrimination include the system of apartheid in South Africa, the exclusion of American women from voting rights prior to the 1920s, and the "Jim Crow" laws in the southern United States prior to 1954. An example of institutionalized discrimination is what can result when a minority group is denied equal access to housing and employment over a long period of time. Being concentrated in low-income neighborhoods with poorly funded schools may result in the inability of the minority group to take advantage of newly opened opportunities even after the restrictions are lifted.

2. **(a)** Thomas's theorem states that if people define situations as real, they are real in their consequences. In other words, people see their world based on what they expect to be true, not always on what actually is true. These prejudiced beliefs can affect the social situation of individuals and groups. For example, if people are told often enough and long enough that they are inferior, they may come to believe it. **(b)** A false definition of a situation may become a self-fulfilling prophecy. For example, if members of a minority group are believed to be incapable of understanding technical information, they will not be given technical training. Because they lack training, they will not be able to get jobs in highly technical fields.

The lack of employment in technical fields then will be used as evidence that the group is unable to understand technical information.

3. Three sources of prejudice and discrimination are stereotyping, scapegoating, and the social environment. Stereotyping involves the use of an oversimplified, exaggerated, or unfavorable generalization about a category of people. Scapegoating is the practice of blaming an innocent person or group of people for one's own troubles. Certain aspects of the social environment, such as vast differences in power between various groups and extreme competition for scarce resources, can lead to prejudice and discrimination.

4. There are six common patterns of minority group treatment. Assimilation occurs when culturally distinct groups are blended into a single group with a common culture and a common identity. Cultural pluralism occurs when the various groups are allowed to keep their own cultural identities. Legal protection involves the taking of official action to ensure that the rights of minority groups are upheld. The pattern of population transfer occurs when members of the minority group are transferred to a different geographic area. Subjugation is a pattern that involves the maintenance of control over a group through the use of force. The most extreme pattern is extermination, which involves the planned destruction of the minority group.

SECTION 3 *(pages 245–253)*

MINORITY GROUPS IN THE UNITED STATES

Section Overview

For the most part, minority groups in the United States have prospered in relation to how closely they adapt to the white Anglo-Saxon Protestant (WASP) image. Those who can more easily adapt are accepted into mainstream American society relatively quickly. For example, northern and western European immigrants from heavily Protestant nations such as Sweden, the Netherlands, and Germany generally gained dominant status within a generation. Other groups—such as African Americans, Hispanic Americans, Native Americans, Asian Americans, and white ethnics—have had more difficulty in gaining acceptance in the United States.

Previewing Key Terms

Section 3 contains the following key term: **white ethnics**. Tell students that white ethnics make up one of the minority groups that they will learn about in Section 3. Then ask students to consider which groups of people might be included in the category of "white ethnics." Write the students' responses on the chalkboard. Then ask a volunteer to turn to the Glossary and read the definition of the term aloud to the class.

Introducing the Section

Begin the section by writing the following questions on the chalkboard: (1) What is a minority group? (2) What are some of the minority groups that are found in the United States? (3) What kinds of problems have minority groups faced? (4) For what kinds of rights have members of minority groups struggled? (5) What strides have members of minority groups made over the years? (6) What problems remain? Assign students, as they read Section 3, to take notes that will help them answer these questions. Have students place their notes in their study notebooks for use later in the chapter.

Suggested Teaching Strategies

1. **Learning from Multimedia Materials (I)** Share with the class one or more of the multimedia materials included in the list of such materials for Chapter 10. Discuss these materials with the class or ask students to prepare reaction papers.
2. **Synthesizing Information (I, II)** Organize the class into five small groups and assign each group one of the five minority groups discussed in the section. Have the members of each group identify how their assigned minority group meets the five characteristics of a minority group discussed in Section 1 of the chapter. Have each group share its conclusions with the class.
3. **Locating Information (I, II)** Assign students to clip articles on racial and ethnic relations in the United States from newspapers and magazines. Arrange the articles on the bulletin board by racial or ethnic group for a class discussion.
4. **Working in Groups (II, III)** Organize the class into small groups and have each group choose one of the minority groups discussed in the section. Have the members of each group work together to create a piece of art that illustrates the struggle of that minority group to achieve equal rights in the United States. Art may take the form of a song, a poem, a painting, a collage, a dance, or so on. Have the groups perform or display their art for the class.

Suggested Enrichment Activities

1. **Exploring Multicultural Perspectives (III)** Have interested students interview older members of the minority groups discussed in this section concerning how the treatment of minority groups has changed over the past few decades. Have the students share their interview findings with the class.
2. **Creating a Time Line (III)** Have interested students conduct library research on the number and kinds of laws passed by Congress from 1960 to 1990 to protect Americans' civil rights. Have the students use this information to make a time line of civil rights legislation.

Suggested Assignments

1. **Understanding Ideas (I)** As homework, have students complete the appropriate Understanding Sociological Ideas Worksheet, found in the *Teacher's Resource Binder*.

2. **Summarizing Information (I)** Have students write a summary of the information presented in the Case Study on textbook page 246.
3. **★Thinking about Sociology: Identifying Assumptions (I)** Have students read the Developing Sociological Imagination feature on textbook pages 254–255 and then complete the assignment under Practicing the Skill.

Closing the Section

Close the section by having students retrieve the notes they wrote in answer to the questions presented in the Introducing the Section activity. Then, one at a time, read the questions aloud and have volunteers supply the answers. Instruct students to fill in any gaps in their note-taking at this time.

Assessing the Section

Have students complete the Section 3 Review.

Answers to Section 3 Review *(page 253)*

Identify *Chinese Exclusion Act:* act passed by Congress in 1882 that prevented Chinese men from bringing their wives and children into the United States and from holding certain types of jobs. Ended Chinese immigration into the United States. In effect from 1882 until 1940; *Tydings-McDuffie Act:* act that limited the number of Filipino immigrants coming into the United States to 50 per year. Passed in 1934; *McCarran-Walter Act:* act that allowed Asians to enter the United States according to national quotas and eligibility for citizenship. Passed in 1952

1. The status of African Americans has improved in several important ways over the years. First, the educational attainment of African Americans has increased, with the percentage of African Americans and whites graduating from high school being nearly identical. Second, over 16 percent of employed African Americans now hold professional or managerial jobs. Third, the number of African Americans elected to public office has jumped from about 200 in 1965 to almost 7,500 today. Many socioeconomic inequalities still exist, however. African Americans are only half as likely as whites to finish four years of college. The average income of African American families is only slightly more than half that of white families. African American families are three times as likely as white families to live below the poverty level. Forty-six percent of African American children live below the poverty level. The unemployment rate among African Americans is 2.2 times higher than the rate among whites. Finally, employed African American women are almost twice as likely as white women to work in service occupations.
2. Students' answers should be based on information taken from the table at the top of textbook page 248.
3. Asian Americans have been particularly successful in achieving economic security and social acceptance and have, as a result, been called a model minority. Many Asian Americans resent the label, however,

because it disregards the fact that the group has faced many hardships on the road to acceptance. These hardships include a history of prejudice, discrimination, and violence, as well as legal discrimination in the form of anti-Asian laws and internment during World War II.

4. In the late nineteenth century, the United States government made Native Americans wards of the government and moved them from their tribal lands to reservations. At this point, the federal government attempted to assimilate Native Americans into the dominant culture. In the process, traditional Native American patterns of subsistence and property distribution were destroyed. Family relationships also were weakened. When it became clear that the Native Americans were not being assimilated, the government changed its approach. Native American groups were granted the right to self-government and Native American land was returned to tribal ownership. Additionally, the Native American groups were provided with financial assistance to help them restore their cultures.

5. White ethnics came to the United States with little money and few skills. They also spoke little English and practiced a religion that differed from that of the dominant culture. For these reasons, white ethnics were not accepted into mainstream society as quickly as were other European immigrants.

Answers to Developing Sociological Imagination (pages 254–255)

Answers will vary, but students should identify and evaluate assumptions made about Native American culture in the reading.

Closing the Chapter

Have students complete the Chapter 10 Review Worksheet, found in the *Teacher's Resource Binder*.

Assessing the Chapter

Have students complete the Chapter 10 Review, found on page 256 of the *Pupil's Edition*.

Give students the Chapter 10 Form A Test and, if desired, the Chapter 10 Reteaching Worksheet and Form B Test, found in the *Teacher's Resource Binder*.

Answers to Chapter 10 Review (page 256)

Reviewing Sociological Terms

1. Subjugation
2. ethnicity
3. ethnic group
4. Assimilation
5. Genocide
6. slavery
7. Cultural pluralism

Thinking Critically about Sociology

1. Scapegoating is the practice of blaming innocent people or groups for one's own troubles. People who

scapegoat gain a sense of superiority at a time when they might be feeling powerless.

2. According to Merton, individuals can combine discriminatory behavior and prejudicial attitudes in four ways. They can have prejudicial attitudes and act in discriminating ways. They can have prejudicial attitudes but not discriminate because of societal pressures. They can discriminate without having prejudicial attitudes simply to go along with societal pressure. Finally, they can have nonprejudicial attitudes and not discriminate.

3. (a) A self-fulfilling prophecy is a prediction that results in behavior that makes the prediction come true. (b) Answers will vary but students should provide an example of a self-fulfilling prophecy.

4. After a long period of being denied access to opportunities for education and training, minority group members are unable to compete for positions of power. Their inferior social status becomes self-perpetuating in that it is used to justify ongoing inequality. Discrimination thus becomes institutionalized.

5. (a) It is difficult to classify people in terms of race because people often possess the traits of more than one race. Intermarriage between the races has produced wide variations within the three main racial groups. (b) For sociologists, the biological or physical characteristics of a racial category are less important than the social reactions to those characteristics and the consequences of the social reactions for individuals in society.

6. (a) Segregation is the physical separation of a minority group from the dominant group. (b) There are two basic types of segregation: de jure segregation and de facto segregation. De jure segregation is segregation that is based on laws. De facto segregation, on the other hand, is segregation that is based on informal norms.

7. Prejudice serves the dominant group in society by providing justification for discrimination and racism and by eliminating the guilt produced by these actions.

Exercising Sociological Skills

1. After a long period of being told that they were a superior "race," and that the Jews were inferior, Hitler's German forces came to believe that the massacre of the Jews was necessary. The brown-eyed children in the experiment adopted a belief in their own superiority and a hatred toward their former friends, the blue-eyed children, after only a few hours of indoctrination.

2. In neighborhood B, the high density of blacks and Asians fostered positive race relations. Strong networks developed within the minority groups and these in turn helped the minorities maintain their cultural identities. There also was an absence of peer pressure against cross-racial friendships since most people had had cross-racial contacts since childhood. In area A, on the other hand, poor race relations grew out of poor economic conditions. Unemployed white youths blamed the minorities for the economic problems experienced by whites in the area.

3. Answers will vary.

Extending Sociological Imagination

1. Answers will vary.
2. Answers will vary.

Answers to Interpreting Primary Sources *(page 257)*

1. Reasons why it might be difficult to collect data on hate crimes include the fact that some victims might choose not to report such crimes; some people might be unaware of what constitutes hate crimes; and police officer discretion in the reporting of such crimes might mean that not all such crimes are recorded as hate crimes.
2. Suggested reasons why hate crimes appear to be on the rise include increased immigration and affirmative action programs that might cause resentment toward minority groups.

CHAPTER 11 *(pages 258–287)*

GENDER, AGE, AND HEALTH

SECTION 1
GENDER

SECTION 2
AGE

SECTION 3
HEALTH

Chapter Overview

Race and ethnicity are not the only factors that affect a person's standing in society. An individual's position in the social structure also is influenced by whether he or she is male or female, young or old, able-bodied or disabled. In general, to be female, old, or a person with a disability is to be in a position of lesser power in society. The degree of that power difference varies from society to society, but it exists to some degree in all societies.

Chapter Objectives

At the conclusion of the chapter, students will be able to

1. Define gender and gender roles, and explain how gender roles affect the life chances of men and women in society.
2. Describe what effects the aging of the population is having on society and the life chances of the elderly.
3. Evaluate the state of health care in the United States.
4. Outline the main provisions of the Americans with Disabilities Act.
5. Discuss some of the special health-care concerns of various segments of society.

Introducing the Chapter

Remind students that in Chapter 10 they examined how race and ethnicity can affect an individual's position in the social structure. Note that most people have little difficulty accepting that both of these factors help to determine life chances in many societies. Then suggest that other factors also can affect access to social rewards and scarce resources. Tell students that Chapter 11 will examine three of these other factors—gender, age, and health.

Chapter 11 Suggested Lesson Plans

Day 1	**Suggested Procedures:** Introducing the Chapter; Section 1 Previewing Key Terms; Introducing the Section **Materials:** PE: pp. 258–269; TM: pp. 73–74
Day 2	**Suggested Procedures:** Section 1 Strategies and Assignments **Materials:** PE: pp. 260–269; TM: pp. 74–75; TRB: Assorted Worksheets
Day 3	**Suggested Procedures:** Section 2 Previewing Key Terms; Introducing the Section; Strategies and Assignments **Materials:** PE: pp. 270–274; TM: pp. 75–76; TRB: Transparency 10, Worksheet
Day 4	**Suggested Procedures:** Section 3 Previewing Key Terms; Introducing the Section; Strategies and Assignments **Materials:** PE: pp. 275–285; TM: pp. 76–78; TRB: Assorted Worksheets
Day 5	**Suggested Procedures:** Closing the Chapter; Assessing the Chapter **Materials:** PE: pp. 286–287; TM: pp. 78–79; TRB: Review Worksheet, Tests, Reteaching Worksheet
Day 6	**Suggested Procedures:** Closing the Unit; Assessing the Unit **Materials:** PE: pp. 288–289; TM: pp. 79–80; TRB: Review Worksheet, Tests, Reteaching Worksheet

---

SECTION 1 *(pages 260–269)*

GENDER

Section Overview

The specific behaviors and attitudes that a society establishes for men and women are called gender roles. Gender roles result from the division of labor that assigns different tasks to men and women in society. Individuals learn proper gender behavior through the socialization process.

Many social scientists are interested in studying gender inequality. One such social scientist is Ernestine Friedl. Friedl claims that power in society is based on who controls the distribution of scarce resources. Because men control the distribution of scarce resources, they hold the greatest degree of power. Conflict theorists are in basic agreement with Friedl's position. According to conflict theorists, gender roles in industrial society are a reflection of male dominance.

Previewing Key Terms

Section 1 contains the following key terms: **gender, gender roles, Equal Rights Amendment (ERA), sexism**. Write these terms on the chalkboard. Then have students develop a definition for each term, based on what they think it means. Write the definitions on the chalkboard and ask a volunteer to record them on a piece of paper. After students have read Section 1, ask them to revise the definitions based on the material presented in the section.

Introducing the Section

Organize the class into four groups: two groups of females and two groups of males. Have one group of females prepare a description of female socialization in the United States and the other group prepare a description of male socialization. Have one group of males prepare a description of male socialization and the other group prepare a description of female socialization. Once the groups have presented their descriptions to the class, discuss how male and female socialization differ. Then explore how male and female perceptions of each other's socialization differ and what effects these differing perceptions might have on gender equality.

Suggested Teaching Strategies

1. **Extending Ideas (I)** Show the class the film *Who You Are and What You Are: Understanding Sex Roles* (rental information can be found in the introductory section of this *Teacher's Manual*), which explores various gender-role related issues. Use the film as the basis of a class discussion of gender and gender roles.
2. **Summarizing Information (I, II)** Have students read the Case Study feature on textbook page 263 and summarize the history of women's experiences in the military.
3. **Conducting a Survey (II, III)** Have students read the Applying Sociology feature on textbook pages 266–267. Then have interested students conduct a survey on gender-based attitudes toward success by following the instructions presented in the feature. Discuss the results in class.

Suggested Enrichment Activities

1. **Exploring Cross-Cultural Perspectives (I)** Have students complete the appropriate Cross-Cultural Perspectives Worksheet, found in the *Teacher's Resource Binder*.

2. **Conducting Library Research (III)** Have interested students conduct library research on some of the problems faced by women in the areas of education, employment, or politics.

Suggested Assignments

1. **Linking the Past to the Present (I)** As homework, have students view one or two syndicated television programs from the 1950s or 1960s (such as *Father Knows Best, Ozzie and Harriet,* or *Leave It to Beaver*). Instruct students to write a short essay that compares the gender-role expectations evident in these programs with the gender-role expectations of today. Have volunteers read their essays aloud to the class for class discussion.
2. **Interpreting Statistics (I)** Have students complete the appropriate Critical Skills Mastery Worksheet, found in the *Teacher's Resource Binder*.
3. **Expressing a Point of View (I)** Have students write a reaction paper on the view of gender inequality put forth by Ernestine Friedl or conflict theorists.

Closing the Section

Close the section by having a volunteer turn to textbook page 260 and read the excerpt on that page from the book *Femininity* by Susan Brownmiller. Then ask volunteers to recount similar anecdotes from their own early childhoods that focus on gender-role socialization. Finally, have students consider how their own gender-role socialization has affected their expectations of adult life.

Assessing the Section

Have students complete the Section 1 Review.

Answers to Applying Sociology *(pages 266–267)*

Answers will vary, but students should conduct the survey according to the directive given in the feature and draw sound conclusions from the data.

Answers to Section 1 Review *(page 269)*

Define *gender:* behavioral and psychological traits considered appropriate for males and females; ***gender roles:*** specific behaviors and attitudes that a society establishes for women and men; ***sexism:*** belief that one sex is by nature superior to the other

Identify *Equal Rights Amendment:* amendment approved by Congress in 1972 proposing equality for the sexes, but defeated when it did not receive ratification by the required number of states

1. **(a)** Gender roles are a function of the division of labor. In all societies, there is some degree of specialization in the performance of necessary tasks. Typically, men and women specialize in different kinds of work. **(b)** In some societies, gender roles are reversed from those found in the United States. Among the Tchambuli, for example, women provide the food and men care for the young. Societies also

vary in the psychological traits typical of men and women. Mead, for example, found that Tchambuli women were bossy and efficient, while Tchambuli men were gossipy and artistic. **(c)** Sociologists argue that if gender roles were based primarily on biology, few variations in gender behavior would exist within or between cultures.

2. Traditionally, females in the United States are expected to be gentle, passive, and polite. They are not supposed to be too aggressive or too adventuresome. Males, on the other hand, are expected to be active, adventuresome, and aggressive rather than passive or gentle.

3. **(a)** Friedl argues that power in society is based on the distribution of scarce resources. Individuals who exchange goods and services with nonfamily members have higher statuses and thus greater power. In most societies, it is the men who control such exchanges. Thus women tend to have less power than do men. **(b)** The evidence Friedl offers to support her argument comes from hunting and gathering societies. In such societies, there is a gender-based division of labor: women collect fruits, nuts, and vegetables; men hunt animals. Because the women provide the majority of the food, they have more power relative to men than do women in more technologically advanced societies. The food that these women provide, however, is distributed within the family. The food collected by men, on the other hand, is shared with people outside the family. As a result, the men retain the greatest amount of societal power.

4. Control theorists believe that gender roles persist in industrial societies simply because of male dominance. Because men control the economy and the government, they have been able to establish laws and customs that protect their privileged status.

5. In the educational realm, women are less likely than men to pursue graduate and professional degrees. In addition, women tend to select college majors that lead to lower-paying jobs. In the area of employment, women workers tend to be concentrated in low-paying, low-status jobs. As a result of this sex segregation in the work place, women earn far less money than men. In the area of politics, women are underrepresented in the upper levels of government.

SECTION 2 (pages 270–274)

AGE

Section Overview

The elderly in industrial societies suffer from discrimination in the form of ageism. Ageism is the belief that one age category is by nature superior to another age category. Although Social Security benefits and other government transfer payments have reduced the level of poverty among the elderly, some segments of the elderly population still suffer from high rates of poverty.

Previewing Key Terms

Section 2 contains the following key terms: **ageism, baby-boom generation, Medicare**. Have students look up each term in the Glossary. Then have them write on a piece of paper what is important about each term with regard to age stratification. Finished papers may be shared with the class.

Introducing the Section

Ask students to turn to the Section 2 Review on textbook page 274. Then write the following sentence on the chalkboard: "Based on the review questions, I expect to learn at least 10 things from this section:"

1. _____
2. _____
3. _____
etc.

Ask students to copy the sentence and to fill in the blanks. When the activity has been completed, ask volunteers to discuss their answers with the class. Instruct students to keep their list of items in their study notebooks for use later in the section.

Suggested Teaching Strategies

1. **Expressing Ideas (I)** Prior to assigning the reading of Section 2, instruct students to write short stories that have as their theme the life of the elderly in contemporary American society. Use the stories as the basis of a class discussion on the aged in society.

2. **Interpreting Graphs (I)** Place Transparency 10, which focuses on age distributions in countries around the world, on an overhead projector and ask the questions contained in the accompanying teacher's notes. Transparencies and accompanying teacher's notes are found in the *Teacher's Resource Binder*.

3. **Practicing Interviewing Skills (I, II)** Invite a representative from the local Social Security office or from the American Association of Retired Persons, Gray Panthers, or other organization designed to assist the elderly to speak to the class on the needs of the aged in the United States. Have students prepare a list of questions beforehand to ask the speaker.

Suggested Enrichment Activities

1. **Linking Theory and Research (I)** Have students complete the appropriate Developing Research Skills Worksheet, found in the *Teacher's Resource Binder*.

2. **Making Oral Presentations (III)** Ask interested students to research and prepare oral presentations on one of the following topics: the effects of world population trends; the debate over long-term health care for the elderly; the future of the Social Security system in the United States; or the work of the American Association of Retired Persons or the Gray Panthers.

3. **Drawing a Line Graph (III)** Have interested students conduct research to draw a line graph showing the percentage of the elderly living in poverty for each decade from 1920 to 1990.

Suggested Assignments

1. **Analyzing Ideas (I)** As homework, have students watch two television programs that contain elderly characters. Ask the students to write a short analysis of the programs that answers the following questions: (a) How are the elderly characters treated by the other characters in the programs? (b) What, if any, ageist attitudes are evident in the programs?

2. **★Thinking about Sociology: Analyzing Sociological Viewpoints (I)** Instruct students to read the Developing Sociological Imagination feature on textbook pages 284–285 and then complete the assignment under Practicing the Skill.

3. **Creating a Bar Graph (III)** Ask interested students to conduct library research on population projections for each decade from the year 2000 to the year 2050. Have students use this information to create a bar graph showing what percentage of the population will be over the age of 65 for each of the decades within the period of consideration. Have students take special note of what the percentage of the population over 65 will be when they themselves reach the age of 65.

Closing the Section

Close the section by having students retrieve the lists of items they prepared during the Introducing the Section activity. Ask volunteers to read items from their lists aloud and have the class discuss how their expectations for learning the section material have been fulfilled.

Assessing the Section

Have students complete the Section 2 Review.

Answers to Section 2 Review (page 274)

Define ageism: belief that one age category is by nature superior to another age category; **baby-boom generation:** approximately 76 million people born in the United States from 1946 through 1964; **Medicare:** government-sponsored insurance plan for the elderly and the disabled

Identify American Association of Retired Persons (AARP): organization of 32 million people that has worked effectively to bring the needs of the elderly to public attention

1. **(a)** One of the ways in which ageism is evidenced in industrial societies is in the stereotypes used to describe the elderly. The elderly often are portrayed as unproductive, cranky, and physically or mentally impaired. **(b)** Ageism in American society is reinforced by the media. In commercials, the elderly are used primarily to promote products associated with illness and death. In the news, features about the elderly typically focus on the negative aspects of aging.

2. **(a)** The world's population is aging. Today there are approximately 332 million people aged 65 and older worldwide. It is estimated that by the year 2000, this number will have grown to more than 426 million. **(b)** There are two basic reasons why the average age

of the United States population is increasing. First, advances in health care and better living conditions have resulted in more people surviving to old age. Second, variations in birth rates have changed the age structure of the United States. As the large baby-boom generation ages, the average age of the population will increase even further.

3. The Social Security system is funded by workers. Current workers pay for the benefits received by current retirees. Declining birth rates and longer life expectancies mean that there are fewer workers available to support growing numbers of retirees.

4. **(a)** Such critics point to statistics that show that the poverty rate among the aged population has dropped from 35 percent in 1960 to slightly more than 12 percent today. **(b)** In reality, the 12 percent figure masks a great deal of variation in living conditions among the different segments of the elderly population in the United States. For instance, almost 34 percent of elderly African Americans and around 21 percent of elderly Hispanic Americans are poor. In comparison, the poverty rate for elderly whites is approximately 10 percent. In addition, many other elderly people live just above the poverty level.

SECTION 3 (pages 275–283)

HEALTH

Section Overview

Health, like gender and age, plays a role in determining equality in industrial societies. As health-care costs climb and as access to medical care declines in rural and inner-city areas, Americans increasingly are expressing concern over the state of the nation's health care. Consequently, health has become an important political issue. Among the topics being discussed are the need for a national health-care system, the rights of Americans with disabilities, and policy issues involving the treatment of AIDS and AIDS victims.

Previewing Key Terms

Section 3 contains the following key terms: **acquired immune deficiency syndrome (AIDS), Medicaid**. Have students look up both of these terms in the Glossary. Then ask: "What is the relationship between AIDS and Medicaid?" *(Medicaid pays a portion of AIDS-related health-care costs.)*

Introducing the Section

Before introducing this section, research the cost of the following medical services in your area: a private hospital room, a semiprivate hospital room, a visit to the doctor's office, a school physical examination, the setting of a broken arm, a blood test, treatment for severe acne, and the delivery of a baby without complications. Then begin the class session by asking students to estimate the cost of each one of these services. Write the students' responses on the chalkboard. Then compare the actual prices with the class estimates. Use the comparisons as a lead-in to a discussion of how health-care costs affect access to medical care.

Suggested Teaching Strategies

1. **Solving Problems (I)** After discussing the forces that affect access to health care in the United States, have students speculate on what can be done to encourage doctors to become general practitioners and to serve in poor inner-city and rural areas of the country.
2. **Seeing Relationships (I)** Show the film *Main Street: He's My Brother,* which explores the challenges and rewards of having a sibling who is disabled. After a class discussion of the film, have students outline the ways in which the Americans with Disabilities Act will improve life for Americans with disabilities.
3. **Learning from Charts (I)** Have students examine the chart on textbook page 280 and write a summary in essay form of the information presented in the chart.
4. **Making Oral Presentations (II, III)** Have interested students conduct research and make oral presentations on some of the technologies that have been developed to improve the lives of Americans with disabilities. Then have the class speculate on what future advances in technology for people with disabilities are still needed.

Suggested Enrichment Activities

1. **Working in Groups (II, III)** Organize interested students into small groups and have them research one of the following topics: the origin and purpose of the Names Project Quilt, the spread of the AIDS epidemic throughout the world, United States funding for AIDS research, the physical and social consequences of AIDS, or the threat posed to American teenagers by the AIDS epidemic. Have the students use this information to present a panel discussion on AIDS to the class.
2. **Practicing Interviewing Skills (III)** Ask interested students to interview public health officials, hospital administrators, or social workers about the health-care needs of the poor. Have the students share their findings with the class.

Suggested Assignments

1. **Organizing Ideas (I)** As homework, have students complete the appropriate Graphic Organizer Worksheet, found in the *Teacher's Resource Binder.*
2. **Conducting Research (III)** Ask interested students to conduct library research on the causes and consequences of some of the catastrophic health epidemics found throughout history, such as the bubonic plague, influenza, or polio. Have students share their information with the class and compare this information with the worldwide implications of the AIDS epidemic.
3. **Drawing a Line Graph (III)** Have interested students research the costs of medical insurance and the percentage of uninsured Americans over the past few

decades and show this information in a line graph. Have students display their graphs to the class and discuss the implications of rising insurance costs.

Closing the Section

Close the section by having students complete the appropriate Understanding Sociological Ideas Worksheet, found in the *Teacher's Resource Binder.*

Assessing the Section

Have students complete the Section 3 Review.

Answers to Section 3 Review *(page 283)*

Define *acquired immune deficiency syndrome (AIDS):* fatal disease caused by a virus that attacks an individual's immune system, leaving the person vulnerable to a host of deadly infections; *Medicaid:* state and federally funded health-insurance program for people with little or no money

Identify *National Health Service:* Great Britain's national health-care program that provides free or nearly free health care to British citizens; established in 1948, the NHS is funded and controlled by the government

1. The two major issues at the center of concern over health care in the United States are the cost of care and access to care. More money is spent on health care in the United States than in any other nation in the world, and costs are increasing. Contributing to rising costs are hospital care, advances in medical technology, and increased testing due to fears of malpractice suits. In addition, access to health care is becoming more difficult for many Americans, despite the fact that there is a "surplus" of physicians. The shortage is due, in large part, to the fact that doctors tend to be concentrated in certain geographic areas and in certain medical specialties.
2. Answers will vary, but students should base their essays on information from textbook pages 277–282.
3. The poor are much more likely than the affluent to experience serious health problems. For instance, poor children have a 50 percent greater chance of dying before their first birthday than children from wealthier families. In addition, people from poor families are absent from school or work almost three times as many days as people from wealthier families. Complicating the situation is the fact that tuberculosis, once very much under control, is now beginning to reappear in poor urban neighborhoods. Also, people from poor families are less likely than people from wealthier families to characterize their health as excellent. Finally, the poor suffer disproportionately from a number of serious diseases and have a lower life expectancy than the wealthier segments of society.

Answers to Developing Sociological Imagination *(pages 284–285)*

Answers will vary, but students should note that Etzioni's position is based both on fact and on opinion. When

Etzioni recounts Callahan's position on medicare assistance for the elderly or discusses the uses of medical technology for the young and old, he is basing his arguments on fact. Much of his discussion of the advisability of reducing other medical-related spending, however, is based on opinion. Before accepting these statements, students should carefully weigh whether they are reasonable. Students also should consider whether Etzioni is offering these suggestions, not in earnest, but as a way to show the absurdity of Callahan's position.

Closing the Chapter

Have students complete the Chapter 11 Review Worksheet, found in the *Teacher's Resource Binder*.

Assessing the Chapter

Have students complete the Chapter 11 Review, found on page 286 of the *Pupil's Edition*.

Give students the Chapter 11 Form A Test and, if desired, the Chapter 11 Reteaching Worksheet and Form B Test, found in the *Teacher's Resource Binder*.

Answers to Chapter 11 Review *(page 286)*

Reviewing Sociological Terms

1. Sexism
2. Medicaid
3. baby-boom generation
4. Gender roles
5. Ageism

Thinking Critically about Sociology

1. According to Ernestine Friedl, power in society is based on the distribution of scarce resources. Individuals who exchange goods and services with nonfamily members have higher statuses and thus greater power. In most preindustrial societies, the money earned by women tends to be used for the maintenance of the family. Little of the money earned by women is invested in money-earning enterprises. Friedl argues that as long as women's economic contributions center on the home, gender inequality will continue to be a problem.
2. The provisions of the Americans with Disabilities Act will help disabled Americans find and keep meaningful employment by prohibiting employers from discriminating against people on the basis of disability.
3. Answers will vary, but students should specify what characterizations of the elderly are reflected in the television commercials they have chosen.
4. **(a)** Among the factors contributing to rising health-care costs in the United States are the increased costs of hospital care, the increased use of advanced medical technologies, and increased testing due to doctors' fears of malpractice suits. **(b)** All Americans are affected—directly or indirectly—by the dramatic rise in health-care costs. Nearly half of the nation's annual medical expenditures are paid for by the government. Rising medical costs mean a bigger chunk out of the federal budget. For businesses, higher medical costs mean that they must either accept lower profits or raise prices. When businesses raise prices, they run the risk of being less competitive. American consumers, however, may be the biggest losers. Approximately 25 percent of all annual health-care expenditures come directly out of the pockets of consumers.
5. AIDS is a fatal disease caused by a virus that attacks an individual's immune system, leaving the person vulnerable to a host of deadly infections. AIDS is transmitted through sexual contact, contaminated blood and tissue, and the use of contaminated needles. The groups at highest risk of acquiring AIDS are homosexual or bisexual men, intravenous drug abusers, persons receiving blood transfusions, the sexual partners of high-risk persons, and the babies of high-risk mothers. **(b)** The federal government has instituted several measures aimed at stopping the spread of AIDS. The government has, for instance, increased funding for AIDS research and sponsored educational programs designed to teach the public about high-risk behaviors. **(c)** AIDS activists and many government officials claim that discrimination against AIDS victims is one of the biggest obstacles to combatting the disease. These people argue that the legal rights of AIDS victims must be protected under the Americans with Disabilities Act. If this were not the case, the fear of losing their jobs or homes would stop people from seeking voluntary AIDS testing. Opponents argue that giving AIDS patients protection under the Americans with Disabilities Act and other legislation provides special rights for homosexuals and other high risk groups while putting the general public at risk.
6. Answers will vary, but encourage students to provide workable, carefully thought out answers to the question.
7. Poor people are more likely than wealthier people to suffer health problems because of crowded and unsanitary living conditions, inadequate diets, and the absence of regular medical care.
8. Passage of the Equal Rights Amendment would not automatically solve the problem of gender inequality because women, like most minority groups, face institutionalized discrimination. While laws can be changed with the stroke of a pen, it takes generations to erase discriminatory social customs.

Exercising Sociological Skills

1. The chart on page 157 tends to support Horner's study, but only weakly. As Horner would predict, women make up less than half of all professional and managerial workers. Most women are concentrated in technical, sales, and administrative support occupations and in service occupations. The percentage of women in managerial and professional specialties is higher, however, than one might expect from Horner's study.
2. Prior to the 1940s, women's participation in the military was limited mainly to nursing, clerical work, and laundry duties. After World War II broke out, the Women's Army Auxiliary Corps was established, paving the way for separate women's corps in all branches of the military. In 1948, women were integrated into the armed services, but only to a proportion of 2 percent and only under certain conditions.

In 1967, the 2 percent cap on female enlistment was lifted and women could fill all but the top ranks in the military. The end of the draft and the establishment of an all-volunteer army contributed to a dramatic rise in the number of military women. Today, women make up 11 percent of the military, and have participated in military actions in Grenada, Libya, Panama, and the Persian Gulf. The last obstacle to women's participation in the military fell recently when combat roles were opened to women.

3. Answers will vary, but students should use the skills presented in the Developing Sociological Imagination feature on textbook pages 284–285 to analyze the viewpoints presented in the articles.

Extending Sociological Imagination

1. Answers will vary.
2. Answers will vary.
3. Answers will vary.

Answers to Interpreting Primary Sources (page 287)

1. Survey results show that 31 percent of all required modifications cost nothing and two-thirds can be done for under $500.
2. Employers can avoid discriminating against people by doing such things as giving job applicants the opportunity to write for interviews rather than telephoning and allowing new hires to use identification other than drivers' licenses.

Closing the Unit

Have students complete the Unit 3 Review Worksheet, found in the *Teacher's Resource Binder.*

Assessing the Unit

Have students complete the Unit 3 Review, found on page 289 of the *Pupil's Edition.*

Give students the Unit 3 Form A Test and, if desired, the Unit 3 Reteaching Worksheet and Form B Test, found in the *Teacher's Resource Binder.*

Answers to Unit 3 Review (page 289)

Reviewing Sociological Ideas

1. **(a)** Social stratification is the ranking of individuals or categories of people on the basis of unequal access to scarce resources and social rewards. **(b)** In a closed system, movement between social strata is impossible. A person is assigned a status at birth and remains at that level throughout life. In an open system, on the other hand, movement between strata is possible. The ease of movement depends on the degree of openness in the system.
2. **(a)** Exogamy is marriage outside of one's social category. **(b)** Endogamy is marriage within one's own social category. **(c)** Endogamy is practiced in caste systems because marriage between members of different castes would make it difficult to assign a status to children.

3. **(a)** Social mobility is the movement of people between or within social classes or strata. **(b)** Among the major structural causes of downward mobility are changes in the economy that alter the demand for labor.
4. **(a)** Ethnicity is the set of cultural characteristics that distinguishes one group from another. **(b)** Ethnic groups are based on cultural characteristics, such as religion, language, customs, and values, whereas race is based on inherited physical characteristics such as skin color. **(c)** According to the classification system, Caucasoids typically have fair skin and straight or wavy hair. Mongoloids have yellowish or brownish skin and distinctive folds on their eyelids. Negroids have dark skin and tightly curled hair.
5. **(a)** Discrimination is the denial of equal treatment to individuals based on their group membership. Societal discrimination can appear as legal discrimination and institutionalized discrimination. Legal discrimination is based on laws and can be eliminated by a simple change in laws. Institutionalized discrimination results from the way a society is structured. It is an outgrowth of former discrimination and is much more difficult to change. **(b)** Prejudice is an unsupported generalization about a category of people. For the dominant members of society, prejudice serves as a justification for discriminatory actions. **(c)** Three sources of prejudice and discrimination are stereotyping, scapegoating, and the social environment. Stereotyping is an oversimplified, exaggerated, or unfavorable generalization about a category of people, while scapegoating is the practice of placing the blame for one's troubles on an innocent individual or group.
6. **(a)** Gender roles are the specific behaviors and attitudes that a society establishes for women and men. **(b)** Gender roles are a function of the division of labor. In all societies, there is some degree of specialization in the performance of necessary tasks. Typically, men and women specialize in different kinds of work.
7. **(a)** Ageism is the belief that one age category is by nature superior to another age category. **(b)** The American Association of Retired Persons helps the elderly in many ways. It is a major lobbyist for aged Americans. Additionally, it operates a credit union and a large health-insurance plan, offers travel and prescription drug discounts, publishes a magazine, produces a weekly television series, and operates a wire service that disseminates information about the elderly.

Synthesizing Sociological Ideas

1. **(a)** Poverty is a standard of living below the minimum level considered decent and reasonable by the society. **(b)** The poor differ from the nonpoor in many important respects. One of the most important differences pertains to health and length of life. The poor have the highest rates of heart disease, diabetes, cancer, tuberculosis, arthritis, anemia, pneumonia, and influenza. Infant mortality is twice as high among the poor as it is among the general population. Thus, life expectancy is much shorter for the poor. The poor

also are at a disadvantage in regard to housing. They must spend a higher proportion of their income on housing costs. Often their housing is inadequate and dangerous. As a result, poor children are more likely to experience environmental hazards such as lead-paint poisoning and fires than are the children of more affluent parents. Educational opportunities for the poor also are limited. Schools in low-income neighborhoods often are not adequately funded. In addition, drop-out rates are higher in poor communities and college is financially impossible for many.

2. **(a)** Most sociologists define social class as a grouping of people with similar levels of wealth, power, and prestige. This definition builds on the work of Max Weber and is broader than the Marxian definition. Marx defined social class in terms of ownership of the means of production. On this basis, society is divided into two classes—the owners of the means of production (the bourgeoisie) and the workers (the proletariat). According to Marx, there is inequality in capitalist societies because the owners of the means of production get all of the profits but the workers do all of the actual work. **(b)** When Marx was writing, in the 1800s, the Industrial Revolution was at its peak. Working and living conditions were terrible for most of the population. The divisions between owners and workers were striking. Today, growth in the professions, the managerial classes, the number of self-employed, and the rise of the service industry have altered the nature of work. In addition, daily control of industry is in the hands of middle and upper management—individuals who are themselves employees. **(c)** Sociologists use three basic methods to assign individuals to social classes: the reputational method, the subjective method, and the objective method. In the first method, individuals in the community are asked to rank other community members based on what they know of their characters and lifestyles. In the second method, individuals estimate their own social classes. In the third method, sociologists use factors such as education, income, and occupation to assign persons to social classes.

3. **(a)** Horizontal mobility refers to movement within a social class, as happens when a person moves from one job to another of equal social ranking. Vertical mobility refers to movement between social classes. This movement can be either upward or downward. **(b)** Intergenerational mobility refers to social class differences that exist between adult children and their parents. It is considered a special form of vertical mobility because it involves movement between social classes.

4. **(a)** A minority group is a category of people who share physical characteristics or cultural practices that result in the group being denied equal treatment.

(b) Answers will vary, but students should base their answers on information taken from textbook pages 245–253.

5. **(a)** Sexism is the belief that one sex is by nature superior to the other. **(b)** Answers will vary, but students might mention that women face gender-based inequality in all major aspects of life. In terms of religion, women make up only a very small percentage of the clergy in the major denominations. In terms of jobs and income, women are concentrated in the lowest paying jobs and earn around 70 percent of what men earn. In the family, women continue to do the bulk of household labor, even when they are employed outside the home.

6. Assimilation is the blending of culturally distinct groups into a single group with a common culture and identity. Cultural pluralism is the policy that allows each group within a society to keep its unique cultural identity. Legal protection involves legal steps to ensure that the rights of minority groups are protected. Population transfer involves the coercive relocation of a minority group by the dominant group. Subjugation is the maintaining of control over a group by force. Subjugation can take the form of slavery or segregation. Extermination is the elimination of a minority group through killing. When the goal of extermination is the intentional destruction of the entire targeted population, it is called genocide.

7. **(a)** As the size of the elderly population increases and as more elderly people live into their 80s, the need for added financial and health-care benefits will place additional strain on the Social Security system. **(b)** Answers will vary, but students might mention that around one-third of elderly African Americans and almost one-fourth of elderly Hispanic Americans are poor. In comparison, elderly whites have a poverty rate of 10 percent. Students also might mention that many elderly live just above the poverty level.

8. Major categories in student outlines should include the costs of health care and access to health care.

9. **(a)** Acquired immune deficiency syndrome is a fatal disease caused by a virus that attacks an individual's immune system, leaving the person vulnerable to a host of deadly infections. **(b)** AIDS is transmitted through sexual contact, contaminated blood and tissue, and the use of contaminated needles. **(c)** The federal government has instituted several measures aimed at stopping the spread of the disease. Among these steps are increased funding for AIDS research and educational programs designed to teach the public about high-risk behavior.

Applying Sociological Imagination

1. Answers will vary.
2. Answers will vary.

UNIT 4 *(pages 290–401)*

SOCIAL INSTITUTIONS

CHAPTER 12
THE FAMILY

CHAPTER 13
THE ECONOMY AND POLITICS

CHAPTER 14
EDUCATION AND RELIGION

CHAPTER 15
SCIENCE AND SPORT

Unit Overview

If a society is to survive over time, certain basic needs must be met. For instance, new members must be added to the population to replace those members who have died or moved away. People must be clothed, sheltered, and fed. Goods and services must be produced and made available to those who need and desire them. The young must be educated and socialized into society. The elderly and the sick must receive care. Order must be maintained and power must be distributed among the members of society. Societies satisfy these needs through social institutions.

A social institution is a system of statuses, roles, norms, and values that is organized to satisfy one or more of the basic societal needs. Sociologists traditionally have recognized five major social institutions: family, economy, politics, education, and religion. In recent years, sociologists have noted the development of several new social institutions in industrialized societies. Two of these emerging social institutions are science and sport. Unit 4 examines each of these social institutions.

Unit Goals

At the end of the unit, students should be able to

1. Discuss family systems and marriage patterns from a cross-cultural perspective.
2. Describe the characteristics of the American family, including courtship and marriage patterns, family disruption, and current trends.
3. Examine the economic institution in terms of economic systems, economic models, and the characteristics of postindustrial America.
4. Examine the political institution in terms of the nature of power and authority, types of government, and the characteristics of the American political system.
5. Explain the functionalist and conflict perspectives on education, and discuss some of the issues in American education.

6. Describe the functions and nature of religion, and identify the characteristics of religion in American society.
7. Discuss science as a social institution, focusing on the rise of modern science and the norms and realities of scientific research.
8. Discuss sport as a social institution, focusing on the institutionalization of sport, the characteristics of modern sport, and issues in American sport.

Unit Skills

Four skills are developed in Unit 4.

★ READING ABOUT SOCIOLOGY: *Understanding Census Data* (Chapter 12; PE pages 314–315; TM page 87)
★ INTERPRETING THE VISUAL RECORD: *Analyzing Editorial Cartoons* (Chapter 13; PE pages 342–343; TM page 92)
★ WRITING ABOUT SOCIOLOGY: *Summarizing Sociological Information* (Chapter 14; PE pages 370–371; TM page 95)
★ THINKING ABOUT SOCIOLOGY: *Determining Fallacies in Reasoning* (Chapter 15; PE pages 396–397; TM page 100)

Suggestions for teaching the skills appear on the TM pages mentioned above. The suggestions are clearly identified by the ★ symbol. Each skill is reinforced in the Chapter Review under Exercising Sociological Skills. Answers to the questions in the textbook's skill features appear in the Answers to Developing Sociological Imagination sections of this Teacher's Manual.

Introducing the Unit

Remind the class that all societies develop social institutions to ensure that basic societal needs are met. If societies did not develop social institutions, social order would break down. To illustrate this point, show to the class the film *Lord of the Flies,* available at video rental stores in either an older black and white version or the newer color version. After the film has been viewed and discussed, tell the class that Unit 4 will explore the range of social institutions found in modern society.

References for Teachers

Birnbaum, Jeffrey H. *The Lobbyists: How Influence Peddlers Get Their Way in Washington.* New York: Times Books, 1992. Behind-the-scenes view of congressional lobbyists representing corporate interests and the power politics of the 101st Congress of 1989–1990.

Collins, Randall, and Coltrane, Scott. *Sociology of Marriage and the Family: Gender, Love, and Property.* Chicago, IL: Nelson-Hall, 1990. Introductory-level college textbook of marriage and the family written from a conflict perspective.

Feigelman, William, ed. *Sociology Full Circle,* 5th ed. New York: Holt, Rinehart and Winston, 1989. Collection of articles and essays on a variety of sociological topics, including social institutions.

Harrington, Michael. *Socialism: Past and Future*. New York: New American Library, 1992. Examines the social, economic, and political impact of socialism.

Jamieson, Kathleen Hall. *Dirty Politics: Deception, Distraction, and Democracy*. New York: Oxford University Press, 1992. Analyzes the ways in which television has affected the political process in the United States.

Kozol, Jonathan. *Savage Inequalities: Children in America's Schools*. New York: Random House, 1991. Argues that the nation's poor will be condemned to inferior schools as long as the quality of education is tied to community affluence.

Larossa, Frank. *Social History of Fatherhood*. Chicago, IL: University of Chicago Press, 1992. Examines how the social role of father has changed throughout history.

Mulkay, Michael. *Sociology of Science: A Sociological Pilgrimage*. Bloomington, IN: Indiana University Press, 1991. Insightful exploration of theory and research into the sociology of science.

Religion in America: Opposing Viewpoints. San Diego, CA: Greenhaven Press, 1989. Anthology of divergent views on the role and influence of religion in American society.

Rogasky, Barbara. *Smoke and Ashes: The Story of the Holocaust*. New York: Holiday House, 1988. Pictorial and written history of the Holocaust.

Scanzoni, L.D., and Scanzoni, J. *Men, Women, and Change: A Sociology of Marriage and the Family*, 3rd ed. New York: McGraw-Hill, 1988. Research- and theory-based discussion of marriage and family life.

Sherrow, Victoria. *Separation of Church and State*. New York: Franklin Watts, 1992. Discusses how the separation of church and state emerged in American society and how it has been challenged in the courts through the years.

Vogler, Conrad C., and Schwarz, Stephen. *Sociology of Sport: An Introduction*. Englewood Cliffs, NJ: Prentice-Hall, 1992. Basic sociological introduction to the social institution of sport.

Readings for Student Enrichment

Adams, Richard. *Watership Down*. New York: Macmillan, 1974. Allegorical examination of human society; enables students to analyze the power of government over individuals.

Buck, Pearl. *The Good Earth*. New York: Pocket Books, 1983. Portrayal of life in China during the last century; allows students to examine family relations from a cross-cultural perspective.

A Family History Handbook. Des Moines, IA: Perfection Learning, 1991. Teaches students how to research and explore their family histories and heritages; helps students develop an appreciation for their family roots.

Golding, William. *Lord of the Flies*. Hauppauge, NY: Barron's Educational Series, 1984. Group of boys stranded on a deserted island create their own system of government; allows students to explore the nature of power.

Michener, James. *The Source*. New York: Fawcett, 1988. Archaeological dig in Israel is used as a vehicle to explore the evolution of Judeo-Christian religion; provides students with insights into the nature and functions of religion.

Potok, Chaim. *The Promise*. New York: Fawcett, 1985. Story of two Jewish boys coming to terms with their faith in the modern world; allows students to examine the influence of religion on social relations.

The Role of the United States in a Changing World: Choices for the 21st Century. Guilford, CT: Dushkin Press, 1993. Presents four alternative "futures" for students to analyze in terms of feasibility and impact; helps students learn how to think critically and independently about foreign policy.

Stein, Herbert, and Foss, Murray. *An Illustrated Guide to the American Economy*. Washington, DC: AEI Press, 1992. Full-color graphs and text combine to help students visualize more than 100 key economic topics; helps students develop a broader understanding of the American economy.

Steinbeck, John. *The Grapes of Wrath*. New York: Penguin Books, 1976. Chronicles the journey of a poverty-stricken family during the Dust Bowl years of the 1930s; allows students to examine the effects of the economy on individuals.

Multimedia Materials

The selected materials listed below may be useful during the study of Unit 4. The following abbreviations are used in the list:

c = color	lvd = laser videodisc
b&w = black & white	sim = simulation
f = film	sw = software
fs = filmstrip	g = game
vhs = videocassette	

Chapter 12

Alcohol and the Family: The Breaking Point (f, vhs; 29 min.) AM. Emphasizes the fact that families of alcoholics are as much in need of professional help as the alcoholics themselves and that seeking such help offers hope for a healthier future.

Alcohol, Children, and the Family (f, vhs; 28 min.) AM. Reviews the developmental needs of children and shows how these needs are not met in families where one or both parents are alcoholics.

And They Lived Happily Ever After? Understanding Teenage Marriage (fs on vhs; 36 min.) GA. Teenagers discuss their expectations of marriage and why early marriages often fail.

Broken Dolls (vhs; 29 min.) EBEC. Demonstrates how abused children often grow up to become child abusers themselves, and how preventing child abuse depends on breaking this cycle.

Child of the Philippines: No Time to Play (vhs; 14 min.) EBEC. Focuses on Cynthia, the eldest of four children in the Cena family of the Philippines, whose responsibilities include hours of work at home each day and a full day of school.

Children of New Zealand: Living in the High Country (vhs; 13 min.) EBEC. Focuses on Malcolm Prouting and his sister, who live with their family on a sheep station in New Zealand.

Coping with Family Crisis: Violence, Abuse, Separation, Divorce (vhs; 57 min.) GA. Presents interviews with people who have experienced family abuse, separation, or divorce.

Families: Will They Survive? (vhs; 20 min.) EBEC. Examines various family forms, including nuclear families and extended families, throughout history.

Family Matters: The Role of the Family in the Middle East (vhs; 25 min.) EBEC. Explores the role of women in Middle Eastern families and the effects of Western influences.

Jen's Place (f, vhs; 26 min.) BF. Teenager Jen is angered to return from summer camp and find that her parents have separated and agreed on a custody arrangement for her without including her in the discussions.

Rajvinder: An East Indian Family (f, vhs; 16 min.) BF. Presents the marriage preparations and wedding of Rajvinder, a young Sikh woman who lives in an East Indian community in North America.

Today's Family: Adjusting to Change (vhs; 28 min.) GA. Discusses the wide variety of family types found in the United States today, including dual-worker families, single-parent families, and stepfamilies.

Who Will Be My Guardian? (vhs; 29 min.) EBEC. Explains how to recognize child abuse and what can be done to combat this serious social problem.

Chapter 13

America's Political Parties: The Democratic Party (vhs; 58 min.) AM. Nationally syndicated columnist Ben J. Wattenberg uses documentary footage and interviews with Democratic leaders to examine the recent history of the Democratic party.

America's Political Parties: The Republican Party (vhs; 58 min.) AM. Former White House staffer David Gergen uses documentary footage and interviews with Republican leaders to explore the recent history of the Republican party.

Balance of Power (sw, sim) SVE. Simulation in which students use research and reasoning skills to direct the balance of power in global politics.

Capitalism (vhs, c; 24 min.) NGS. Follows the development of capitalism from the Industrial Revolution in England to the United States today.

Communism (vhs, c; 27 min.) NGS. Traces the system of communism from Marx and Engels to the former Yugoslavia.

Communism and the Cold War (lvd) CMFV. Examines the events that led to the collapse of communism in Eastern Europe and the end of the Cold War.

If I'm Elected: Modern Campaign Techniques (vhs; 25 min.) CE. Behind-the-scenes documentary that examines how and why modern political campaigns have become a science of manipulation.

Lobbying: A Case History (vhs; 18 min.) EBEC. Shows how interest groups mobilize support for a cause and attempt to influence Washington legislators to accept their point of view.

Political Parties in America: Getting the People Together (vhs; 20 min.) EBEC. Examines all levels of political parties in the United States and explains how and why political parties function.

The Price of Power: Money in Politics (vhs; 25 min.) CE. Absorbing documentary that investigates where political candidates get their money and analyzes the role of money in local, state, and national elections.

The Rise and Fall of the Soviet Union (vhs, c, b&w; 124 min.) SSSS. Uses documentary footage to present a historical overview of the Soviet Union.

The Road to the White House '92 (vhs, c; 90 min.) SSSS. Bernard Shaw and Catherine Crier chronicle the 1992 presidential campaign.

72 Hours to Victory: Behind the Scenes with Bill Clinton (vhs; 50 min.) CSS. Ted Koppel narrates this behind-the-scenes look at the 72 hours before the election of Bill Clinton to the presidency.

Socialism (vhs, c; 25 min.) NGS. Examines the history and practice of socialism.

The Soviet World in Transition (3 fs; 21 min. each) NGS. Presents the formation of the USSR, the eras of Stalin through Gorbachev, the breakup of the country in the 1990s, and prospects for the future.

What Is Capitalism? (fs on vhs; 36 min.) GA. Presents a historical perspective on capitalism, from the theories of Adam Smith to the present operation of a free market based on supply and demand.

Chapter 14

Faith and Belief: Five Major World Religions (vhs, c; 21 min.) ZM. Introduction to the origins and principal beliefs of Judaism, Christianity, Islam, Hinduism, and Buddhism.

Inner City vs. *Suburban Schools* (vhs, c; 28 min.) FHS. Specially adapted Phil Donahue program that explores the problems found in inner-city schools and what can be done to solve the inequalities between inner-city and suburban schools

Islam: The Faith and the People (vhs; 20 min.) CSS. Explores the meaning of Islam, why it is embraced by so many people, and why it is feared by some.

Is There Life after High School? Planning Your Future (fs on vhs; 45 min.) GA. Overview of the options available to students, based on a four-stage assessment of preferences, abilities, geographic considerations, and definitions of success.

Look Before You Leap: The Dropping-Out Crisis (vhs; 30 min.) CE. Emphasizes the importance of staying in school by focusing on the diminished opportunities available to people who drop out.

Putting High School to Work (vhs; 30 min.) CE. Helps students develop a plan of study in high school that will help them to achieve their personal and occupational goals later in life.

Sects and Violence: Fragmentation Within Religions (vhs; 25 min.) EBEC. Examines the three major religions of the Middle East and shows how they have fragmented into smaller sects that compete for influence.

Textbooks and Dreams (vhs; 15 min.) BF. Examines the varied school systems available in Africa, from outdoor rural schools to schools with modern facilities, and explores why many African children do not have the opportunity to attend school.

Why School Is Important (vhs) CE. Identifies the negative consequences of dropping out of school.

The Age of Enlightenment (vhs; 30 min.) CSS. Describes the contributions of Newton, Locke, Rousseau, and others of the Enlightenment period while examining the relationship between natural laws and human existence.

Can Science Build a Champion Athlete? (vhs, c; 60 min.) FHS. Nova documentary that examines the technologies that have been developed to enhance athletic performance and the excesses to which science can go in the pursuit of athletic excellence.

Discovering the Scientific Method: Snigs ... Flirks ... Blorgs (sw) FM. Software that helps students develop an appreciation for the scientific method through numerous problem-solving exercises.

The Human Race (vhs, c; 15 min.) FHS. Imaginative view of a future society in which athletes become testing grounds for drug companies trying to overcome the limitations of the human body through drugs and medical enhancements.

Into the Unknown: A Voyage Simulation (sim) FM. Simulation that involves students in the experiences of a ship's voyage of discovery during the Age of Exploration.

Only the Ball Was White (vhs, c, b&w; 30 min.) SSSS. Documents the participation of African Americans in baseball before the sport was integrated and pays tribute to the men who were members of the Negro Leagues.

Steroids: Shortcut to Make-Believe Muscles (vhs; 35 min.) EBEC. Uses on-camera interviews with athletes, health educators, and medical professionals to explore the problem of anabolic steroid abuse.

The Steroid Trap: Turning Winners into Losers (vhs; 65 min.) GA. Examines who uses steroids and why, how steroids work, and the short-term and long-term effects of steroid abuse.

Time Tables of History: Science & Innovation (sw) SVE. Presents a time table of major scientific developments consisting of over 6,000 stories on a variety of science and technology subjects.

CHAPTER 12 *(pages 292–317)*

THE FAMILY

SECTION 1
THE FAMILY IN CROSS-CULTURAL PERSPECTIVE

SECTION 2
THE AMERICAN FAMILY

Chapter Overview

The family is a universal phenomenon. In all societies, no matter how small, the family serves as the basic social unit.

The form that the family takes, however, varies widely from society to society and even within a single society over time. Family organization is determined by how a society or group within society answers four basic questions: (1) How many marriage partners may a person have? (2) Who will live with whom? (3) How will family membership be determined? (4) Who will make the decisions in the family?

The traditional American family—with the father as sole breadwinner and the mother as the stay-at-home caretaker of the children—is only one possible form of family organization. A variety of family forms and marriage, residential, descent, and authority patterns are found cross-culturally. And even in the United States and other industrialized nations, new family forms have emerged. Dual-earner families, divorce, one-parent families, and stepfamilies, for instance, have become common features of Western family life.

Chapter Objectives

At the conclusion of the chapter, students will be able to

1. Explain how norms influence the ways in which marriage and family patterns around the world are organized.
2. Identify which basic societal needs are satisfied by the family institution.
3. Analyze the ways in which family life can be disruptive for family members.
4. Describe some of the trends in American family life currently being examined by sociologists.

Introducing the Chapter

Prior to assigning the reading of Chapter 12, list on the chalkboard the four questions that determine family organization: (1) How many marriage partners may a person have? (2) Who will live with whom? (3) How will family membership be determined? (4) Who will make the decisions in the family? Ask students to describe the variety of ways in which each question might be answered.

After students have mentioned several options for each question, reinforce the idea that the traditional American family of two parents with the father as breadwinner and the mother as homemaker is only one possible form that the family may take. Tell students that Chapter 12 will introduce them to the wide variety of marriage and family forms found in the United States and around the world.

Chapter 12 Suggested Lesson Plans

Day 1	**Suggested Procedures:** Introducing the Unit; Introducing the Chapter; Section 1 Previewing Key Terms; Introducing the Section **Materials:** PE: pp. 290–300; TM: pp. 81–85
Day 2	**Suggested Procedures:** Section 1 Strategies and Assignments **Materials:** PE: pp. 294–300; TM: pp. 85–86; TRB: Assorted Worksheets

Day 3	**Suggested Procedures:** Section 2 Previewing Key Terms; Introducing the Section; Strategies and Assignments **Materials:** PE: pp. 301–315; TM: pp. 86–88; TRB: Transparency 11, Assorted Worksheets
Day 4	**Suggested Procedures:** Closing the Chapter; Assessing the Chapter **Materials:** PE: pp. 316–317; TM: pp. 88–89; TRB: Review Worksheet, Tests, Reteaching Worksheet

SECTION 1 *(pages 294–300)*

THE FAMILY IN CROSS-CULTURAL PERSPECTIVE

Section Overview

A family is a group of people who are related by marriage, blood, or adoption and who live together and share economic resources. The two basic family forms are nuclear families and extended families. Nuclear families include families of orientation and families of procreation.

Marriage refers to the complex of norms that specify the ways in which family structure should be organized. Among the most important norms are those governing marriage partners, residence patterns, descent patterns, and authority patterns.

In all societies, the family performs certain functions. It regulates sexual activity, produces new members for the society, socializes children, and provides economic and emotional security. In industrialized societies, many of these traditional functions have been taken over by other social institutions.

Previewing Key Terms

Section 1 contains the following key terms: **social institution, family, nuclear family, family of orientation, family of procreation, extended family, kinship, marriage, monogamy, polygamy, polygyny, polyandry, patrilocality, matrilocality, bilocality, neolocality, patrilineal descent, matrilineal descent, bilateral descent, patriarchal system, matriarchal system, egalitarian system, incest taboo.** Ask students to choose 15 of the key terms in the list and create a Word Search puzzle using each of the terms. Then have students exchange papers and complete the puzzles. Students then may place the puzzles in their notebooks for later review.

Introducing the Section

Begin by telling students that, in recent years, many people in the United States have become concerned about the fate of the American family. Some people even fear that the family system is undergoing so much change that it eventually will collapse. Then invite students to comment on this view. Next, tell students that sociologists believe that the institution of the family is likely to survive. Sociologists base this belief on the fact that the family is the basic social unit in every known society throughout the world. The form that the family takes, however, varies from society to society and even in the same society over time. Then show the film *Families: Will They Survive?* (rental information can be found in the introductory section of this *Teacher's Manual*), which examines family forms found throughout history. Use the film as an introduction to the family in cross-cultural perspective, the focus of Section 1.

Suggested Teaching Strategies

1. **Making Comparisons (I)** Have students read Section 1 and then differentiate in writing between the following sets of concepts: family and kinship; nuclear and extended families; family of orientation and family of procreation; monogamy and polygamy; polygyny and polyandry; patrilocality, matrilocality, bilocality, and neolocality; patrilineal, matrilineal, and bilateral descent; patriarchal, matriarchal, and egalitarian systems. Discuss the differences in class.
2. **Interpreting Ideas (I)** To help students understand the concept of kinship, have them make a chart identifying as many of their primary, secondary, and tertiary relatives as they can. Poll the class to see how many of the possible 191 categories of relatives the students can name within their own family.
3. **Practicing Interviewing Skills (I, II)** Invite one or more foreign-born individuals to talk to the class about marriage and family patterns in other parts of the world. Have students prepare beforehand a list of questions to ask the speaker.
4. **Working in Groups (II, III)** Organize the class into four small groups and assign each group one of the functions of the family discussed in the section. Ask the groups to research how their assigned functions are fulfilled in (a) preindustrial societies and (b) postindustrial societies. Have the groups share their findings with the class.

Suggested Enrichment Activities

1. **Exploring Cross-Cultural Perspectives (I)** Have students complete the appropriate Cross-Cultural Perspectives Worksheet, found in the *Teacher's Resource Binder*.
2. **Making Oral Presentations (III)** Have interested students research and prepare oral presentations on marriage patterns in specific preindustrial societies.

Suggested Assignments

1. **Organizing Ideas (I)** As homework, have students complete the appropriate Graphic Organizer Worksheet, found in the *Teacher's Resource Binder*.
2. **Dramatizing Sociology (II, III)** Organize interested students into two groups. Ask one group to research family life in colonial America, and ask the other group to research family life during the Industrial Revolution. Then have each group write and present short skits depicting family life during the respective time periods.

Closing the Section

Close the section by having students complete the appropriate Understanding Sociological Ideas Worksheet, found in the *Teacher's Resource Binder*.

Assessing the Section

Have students complete the Section 1 Review.

Answers to Section 1 Review *(page 300)*

Define *social institution:* system of statuses, roles, values, and norms that is organized to satisfy one or more of the basic needs of society; ***family:*** group of people who are related by marriage, blood, or adoption and who live together and share economic resources; ***nuclear family:*** family form that consists of one or both parents and their children; ***family of orientation:*** nuclear family into which a person is born; ***family of procreation:*** nuclear family consisting of an individual, his or her spouse, and their children; ***extended family:*** family form that consists of three or more generations of a family sharing the same residence

1. **(a)** Societies vary in terms of the number of marriage partners an individual can have. Societies that practice monogamy allow people to have only one marriage partner. Societies that practice polygamy allow people to have multiple spouses. Polygyny—the marriage of one man to multiple wives—and polyandry—the marriage of one woman to multiple husbands—are types of polygamy. **(b)** Family patterns also vary in terms of residential rules. Some societies practice patrilocality and require newly married couples to live with or near the husband's family. Societies that practice matrilocality require newlyweds to live with or near the wife's family. In other societies, the newlyweds can choose to live near either the husband's or the wife's family, a system called bilocality. Finally, some societies, especially industrialized societies, practice neolocality and allow newlyweds to live apart from both sets of parents. **(c)** Societies also differ in terms of the way family descent is traced. Those that trace kinship through the father's family are patrilineal. Those that trace kinship through the mother's family, on the other hand, are matrilineal. Those that trace kinship through both the mother's and the father's families are bilateral. **(d)** There are three possible patterns of authority in families. In patriarchal systems, fathers hold most of the power. In matriarchal systems, mothers hold most of the power. In egalitarian systems, authority is shared by both mother and father.
2. The family has four central functions. It regulates sexual activity, enforcing an incest taboo that forbids sexual relations between certain relatives. Families also reproduce societal members, replacing those who die or move away. Within this function, they set up rules concerning childbearing and parenting obligations. Families also socialize children, teaching them the values and norms of society. Finally, families act as the basic economic units of societies. Basic needs are met through the division of labor among family members.

SECTION 2 *(pages 301–313)*

THE AMERICAN FAMILY

Section Overview

The great majority of Americans marry. Nevertheless, marital happiness appears to be on the decline. The family may be disrupted through violence or divorce. Although family violence once was thought to be a problem of the lower classes, sociologists now know that such violence occurs among all social classes and races. Divorce rates, on the other hand, vary among different segments of the population. In general, divorce rates are affected by factors such as age at marriage, race, ethnicity, and education.

Sociologists have noted a number of trends in American family life. These trends include delayed marriage, delayed childbearing, and increases in the number of dual-earner families, one-parent families, and remarriages.

Previewing Key Terms

Section 2 contains the following key terms: **homogamy, heterogamy, voluntary childlessness**. Have students write three sentences, one key term per sentence, based on what they think the terms mean. Then have them look up the definitions in the Glossary and revise their sentences as needed.

Introducing the Section

Begin by asking students if they have ever seen episodes of the television programs "Father Knows Best," "Leave It to Beaver," or "Ozzie and Harriet." If so, have students describe how family life is portrayed in these programs. Then ask: "Do you think these television programs are an accurate portrayal of family life in the 1950s and 1960s?" Next have students suggest ways in which family life in the 1990s differs from how it is portrayed on these television programs. Emphasize the fact that, although the family now exists in many forms, the family institution is an enduring feature of American society.

Suggested Teaching Strategies

1. **Writing Case Studies (I)** Ask students to read the Applying Sociology feature on textbook pages 306–307. After discussing the feature, ask students to develop additional case studies that describe other trends in American family life. Use the case studies as the basis of a class discussion on the changing American family.
2. **Interpreting Charts (I)** Place Transparency 11, which focuses on median ages at marriage in the United States, on an overhead projector and ask the questions contained in the accompanying teacher's notes. Transparencies and accompanying teacher's notes are found in the *Teacher's Resource Binder*.
3. **Learning from Films (I)** Show the class the film *Today's Family: Adjusting to Change* (rental information can be found in the introductory section of this

Teacher's Manual). Use the film as the basis of a class discussion on trends in American family life, including dual-worker families, single-parent families, and stepfamilies.

4. **Conducting a Debate (II, III)** Have students read the Interpreting Primary Sources feature on textbook page 317. Then organize the class into three groups: one group to argue for government and business assistance for working parents, one group to argue against such assistance, and a larger group to act as an audience. Have the debate teams conduct additional research before engaging in the debate.

Suggested Enrichment Activities

1. **Developing Research Skills (I)** Have students complete the appropriate Developing Research Skills Worksheet, found in the *Teacher's Resource Binder.*
2. **Developing Interviewing Skills (III)** Have interested students interview people working in the area of family violence. Interviewees might include police officers, social workers, attorneys, alcohol-abuse counselors, and personnel at shelters for abused women and children. Have the students report their findings to the class.

Suggested Assignments

1. **Determining Cause and Effect (I)** As homework, have students complete the appropriate Critical Skills Mastery Worksheet, found in the *Teacher's Resource Binder.*
2. **★Reading about Sociology: Understanding Census Data (I)** Instruct students to read the Developing Sociological Imagination feature on textbook pages 314–315 and then complete the assignment under Practicing the Skill.
3. **Working in Groups (II, III)** Organize the class into small groups. Assign each group the task of collecting pictures and articles that focus on a different trend in American family life. After discussing the articles in class, use the articles and pictures to create a bulletin board.

Closing the Section

Close the section by having students conduct a poll in which they ask five people (friends, neighbors, family members) the following question: "What do you think is the greatest challenge facing American families today?" Tally the results in class, and have students brainstorm solutions to the challenges facing today's families.

Assessing the Section

Have students complete the Section 2 Review.

Answers to Applying Sociology (pages 306–307)

Answers will vary, but students' case studies should be based on the family patterns discussed in the section.

Answers to Section 2 Review (page 313)

Define *homogamy:* marriage between individuals who have similar social characteristics; ***heterogamy:*** marriage between individuals who have different social characteristics

1. There are several common characteristics among marriages that are happy. These characteristics are having parents who are successfully married; having known each other for at least two years prior to marriage; marrying at an older age; holding traditional values; having a conflict-free engagement; being of the same race and religion; having a college education; and having parental approval of the marriage. Two additional factors affect marital satisfaction: gender and the presence of children. In general, men are more satisfied with marriage than are women. And, couples with no dependent children are more satisfied than parents.

2. **(a)** In the past, family violence was thought to be confined to the lower classes. This largely was the result of the way in which the statistics on family violence were collected. Such statistics relied on police and hospital records. Since the police and the hospitals were more likely to deal with family violence involving the lower classes, these families were more likely to be represented in the statistics. **(b)** Family violence appears to have decreased somewhat in recent years. This can be attributed to changes in public attitudes. People are more aware of what represents abusive and unacceptable behavior and are more likely to report it. In addition, there are more programs designed to treat family violence.

3. Divorce rates vary among various segments of the population. For example, rates vary by age at first marriage. Those who marry during their teen years have a much greater chance of divorce than people who marry after the age of 20. Education also affects the rate of divorce—couples with college educations are less likely to divorce than are couples who have not attended college. Rates also vary by race and ethnicity. African American women are more likely than white women to be divorced or separated, while Hispanic American women are less likely than white women to be divorced.

4. Several trends in family life have been noted in recent years. First, people now are delaying marriage and marrying at older ages. Accompanying the delay in marriage is a delay in childbearing. Women now are waiting longer to have their first child. Additionally, the number of childless couples has been on the rise. A third trend is the increase in female labor force participation and in the number of dual-earner families. A fourth major trend involves an increase in the number of single-parent families. Finally, remarriages and stepfamilies have been on the rise over the years.

Answers to Developing Sociological Imagination (pages 314–315)

1. **(a)** The subject of the chart on page 315 is the marital status of the United States population from 1920 to 1950. **(b)** The chart on page 315 differs from the chart on page 314 in that the latter covers the period from 1960 to 1990.
2. **(a)** According to the chart on page 315, the proportion of the population that was divorced more than

doubled between 1920 and 1950. **(b)** The proportion of the population that was divorced tripled between 1960 and 1990. **(c)** Females are more likely than males to be divorced.

3. **(a)** The proportion of the population that was single decreased between 1920 and 1950. **(b)** The proportion of the population that was single increased between 1960 and 1990. **(c)** Men are more likely than women to be single.

Closing the Chapter

Have students complete the Chapter 12 Review Worksheet, found in the *Teacher's Resource Binder.*

Assessing the Chapter

Have students complete the Chapter 12 Review, found on page 316 of the *Pupil's Edition.*

Give students the Chapter 12 Form A Test and, if desired, the Chapter 12 Reteaching Worksheet and Form B Test, found in the *Teacher's Resource Binder.*

Answers to Chapter 12 Review (page 316)

Reviewing Sociological Terms

1. Marriage
2. family
3. Polyandry
4. neolocality
5. incest taboo
6. patriarchal system

Thinking Critically about Sociology

1. **(a)** Some people predict the collapse of the nuclear family because the traditional family form has undergone dramatic changes over the past several decades. **(b)** Social scientists believe that the family institution will survive. The fact that it exists in all known societies and that it takes various forms indicates that it is a highly valued and important social institution.

2. An individual can be a member of two nuclear families at the same time if he or she is married. In such cases, the individual belongs both to the family into which he or she was born—the family of orientation—and to the family created at marriage—the family of procreation.

3. **(a)** No true matriarchal societies exist in the world today. **(b)** Even in societies that practice matrilineal descent, authority rests with the mother's brothers.

4. According to the table on page 308, the years 1950 and 1960 had the youngest median ages at marriage for both men and women.

5. Some of the factors that have contributed to the increases in heterogamy are higher college enrollments, increased geographic mobility, and increased female labor force participation. All of these factors increase the contacts between people of differing social backgrounds.

6. **(a)** Several factors have contributed to the increase in the divorce rate. First, the laws regulating divorce have become less complex and the costs of obtaining a divorce have decreased. Second, increased

employment has resulted in decreased economic dependence among women. Third, attitudes toward divorce have become more tolerant. Finally, the expectations placed on marriage have become too great, making it more difficult to maintain high levels of satisfaction. **(b)** African Americans are more likely than whites to be divorced.

7. Voluntarily childless couples have high levels of education and income, are nonreligious, have egalitarian attitudes, and share household tasks. They also use more effective methods of birth control than those who plan to have children.

8. **(a)** Two major reasons appear to account for the high rates of poverty among female-headed households. First, many women did not work when their children were young and must take low-paying jobs after divorce to support their children. Second, not all fathers who are ordered by the courts to make child-support payments actually do so. **(b)** Becoming part of a stepfamily involves a period of adjustment for all family members involved. Marital partners, for instance, must now take on new parenting roles, which often are a source of conflict between stepparents and stepchildren. Similarly, stepparents may resent not being treated like biological parents. In addition to adjusting to new stepparents, stepchildren often must adjust to having new grandparents or siblings. This also may involve learning to share a parent's affections with other children in the home.

Exercising Sociological Skills

1. **(a)** The home life of the Arrows changed because the rising cost of living made it difficult for the family to survive on one income and because Marie grew restless staying at home once the children were at school. **(b)** At first, Allen Stone found it difficult to adjust to his divorce. He had trouble meeting the demands of single parenting and maintaining a satisfactory level of involvement in his job. Additionally, he found the advice of his friends and relatives to be a strain. Eventually, however, he and his son developed a workable routine for household chores. And, Allen began to find enough time to participate in his son's school activities.

2. Many adult children of alcoholics become alcoholics themselves. They also may have difficulty trusting other people and developing healthy relationships. Some children of alcoholics turn to drug use or to crime. Other people are haunted by the fearful experiences of their childhoods.

3. **(a)** The percentage of widowed females reached 12 percent in 1930. **(b)** The percentage of widowed males reached 5.2 percent in 1920.

Extending Sociological Imagination

1. Answers will vary.
2. Answers will vary.

Answers to Interpreting Primary Sources (page 317)

1. The number of two-career families is likely to increase in the future because of the need for skilled workers,

the desire of women to remain viable in the work force, and the extremely low number of young women who are planning to become full-time homemakers in the future.

2. Some of the things that American companies are doing to help working parents include on-site child care, financial aid or referral services for child care, job sharing, part-time work with benefits, maternity leave, leave for adoptive parents or employees with elderly relatives who are sick, flexitime, telecommuting, and flexible combinations of benefits, which are called "cafeteria" plans.

CHAPTER 13 *(pages 318–345)*

THE ECONOMY AND POLITICS

SECTION 1
THE ECONOMIC INSTITUTION
SECTION 2
THE POLITICAL INSTITUTION

Chapter Overview

When the world was populated by small bands of people, the family was the main authority in society. The family institution coordinated all economic activities and established the rules of society. Today, in a world where events in one nation can dramatically affect events in other nations and where powerful nations compete with one another for influence, ultimate power no longer rests with the family institution.

In place of the family, various other institutions that attempt to coordinate the activities of millions of people have gained prominence. The economy and politics are two of the most important of these institutions. The economic and political institutions ensure that the economic activities of individuals are controlled and that order is maintained in society.

The forms that economic and political institutions take vary widely from society to society. In some societies, these institutions are influenced by a belief in human freedom. In other societies, these same institutions greatly limit human freedom.

Chapter Objectives

At the conclusion of the chapter, students will be able to

1. Explain how preindustrial, industrial, and postindustrial societies differ in terms of which sector of the economy is being emphasized.
2. Describe the characteristics of pure capitalism and pure socialism, and determine what factors affect how

closely the United States economy follows the capitalist model.
3. Recognize how the exercise of power varies by type of government.
4. Discuss the characteristics of the American political system.

Introducing the Chapter

Remind the class that social structure is an integrated system. Change in one part of the social system therefore produces changes in other parts. In no aspect of society is this more evident than in the areas of economics and politics. History has shown that as societies modernize and move toward capitalism, their political systems become more democratic.

To illustrate the interconnection between economics and politics, discuss with the class the social changes that took place in the former Soviet Union and the People's Republic of China during the late 1980s. Both nations were attempting to modernize their economies. As a result, pressures for democratic reform arose. Point out to the students that the source of pressure was very different in the two countries. In the former Soviet Union, pressure for democratization had come from the top leaders in the form of *perestroika* and *glasnost*. In the People's Republic of China, on the other hand, the call for democratic reform had come from the people and the government had responded with bloodshed and repression. Note that today, the former Soviet Union is well on its way toward democratization, while the People's Republic of China is struggling for ways to modernize its economy without democratizing its government. Close the discussion by noting that Chapter 13 will examine the economic and political institutions from a cross-cultural perspective.

Chapter 13 Suggested Lesson Plans

Day 1	**Suggested Procedures:** Introducing the Chapter; Section 1 Previewing Key Terms; Introducing the Section **Materials:** PE: pp. 318–329; TM: pp. 89–90
Day 2	**Suggested Procedures:** Section 1 Strategies and Assignments **Materials:** PE: pp. 320–329; TM: pp. 90–91; TRB: Worksheet
Day 3	**Suggested Procedures:** Section 2 Previewing Key Terms; Introducing the Section; Strategies and Assignments **Materials:** PE: pp. 330–343; TM: pp. 91–93; TRB: Transparency 12, Assorted Worksheets
Day 4	**Suggested Procedures:** Closing the Chapter; Assessing the Chapter **Materials:** PE: pp. 344–345; TM: pp. 93–94; TRB: Review Worksheet, Tests, Reteaching Worksheet

SECTION 1 (pages 320–329)

THE ECONOMIC INSTITUTION

Section Overview

The economic institution is the system of roles and norms that governs the production, distribution, and consumption of goods and services in a society. All economic systems contain three sectors: the primary sector, the secondary sector, and the tertiary sector. Which sector is emphasized depends on whether the society has a preindustrial, industrial, or postindustrial economy.

Industrial and postindustrial societies can be categorized by the type of economic model that they follow. Sociologists recognize two basic economic models: capitalism and socialism. The United States follows the capitalist model but does not mirror it. Four factors account for this fact: the rise of corporate capitalism, the globalization of the economy, the role of government in regulating the economy, and the changing nature of work in postindustrial society.

Previewing Key Terms

Section 1 contains the following key terms: **economic institution, factors of production, primary sector, secondary sector, tertiary sector, capitalism, socialism, law of supply, law of demand, communism, corporation, oligopoly, protectionism, free trade, public goods**. Ask each student to prepare a crossword puzzle using these terms and their definitions. Definitions can be found in Section 1 or in the Glossary. Then have the students exchange papers and complete the puzzles.

Introducing the Section

Write the following hypothetical scenario on the chalkboard: "You have a $20 bill in your pocket. You are hungry and want to buy lunch. But you also want to go to the movies and still have money left over for a new compact disc. Moreover, today is your sister's birthday and you must buy her a gift." Then ask: "What would you do if you found yourself in this situation?" Tell students that they have just encountered the problem of limited resources. They simply do not have enough resources to do everything that they want to do. Tell students that having limited resources means that they must make decisions. Next explain that societies also have to make decisions about how to use their limited resources. Societies do this by answering three basic questions: (1) What goods and services should be produced? (2) How should these goods and services be produced? (3) For whom should these goods and services be produced? Section 1 focuses on the ways in which these three questions are answered by societies around the world.

Suggested Teaching Strategies

1. **Categorizing Ideas (I)** Create on the chalkboard a blank chart with the column headings "primary sector," "secondary sector," and "tertiary sector" and the row headings "preindustrial systems," "industrial systems," and "postindustrial systems." Ask students to suggest examples of economic activities for each category in the chart. As examples are mentioned, write them in the appropriate category. Then discuss why different sectors of the economy are emphasized in each economic system.

2. **Comparing Ideas (I)** After discussing economic models, have students write a short essay in which they compare the pure capitalist system and the pure socialist system in terms of how they answer the three basic economic questions of what to produce, how to produce, and for whom to produce.

3. **Conducting a Debate (II, III)** After discussing with the class the concepts of protectionism and free trade, organize the students into three groups. Have one group argue in favor of protectionism, have another group argue in favor of free trade, and have the largest group act as an audience. Instruct the debate teams to conduct additional research before engaging in the debate.

Suggested Enrichment Activities

1. **Developing Research Skills (I)** Have students complete the appropriate Developing Research Skills Worksheet, found in the *Teacher's Resource Binder*.

2. **Extending Ideas (III)** Have interested students conduct library research to gather additional information on how the rise of corporate capitalism, the globalization of the economy, the role of government in regulating the economy, and the changing nature of work in postindustrial society have affected the free enterprise system in the United States.

Suggested Assignments

1. **Summarizing Information (I)** As homework, have students locate and summarize two newspaper or magazine articles that examine economic issues in a nation other than the United States.

2. **Comparing Viewpoints (III)** The subject of government regulation of business is widely debated in the United States today. Organize interested students into two groups and have them investigate both sides of the issue. Suggest to the students that they interview relatives or acquaintances who own or manage businesses. Students also might contact consumer or environmental groups for information. Have the groups use this information to debate the issue of government regulation.

Closing the Section

Close the section by having students prepare a quiz on the information contained in Section 1. Ask students to write 10 questions on one side of a piece of paper and the answers to these questions on the other side. When the quizzes are complete, have students exchange papers and answer the questions.

Assessing the Section

Have students complete the Section 1 Review.

Answers to Section 1 Review *(page 329)*

Define *economic institution:* system of roles and norms that governs the production, distribution, and consumption of goods and services; *factors of production:* resources that can be used to produce and distribute goods and services; *law of supply:* principle that states that producers will supply more products when they can charge higher prices and fewer products when they must charge lower prices; *law of demand:* principle that states that the demand for a product increases as the price of the product decreases. On the other hand, the demand for a product decreases as the price increases; *oligopoly:* situation that exists when a few people control an industry; *protectionism:* use of trade barriers to protect domestic manufacturers from foreign competitors; *free trade:* trade between nations that is unrestricted by trade barriers; *public goods:* goods and services that the government provides for everyone in the society

1. **(a)** The primary sector deals with the extraction of raw materials from the environment. The secondary sector deals with the manufacture of goods from raw materials. The tertiary sector is involved in the provision of services. **(b)** Labor in preindustrial societies is heavily concentrated in the primary sector. In industrial societies, the emphasis shifts to the secondary sector. In postindustrial societies, the tertiary sector becomes the most important area of the economy.
2. **(a)** In a pure capitalist system, the economy is regulated by self-interest and market competition. Self-interest leads consumers to try to purchase the goods and services they desire at the lowest prices possible. Producers, on the other hand, are guided by self-interest to undertake only those business ventures that have the potential to make a profit. **(b)** In a pure socialist system, the economy is controlled by social need, rather than by self-interest, and by centralized government planning, rather than by market forces. What to produce is determined by the needs of society. How to produce is determined by central planners. For whom to produce is determined by need rather than by the ability to pay.
3. **(a)** The rise of corporate capitalism has changed the relationship between business ownership and control. Early capitalists managed the day-to-day affairs of the businesses they owned. Today, few corporate stockholders participate in daily business operations. Also, most American corporate stocks are owned by other corporations. **(b)** The globalization of the economy has made nations economically interdependent. As a result, the economic policies of one nation often affect the policies of other nations. **(c)** Population growth and the rise of corporate capitalism have led the government to take on more responsibility for the economy. The government has taken action to regulate economic activity, to protect consumers, to provide public goods, and to promote economic well-being. **(d)** Automation and increased efficiency have reduced the number of workers needed to meet the demand in manufacturing. The demand for workers has increased in the service sector. This has led the government and business leaders to call for a strengthened commitment to quality education.

SECTION 2 *(pages 330–341)*

THE POLITICAL INSTITUTION

Section Overview

The political institution is the system of roles and norms that governs the distribution and exercise of power in society. Power can be legitimate or illegitimate. According to Max Weber, legitimate power, which is called authority, can take three forms: traditional authority, charismatic authority, or rational-legal authority.

How political authority is exercised varies by type of government. Sociologists recognize two basic types of government: democratic systems and authoritarian systems. In a democracy, power is exercised through the people. In an authoritarian system, power rests with the state. The American political system is a democracy.

Previewing Key Terms

Section 2 contains the following key terms: **power, state, political institution, legitimacy, authority, traditional authority, charismatic authority, rational-legal authority, coercion, democracy, monarchy, constitutional monarchy, democratic socialism, authoritarianism, absolute monarchy, dictatorship, junta, totalitarianism, political party, interest group, power-elite model, pluralist model**. Have students choose 15 of the key terms and prepare 15 riddles, using the chosen terms as answers. For example: "I am the primary political authority in society. What am I?" *(state)* Tell students to write their riddles on one side of the paper and the answers on the other side. Completed sets of riddles can be exchanged among students and answered. Then have students put their papers in their study notebooks for later review.

Introducing the Section

Tell students that they are going to practice their outlining skills in this section. First, ask a volunteer to copy the headings and subheadings in Section 2 on the chalkboard. Then have the class provide the important details that should appear under each item in the outline. Have students copy the final outline into their notebooks for later review.

Suggested Teaching Strategies

1. **Comparing Ideas (I)** After discussing types of governments, have students write a short essay in which they compare democratic systems and authoritarian systems in terms of how they exercise power. Ask volunteers to read their essays aloud to the class.
2. **Analyzing Viewpoints (I)** Have students complete the appropriate Critical Skills Mastery Worksheet, found in the *Teacher's Resource Binder*. Then use the worksheet as the basis of a class discussion on the ways in which the mass media has changed the nature of politics in the United States.

3. **Interpreting Charts (I)** Place Transparency 12, which focuses on the 1992 presidential election, on an overhead projector and ask the questions contained in the accompanying teacher's notes. Transparencies and accompanying teacher's notes are found in the *Teacher's Resource Binder*.

4. **Solving Problems (I)** Tell students that the United States has one of the lowest voter participation rates of any industrialized nation in the world. Then have them examine the chart on textbook page 340 and consider the following questions: "Why is low voter participation harmful to a democracy such as the United States?" "What can be done to increase the rate of voter participation in the United States?"

5. **Using Sociological Imagination (II, III)** After students have read the Case Study on textbook page 338, have selected students research Abraham Lincoln's political platform and then rework that platform and Lincoln's image to fit today's made-for-media campaign style.

Suggested Enrichment Activities

1. **Exploring Cross-Cultural Perspectives (I)** Have students complete the appropriate Cross-Cultural Perspectives Worksheet, found in the *Teacher's Resource Binder*.

2. **Making Oral Presentations (III)** Have interested students conduct research and prepare oral presentations on one of the following topics: the current political platform of the Democratic party or the Republican party, the impact of various interest groups on legislation, or the rise of political action committees over the years.

Suggested Assignments

1. **Organizing Ideas (I)** As homework, have students complete the appropriate Graphic Organizer Worksheet, found in the *Teacher's Resource Binder*.

2. **Understanding Ideas (I)** Have students read the Applying Sociology feature on textbook pages 332–333 and answer the accompanying questions.

3. **★Interpreting the Visual Record: Analyzing Editorial Cartoons (I)** Instruct students to read the Developing Sociological Imagination feature on textbook pages 342–343 and then complete the assignment under Practicing the Skill.

Closing the Section

Close the section by having students complete the appropriate Understanding Sociological Ideas Worksheet, found in the *Teacher's Resource Binder*.

Assessing the Section

Have students complete the Section 2 Review.

Answers to Applying Sociology *(pages 332–333)*

1. Under Boris Yeltsin, price controls on most Russian consumer goods have been lifted. Also, the ruble trades freely, and thousands of state-run enterprises have been transformed into privately owned businesses. However, problems still remain. For example, half of Russia's population now lives below the poverty level, industrial production has dropped, and inflation has soared.

2. Experts fear that Russia will slip back into communism if it does not receive sufficient economic aid.

3. Answers will vary, but students should use sound reasoning to support their positions.

Answers to Section 2 Review *(page 341)*

Define *power:* ability to control the behavior of others, with or without their consent; ***state:*** primary political authority in society; ***political institution:*** system of roles and norms that governs the distribution and exercise of power in society; ***coercion:*** power that is exercised through force or the threat of force; ***monarchy:*** type of government in which one person rules. The ruler typically comes to power through inheritance; ***constitutional monarchy:*** government in which the ruler is nothing more than a symbolic head of state; ***democratic socialism:*** combination of a democratic government and a socialist economy

1. **(a)** Legitimacy of power refers to whether those in power are viewed as having the right to control, or govern, others. **(b)** The three forms of legitimate power outlined by Weber are traditional authority, charismatic authority, and rational-legal authority. Traditional authority is power that is legitimated by long-standing custom. Charismatic authority is power that is legitimated by the personal characteristics of the individual exercising the power. Rational-legal authority is power that is legitimated by formal rules and regulations.

2. **(a)** In a democracy, power is exercised through the people, who have the right to participate in the political decision-making process. The following conditions are needed for a democracy to thrive: industrialization and literate, urban populations that expect to have a voice in the political process; access to information; limits on government powers; and shared values. **(b)** In authoritarian governments, power rests firmly with the state. Members of such societies have little or no say in the political decision-making process. There are several different forms of authoritarian governments: absolute monarchies, dictatorships, juntas, and totalitarian states. An absolute monarchy is an authoritarian system in which the hereditary ruler holds absolute power. A dictatorship is an authoritarian system in which power is in the hands of a single individual. A junta is a system in which political power has been seized from the previous government by force. A totalitarian system is one in which government leaders accept few limits on their authority. The lives of the members of such societies are rigidly controlled.

3. There are four topics of primary interest to sociologists who study the American political system: political parties, interest groups, political participation, and the question of who rules America. Student essays should summarize the information presented on textbook pages 336 and 339–341.

Answers to Developing Sociological Imagination *(pages 342–343)*

1. The central figures are Fidel Castro, the leader of Cuba, and Deng Xiaoping, the leader of the People's Republic of China.
2. Dinosaurs are used to represent the central figures.
3. **(a)** The drawing of Castro is a caricature because it exaggerates his beard and his cap. **(b)** The hammer and sickle are used to represent Castro's political system.
4. The cartoon is about communism.
5. **(a)** The message of the cartoon is that communism is obsolete. **(b)** The cartoonist believes that the leaders of Cuba and China should democratize their nations.

Closing the Chapter

Have students complete the Chapter 13 Review Worksheet, found in the *Teacher's Resource Binder*.

Assessing the Chapter

Have students complete the Chapter 13 Review, found on page 344 of the *Pupil's Edition*.

Give students the Chapter 13 Form A Test and, if desired, the Chapter 13 Reteaching Worksheet and Form B Test, found in the *Teacher's Resource Binder*.

Answers to Chapter 13 Review *(page 344)*

Reviewing Sociological Terms

1. corporation
2. political institution
3. economic institution
4. Communism

Thinking Critically about Sociology

1. **(a)** The law of supply states that producers will supply more products when they can charge higher prices and fewer products when they must charge lower prices. The law of demand states that the demand for a product increases as the price of the product decreases. On the other hand, the demand for a product decreases as the price increases. The law of supply holds that producers will provide more goods when they can charge higher prices. **(b)** If consumers are not willing to pay the price producers are asking for their goods, the producers will be forced to lower their prices. If producers cannot lower their prices and still make a profit, they will go out of business. If consumers demand more products than are available, producers can raise their prices somewhat without decreasing demand.
2. The government performs four economic functions. First, the government regulates economic activity through laws aimed at promoting fair business competition, preventing the abuse of workers, and minimizing negative side effects. The government also has established federal agencies to monitor business activities. Second, the government attempts to protect the rights and health of consumers. Third, the government provides public goods such as education, highways, and national defense to be used by all citizens. Fourth, the government attempts to promote economic well-being by redistributing tax revenues to individuals and businesses that need assistance.
3. The structured overview should match the format presented on textbook page 41.
4. **(a)** An oligopoly is the situation that exists when a few people control an industry. **(b)** Oligopolies limit competition by reducing the number of producers competing for business. Less competition means a larger share of the market for each firm in the oligopoly.
5. **(a)** When power is exercised with the consent of the people being governed, it is considered legitimate. Power is considered illegitimate, on the other hand, when it is exercised against the will or without the approval of those being controlled. **(b)** Examples of traditional authority include the royal family of Great Britain, the pope, tribal chieftains, and queens. Examples of charismatic authority include Jesus, Buddha, Hitler, and cult leader Jim Jones. Examples of rational-legal authority include the president of the United States, governors, police officers, and tax collectors. **(c)** Answers will vary.
6. Factors of production are the resources available to produce goods and services. Such resources include land, water, plants, animals, the sun and wind, human labor, money, tools, buildings, and machinery. Because preindustrial societies rely on human and animal labor, technology remains at a low level. Low levels of technology mean that food production is inefficient, thus requiring the majority of the population to engage in the production of food. In industrial societies, the emphasis shifts to the secondary sector. The shift is brought about by the introduction of machines and the development of new sources of energy. Machines and new energy sources produce greater agricultural yields that free people from the land and allow them to engage in varied jobs in return for wages. In postindustrial societies, the tertiary sector becomes the most important area of the economy. Several factors account for this. First, because technological innovations lead to more efficient production techniques, the number of available jobs in the secondary sector declines. Second, the emphasis on knowledge and the collection and distribution of information create a demand for jobs in administration, management, the professions, and so on. Third, the higher standard of living characteristic of industrial societies increases the demand for services.
7. **(a)** The globalization of the economy means that the goods and services produced in or by one country are traded around the world. Sometimes companies will produce goods in foreign countries because of lower labor costs. Thus, corporations within each nation compete not only with each other but also with corporations in other nations. Some people argue that governments should protect their economies from foreign competition. Opponents of protectionism, on the other hand, argue that free trade is one of the cornerstones of the free enterprise system. **(b)** Tax breaks and lower wage rates have encouraged many United States corporations to produce their goods abroad. As a result, many United States manufacturing jobs have been lost. This loss has been partially filled by service jobs.

8. Sociologists recognize two basic types of governments: democratic systems and authoritarian systems. In a democracy, power is exercised through the people, who have the right to participate in the political decision-making process. In authoritarian governments, power rests firmly with the state. Members of such societies have little or no say in the political decision-making process.

Exercising Sociological Skills

1. Answers will vary, but students should use the skills presented in the Developing Sociological Imagination feature on textbook pages 284–285 in making their analyses.
2. The mass media has changed the nature of presidential elections in several ways. First, the influence of political parties has declined. Second, the media's role in candidate selection has increased. Third, the appearance of candidates on television has become a major criterion in elections. Finally, campaign styles have been adapted to the characteristics required by the media.
3. Answers will vary, but students should use the skills presented in the Developing Sociological Imagination feature on textbook pages 342–343 to analyze the cartoons they have chosen.

Extending Sociological Imagination

1. Answers will vary.
2. Answers will vary.

Answers to Interpreting Primary Sources *(page 345)*

1. Authoritarian personalities share the belief that the only possible source of happiness lies in submitting oneself to outside forces that are of a higher nature than oneself.
2. The Germans were told repeatedly that the individual is not as important as the group. They also were told to submit to the Nazi ideology and to feel proud to participate in Hitler's supposed strength and glory.

CHAPTER 14 *(pages 346–373)*

EDUCATION AND RELIGION

SECTION 1
THE SOCIOLOGY OF EDUCATION

SECTION 2
THE SOCIOLOGY OF RELIGION

Chapter Overview

Education and religion, like all social institutions, arose in response to basic human needs. If societies are to sur-vive over time, children must be provided with the knowledge they need to inherit the world of their elders and all members must be afforded the emotional strength they need to face the challenges of life and death. Consequently, all societies develop educational and religious institutions.

The form that education takes varies widely from society to society. The educational process may be as simple as a few tribal elders passing on their ancient lore to apprenticed youth or as complex as any bureaucracy found in modern society.

The social institution of religion also is found in many forms around the world. In some societies, people seek answers to life's mysterious questions through the worship of one all-powerful God. In other societies, these answers are sought in nature or through the worship of ancestors.

Chapter Objectives

At the conclusion of the chapter, students will be able to

1. Compare the views of functionalist sociologists and conflict sociologists concerning the role of education in society.
2. Discuss current issues in American education, such as educational reform, violence in the schools, and bilingual education.
3. Identify the basic societal needs served by religion, and determine how the nature of religion varies cross-culturally.
4. Describe the distinctive features of religion in American society.

Introducing the Chapter

Remind the students that all social institutions exist to meet basic human needs in society. Then ask students to suggest some of the basic needs met by education and by religion. List the needs on the chalkboard as they are mentioned. Next, tell students that education and religion do not exist in isolation—they are part of the larger social structure. Thus education and religion affect and are affected by the other social institutions. Ask students to suggest some of the ways in which education (a) affects and (b) is affected by the institutions of the family, the economy, and politics. Then follow the same procedure for religion. Be sure that the students mention both positive and negative influences.

Chapter 14 Suggested Lesson Plans

Day 1	**Suggested Procedures**: Introducing the Chapter; Section 1 Previewing Key Terms; Introducing the Section **Materials**: PE: pp. 346–360; TM: pp. 94–95
Day 2	**Suggested Procedures:** Section 1 Strategies and Assignments **Materials:** PE: pp. 348–360; TM: pp. 95–96; TRB: Transparency 13, Assorted Worksheets

Day 3	**Suggested Procedures:** Section 2 Previewing Key Terms; Introducing the Section; Strategies and Assignments **Materials:** PE: pp. 361–371; TM: pp. 96–97; TRB: Assorted Worksheets
Day 4	**Suggested Procedures:** Closing the Chapter; Assessing the Chapter **Materials:** PE: pp. 372–373; TM: pp. 97–99; TRB: Review Worksheet, Tests, Reteaching Worksheet

SECTION 1 (pages 348–360)

THE SOCIOLOGY OF EDUCATION

Section Overview

Education is the system of roles and norms that ensures the transmission of knowledge, values, and patterns of behavior from one generation to the next. Sociologists who study education tend to focus on schooling.

According to functionalist sociologists, education serves to maintain the stability and smooth operation of society by transmitting culture, increasing social integration, creating knowledge, and channeling people into occupations. Conflict theorists, on the other hand, argue that education serves to maintain social inequality by teaching obedience to authority and by tracking students into different educational programs. In addition, conflict theorists believe that socioeconomic differences in academic achievement reflect the unequal distribution of power and resources in society.

Educational issues have long held the attention of the American public. Among the contemporary issues being discussed are educational reform, violence in the schools, and bilingual education.

Previewing Key Terms

Section 1 contains the following key terms: **education, schooling, mandatory education, hidden curriculum, tracking, bilingual education**. Have students write a definition for each term, based on what they think it means. Then have students look up each term in the Glossary and revise their original definitions based on what they have learned.

Introducing the Section

Ask students to use what they have learned thus far about theoretical perspectives to suggest what the functionalist perspective and the conflict perspective on education might be. Write these suggestions on the chalkboard and have students give reasons for the suggestions they have made. Then have a volunteer locate this information on textbook pages 349 and 351 and read the information aloud to the class. Remind students that neither of these perspectives is "correct" per se, but rather they each provide a way to view education as a social institution.

Suggested Teaching Strategies

1. **★Writing about Sociology: Summarizing Sociological Information (I)** Prior to assigning the reading of Section 1, have students read the Developing Sociological Imagination feature on textbook pages 370–371 and complete the assignment under Practicing the Skill. Once students understand the technique, have them apply the new skill by summarizing the information presented in Section 1.

2. **Comparing Sociological Perspectives (I)** Remind students that theoretical perspectives outline certain assumptions about the nature of social life. These assumptions determine the general research interests that can be examined using the perspective. Then ask students to list the assumptions about society central to functionalist theory. Write the assumptions on the chalkboard, leaving space to the right of the list. Next have students list the assumptions central to conflict theory. Write these assumptions on the chalkboard, again leaving space to the right of the list. Now ask students to describe the functionalist view of education. List the main points of the view alongside the assumptions. Then do the same thing for the conflict view. By referring to the lists, discuss with the class how theoretical assumptions limit the focus of social research.

3. **Interpreting Charts (I)** Place Transparency 13, which focuses on the relationship between education and income, on an overhead projector and ask the questions contained in the accompanying teacher's notes. Transparencies and accompanying teacher's notes are found in the *Teacher's Resource Binder*.

4. **Seeing Relationships (II)** After students have read the Applying Sociology feature on textbook pages 352–353 and the Case Study on textbook page 358, invite someone who is involved in teaching recent immigrants or adult illiterates to read English to speak to the class about the importance of literacy. Prior to the presentation, have students research the problems of adult illiteracy or English-as-a-second-language education and prepare questions to ask the speaker.

Suggested Enrichment Activities

1. **Exploring Cross-Cultural Perspectives (I)** Have students complete the appropriate Cross-Cultural Perspectives Worksheet, found in the *Teacher's Resource Binder*.

2. **Conducting Research (III)** Have interested students conduct library research on one of the following topics: the history of education in the United States, the use of computers in education, or the system of education in a nation other than the United States. Have students present their findings to the class.

Suggested Assignments

1. **Drawing Conclusions (I)** As homework, have students complete the appropriate Developing Research Skills Worksheet, found in the *Teacher's Resource Binder*.

2. Conducting a Debate (II, III) Have interested students research the "examination wars" in Japan. Then organize the students into two groups and have them debate the following statement: "Examination wars should be made a part of the American educational system." Have the class critique the debate.

Closing the Section

Close the section by having students brainstorm solutions to the problem of violence in the schools. List these suggestions on the chalkboard and have the students review them for soundness and feasibility. Consider having volunteers write an editorial based on these suggestions for submission to the school newspaper.

Assessing the Section

Have students complete the Section 1 Review.

Answers to Applying Sociology *(pages 352–353)*

1. Developing a command of the English language, in written and spoken form, was the most important academic skill needed for Mary's progress in school.

2. Mary's father saw education as a way for his children to achieve what he had not been able to achieve. Education was considered to be the passport to the future. Today, education still is a means to upward intergenerational mobility for many Americans.

3. According to the excerpt, the educational institution values individual achievement through friendly competition. The structure of the organization typically is not flexible enough to accommodate individual differences in learning style, but Mary's teacher appears to have accommodated the special needs of the immigrant students. The role of teacher is seen as one of dedication and concern.

Answers to Section 1 Review *(page 360)*

Define *education:* system of roles and norms that ensures the transmission of knowledge, values, and patterns of behavior from one generation to the next; *schooling:* formal education, which involves instruction by specially trained teachers who follow officially recognized policies; *mandatory education:* enforced schooling; *hidden curriculum:* transmission by schools of cultural goals not openly acknowledged

1. Sociologists who follow the functionalist perspective view education as a force for the stability and smooth operation of society. Sociologists who follow the conflict perspective, on the other hand, view education as a way of creating and maintaining unequal access to positions of power in society.

2. There are three major contemporary issues in education. The first issue concerns educational reform. Reports reveal that American students are falling behind the students of other industrialized nations in math, science, and literacy skills. In response, many states have increased graduation requirements, raised the requirements for teachers, and raised teacher salaries. However, most experts agree that much work remains to be done. A second issue involves violence in the schools. Although no national statistics exist to indicate whether school violence is on the rise, most experts agree that violent episodes increasingly involve deadly weapons. Violence has become such an important issue that many schools around the nation have installed security devices in an effort to keep weapons out of the schools. In addition, thousands of schools around the nation now have implemented some sort of violence-prevention program. A third issue involves bilingual education. Approximately 2 million students currently are enrolled in some type of bilingual program. Some people support bilingual education because it allows foreign-born students to make continued academic progress while they are learning English. Others oppose such programs because they believe the programs prevent foreign-born students from being assimilated into American culture.

SECTION 2 *(pages 361–369)*

THE SOCIOLOGY OF RELIGION

Section Overview

Religion is the system of roles and norms organized around the sacred realm that binds people together in social groups. Although religion exists in varied forms around the world, all religions are composed of three elements: rituals, belief systems (such as animism, theism, and ethicalism) and organizational structures (such as ecclesia, denominations, sects, and cults).

Religion in American society is characterized by pluralism and by the high value placed on religious beliefs. For the protection of all religions, the United States Constitution guarantees separation of church and state. While participation in mainstream religions has been decreasing in recent decades in the United States, participation in fundamentalist Christianity has been on the rise.

Previewing Key Terms

Section 2 contains the following key terms: **sacred, profane, religion, ritual, animism, shamanism, totemism, theism, monotheism, polytheism, ethicalism, ecclesia, denomination, sect, cult, religiosity**. Have students use the Glossary to differentiate in writing between the following sets of concepts: sacred and profane; religion and religiosity; animism, shamanism, and totemism; monotheism, polytheism, and ethicalism; and ecclesia, denomination, sect, and cult. Discuss the differences in class.

Introducing the Section

Ask students to bring to class photographs and newspaper or magazine articles about religious practices that are found in various countries throughout the world. Have volunteers display their images and summarize the articles for the class. Then tell students that Section 2 focuses on the elements of religion that vary throughout the world and the functions that all religions have in common.

Suggested Teaching Strategies

1. **Learning from Films (I)** Show the class the film *Faith and Belief: Five Major World Religions* (rental information can be found in the introductory section of this *Teacher's Manual).* Use the film as the basis of a class discussion on the functions of religion.

2. **Seeing Relationships (I)** Have students examine the chart on text page 367. Then, based on the information in the chart, have students write two generalizations about religion in American society. Ask volunteers to read their generalizations aloud to the class for class discussion.

3. **Working in Groups (II, III)** Organize the class into three groups and assign each group one of the following belief systems: animism, theism, ethicalism. Tell the members of each group that they are to research a religion that is based on their assigned belief system. Have the groups report their findings to the class.

Suggested Enrichment Activities

1. **Understanding Ideas (I)** Have students complete the appropriate Understanding Sociological Ideas Worksheet, found in the *Teacher's Resource Binder.*

2. **Conducting a Debate (II, III)** Have students read the Interpreting Primary Sources feature on textbook page 373. Then organize the class into three groups: one group to argue in favor of religious lobbies, one group to argue against religious lobbies, and a larger group to act as an audience. Have the debate teams conduct additional research on religious lobbies before engaging in the debate.

Suggested Assignments

1. **Organizing Ideas (I)** As homework, have students complete the appropriate Graphic Organizer Worksheet, found in the *Teacher's Resource Binder.*

2. **Exploring Multicultural Perspectives (III)** Have interested students research religious holidays that are celebrated by various religious groups in the United States or around the world. Ask students to research the origins of the holiday, how it is celebrated, and what its meaning is to the people of today who celebrate it.

Closing the Section

Close the section by having students complete the appropriate Critical Skills Mastery Worksheet, found in the *Teacher's Resource Binder.* Then have volunteers read the essays they have written in response to the worksheet directive and use the essays as the basis of a discussion on the functions of religion.

Assessing the Section

Have students complete the Section 2 Review.

Answers to Section 2 Review *(page 369)*

Define *religion:* system of roles and norms organized around the sacred realm that binds people together in social groups; ***animism:*** belief system in which spirits are active in influencing human life; ***shamanism:*** belief system in which spirits communicate with only one person

in the group, who is acknowledged to be a specialist; ***totemism:*** belief in a kinship between humans and animals or natural objects; ***theism:*** belief in a god or gods; ***monotheism:*** belief in one god; ***polytheism:*** belief in a number of gods; ***ethicalism:*** belief that moral principles have a sacred quality

1. The sacred is anything that is considered to be part of the supernatural world and that inspires awe, respect, and reverence. The profane, on the other hand, is anything considered to be part of the ordinary world and thus familiar and common.

2. **(a)** Religion has three important functions. First, religion strengthens the bond between societal members, thus increasing social cohesion. Participating in religious rituals and sharing religious beliefs create a sense of belonging among people. A second major function of religion is to encourage conformity to social norms. Norms surrounding important social issues often not only are formalized as laws but also are supported by religious doctrine. Religion also provides formalized ways for individuals to relieve their guilt for disobeying norms and laws. Finally, religion provides emotional support for people during difficult times and provides answers to questions of life and death that cannot be answered by science or common sense. Such answers lend strength and calm as people approach the unknown. **(b)** The three basic elements of religion are rituals, belief systems, and organizational structures. Rituals are established patterns of behavior through which believers experience the sacred. Rituals unite believers, reinforce faith, and often mark major life events such as birth, marriage, or death. Belief systems are composed of sets of beliefs used to provide guidelines for behavior. There are three major belief systems. Animism is a belief system in which spirits are active in influencing human life. Theism is the belief in a god or gods. Ethicalism is a belief system in which moral principles have a sacred quality. There are four types of organizational structures: ecclesia, denominations, sects, and cults. An ecclesia is a type of religious organization to which people belong simply because of their birth. Denominations are formal, bureaucratic organizations, involving trained officials, to which a substantial proportion of the population belong. Sects are relatively small organizations that have split off from a denomination because of differences in doctrine. Cults are religious groups that are founded on the revelations of a person believed to have special knowledge.

3. Student essays should include the information presented on textbook pages 366–369.

Answers to Developing Sociological Imagination *(pages 370–371)*

Answers will vary, but students' summaries should be based on the topic sentences culled from each paragraph in the reading.

Closing the Chapter

Have students complete the Chapter 14 Review Worksheet, found in the *Teacher's Resource Binder.*

Assessing the Chapter

Have students complete the Chapter 14 Review, found on page 372 of the *Pupil's Edition*.

Give students the Chapter 14 Form A Test and, if desired, the Chapter 14 Reteaching Worksheet and Form B Test, found in the *Teacher's Resource Binder*.

Answers to Chapter 14 Review *(page 372)*

Reviewing Sociological Terms

1. Schooling
2. Religiosity
3. ritual
4. ecclesia
5. tracking

Thinking Critically about Sociology

1. **(a)** Religion strengthens the bonds among people and increases the cohesion of the society. It also encourages people to obey important norms and laws. And, religion provides both emotional support in times of stress and answers to the great mysteries of life. **(b)** Because it encourages strict conformity to religious doctrine, religion sometimes blocks the discussion of beliefs and ideas contrary to the existing doctrine. The inability to consider and discuss new ideas and beliefs can interfere with social change and social progress.

2. Functionalists believe that education serves as an agent of social control in order to produce citizens who share a common set of values. This helps ensure that society will operate smoothly. Conflict theorists, on the other hand, believe that the social control function of education serves to produce citizens who will accept the basic inequalities of society and who will not question the existing order.

3. **(a)** Religion in the United States is characterized by pluralism, separation of church and state, and by the high value placed on it by the American people. **(b)** The American Constitution formalized the separation of church and state to ensure that no one religion is endorsed as the official one at the expense of other religions.

4. According to the table on page 356, at each level of education, the average income of women is lower than the average income of men.

5. **(a)** Schools foster the creation of knowledge by providing the tools and techniques that people can use to develop new approaches and new solutions to problems. Schools also inspire intellectual inquiry and cultivate the critical thinking skills that help create new knowledge. **(b)** Corporations often fund research because research can lead to inventions and new applications of knowledge that can be used to increase corporate profits.

6. **(a)** Animism, theism, and ethicalism differ in the objects or entities considered most sacred and powerful. In animism, the spirits of animals and natural objects are considered sacred and powerful. In theism, a god or gods is considered sacred and powerful. In ethicalism, guiding principles such as truth are thought to have sacred qualities. **(b)** There are two

subtypes of animism: shamanism and totemism. In shamanism, the spirits are thought to communicate with one spiritual leader, called a shaman. This person is believed to be able to cure the sick, predict the future, and see things that are occurring at a distance. Totemism involves a belief in the kinship between humans and animals or natural objects. These animals or natural objects are considered sacred because they represent the group's kin and ancestors. The belief system of theism also contains two subtypes: monotheism and polytheism. Monotheism involves the belief in one god. Polytheism, on the other hand, involves the belief in a number of gods.

7. **(a)** Conflict theorists believe that socioeconomic status affects educational achievement in several ways. First, parents' expectations for their children vary depending on social class. Higher-status families assume that their children will achieve in school and reward them for educational success. Lower-status families want their children to be successful but are not convinced that education is the key to success. They instead encourage their children to begin working after high school rather than going on to college. Second, higher-status families are better able than lower-status families to provide resources that encourage learning, such as books, toys, and trips. Finally, the expenses involved in keeping a child in school are more easily met by higher-status families. **(b)** Conflict theorists believe that tracking is a way in which the wealthy and powerful maintain their positions in society while keeping the disadvantaged and the poor in inferior positions. Typically, children of the lower classes are assigned to tracks that prepare students for lower-status, lower-paying blue-collar jobs. Children of the middle and upper classes more typically are assigned to tracks that lead to college and, hence, higher paying and more prestigious occupations.

8. Although over 90 percent of Americans express a religious preference, only about 70 percent are affiliated with some religious organization. One may conclude from this information that Americans believe religion is an important part of life, but that it need not be expressed by formal affiliation with religious organizations.

Exercising Sociological Skills

1. **(a)** Learning a common language opened up the culture—the history, the myths, the values—to the foreign-born students. The common language helped give the immigrant students a common identity. **(b)** Immigrant parents could benefit from schools indirectly, in that their children could help them learn English and the norms of their adopted culture.

2. Illiteracy programs are not reaching the entire population in need of assistance. There are two primary reasons for this. First, there is a misconception that illiteracy no longer is a problem. This is because the definition of functional literacy has changed. Earlier in our history, literacy was based on a fourth-grade reading level. A ninth-grade reading level now is used as the guideline for literacy. Many people do not meet the higher standards. Second, many people hide their

illiteracy because of embarrassment and thus do not seek out programs that could help them.

3. Answers will vary. Students should use the skills presented on textbook pages 370–371 to summarize the information presented on textbook pages 357 and 359–360.

Extending Sociological Imagination

1. Answers will vary.
2. Answers will vary. Students' charts should include information presented on textbook pages 365–366.

Answers to Interpreting Primary Sources *(page 373)*

1. The fundamentalists concentrate on heated political issues such as school prayer, abortion, and pornography. They have been able to motivate their supporters to send millions of messages to Washington through letters and telephone calls. The "peace and justice" groups have not been as successful in mobilizing their supporters. These groups tend to focus on underlying social and economic problems that are less emotional. The "peace and justice" cluster is, however, able to influence key congressional committees through its mainline church-based organizations.
2. The author believes that religious lobbies counterbalance oligarchic leadership because much of the lobbying strength lies in the ability to mobilize supporters on a widespread basis.

CHAPTER 15 *(pages 374–399)*

SCIENCE AND SPORT

SECTION 1
SCIENCE AS A SOCIAL INSTITUTION

SECTION 2
SPORT AS A SOCIAL INSTITUTION

Chapter Overview

Society is constantly changing. Consequently, the institutional structure of society also changes. Not only do old institutions take on new characteristics, but new institutions develop. Two institutions that have gained increasing importance are science and sport.

Our lives are touched on a daily basis by the effects of science. Our health; our immediate environment; the way we learn, communicate, and travel; what goods and services we produce and how we produce them; and our vision of the future are influenced by science. So great is the influence of science on society that the level of scientific literacy among adults and children has become an issue of public debate.

Sport also invades our daily lives. Annually, people in the United States spend billions of dollars on sports-related equipment and activities. Many of us are obsessed with our bodies, our health, and our athletes. And on television, sporting events are among the most popular form of programming. Sports are so popular with Americans that cable television is willing to provide 24-hour-a-day, 7-day-a-week sports coverage.

Chapter Objectives

At the conclusion of the chapter, students will be able to

1. Identify the factors that led to the institutionalization of science.
2. Explain how the norms of scientific research differ from the realities of scientific research.
3. Identify and describe the seven characteristics that distinguish sport as a social institution.
4. Compare the functionalist perspective and the conflict perspective on sport.
5. Discuss the sociological findings concerning racial discrimination in organized sports and the state of women's athletics.

Introducing the Chapter

After noting that all social institutions exist to meet basic needs in society, ask students to suggest some of the basic needs that are met by science. List the needs on the chalkboard as they are mentioned. Then repeat the exercise for sport. After the lists are completed, ask students to consider how the institutions of science and sport relate to the other social institutions. For instance, in what ways do they assist the other social institutions in meeting the basic needs of society? Conversely, in what ways do they lessen the impact of the other social institutions?

Chapter 15 Suggested Lesson Plans

Day 1	**Suggested Procedures:** Introducing the Chapter; Section 1 Previewing Key Terms; Introducing the Section **Materials:** PE: pp. 374–385; TM: pp. 99–100
Day 2	**Suggested Procedures:** Section 1 Strategies and Assignments **Materials:** PE: pp. 376–385; TM: pp. 100–101; TRB: Assorted Worksheets
Day 3	**Suggested Procedures:** Section 2 Previewing Key Terms; Introducing the Section; Strategies and Assignments **Materials:** PE: pp. 386–397; TM: pp. 101–103; TRB: Assorted Worksheets
Day 4	**Suggested Procedures:** Closing the Chapter; Assessing the Chapter **Materials:** PE: pp. 398–399; TM: pp. 103–104; TRB: Review Worksheet, Tests, Reteaching Worksheet

SECTION 1 *(pages 376–385)*

SCIENCE AS A SOCIAL INSTITUTION

Section Overview

Science is the pursuit of knowledge through systematic methods. Science as a social institution is a relatively recent phenomenon. The process of institutionalization has taken centuries, however. Among the factors that led to the development of science as a social institution are the Renaissance, the growth in knowledge concerning mining and metallurgy, the Age of Exploration, the Protestant Reformation, and the Industrial Revolution. The sociological perspective that examines how scientific knowledge develops is called the sociology of science.

According to sociologist Robert K. Merton, the modern scientific community supposedly is guided by four norms. These norms are universalism, organized skepticism, communalism, and disinterestedness. In reality, however, scientists often fall far short of practicing these ideals. Among the problems that affect modern science are fraud, competition, the Matthew effect, and conflicting views of reality.

Previewing Key Terms

Section 1 contains the following key terms: **science, sociology of science, norm of universalism, norm of organized skepticism, norm of communalism, norm of disinterestedness, Matthew effect, paradigm**. Have students prepare a crossword puzzle using these terms and their definitions, found in the Glossary or in Section 1. Students may then exchange papers and complete the puzzles.

Introducing the Section

Tell students that science as a social institution is a relatively recent phenomenon, even though the process of institutionalization has taken centuries. Then ask students to suggest why this may be so. Tell them that many historical factors worked together to provide a climate in which science could become a social institution. Then assign the reading of Section 1.

Suggested Teaching Strategies

1. **Seeing Relationships (I)** Have students summarize the factors that led to the institutionalization of science.
2. **Analyzing Viewpoints (I)** Have students read the Applying Sociology feature on textbook pages 382–383. Discuss the first two questions that accompany the feature in class. Then have students complete the

essay directive in question 3 and have volunteers read their essays to the class for class discussion.
3. **Extending Ideas (II, III)** Although science is a central feature of the modern world, conflicts between the mainstream scientific community and supporters of other belief systems still occur. Some fundamentalist religious groups, for instance, hold views that differ from those supported by mainstream science. Have groups of interested students research some of the areas of contention and report their findings to the class.

Suggested Enrichment Activities

1. **Classifying Sociological Methods (I)** Have students complete the appropriate Developing Research Skills Worksheet, found in the *Teacher's Resource Binder.*
2. **Gathering Information (III)** Have interested students interview members of the scientific community concerning the norms of science versus the realities of scientific research. If members of the scientific community are not available for interview, have students write to scientists at universities or research institutes requesting their views on problems affecting scientific research.

Suggested Assignments

1. **Organizing Ideas (I)** As homework, have students complete the appropriate Graphic Organizer Worksheet, found in the *Teacher's Resource Binder.*
2. ★**Thinking about Sociology: Determining Fallacies in Reasoning (I)** Instruct students to read the Developing Sociological Imagination feature on textbook pages 396–397 and then complete the assignment under Practicing the Skill.

Closing the Section

Close the section by having students write a 10-question quiz on the information in the section. Have them write their questions on one side of the page and the answers on the other side. The quizzes then can be exchanged and answered. If students have difficulty with any of the material in the quizzes, offer clarifications at this time.

Assessing the Section

Have students complete the Section 1 Review.

Answers to Applying Sociology *(pages 382–383)*

1. The author believes that science education should involve a "hands-on" approach because children continually try to make sense of their environment through experience and experimentation.
2. Reforms are being made in science education. Project 2061 is an attempt to define what science literacy is by setting out a general set of goals for twelfth-graders, including knowledge of key concepts and principles of science. The Scope, Sequence, and Coordination Project calls for spreading the teaching of all the traditional disciplines over six full years, with the connections among them emphasized.
3. Answers will vary, but students should use sound reasoning to support the viewpoints they have chosen.

Answers to Section 1 Review *(page 385)*

Define *science:* pursuit of knowledge through systematic methods; *sociology of science:* sociological perspective that examines how scientific knowledge develops; *paradigm:* set of shared concepts, methods, and assumptions that makes up the scientific reality at any point in time

Identify *Piltdown man:* bones found in a gravel pit in England in 1912 that were supposed to be the "missing link" between apes and humans, later discovered to be part of a scientific hoax; *Robert K. Merton:* sociologist who found that honors and recognition tend to go to those scientists who have already achieved recognition, called by Merton the "Matthew effect"; *Thomas S. Kuhn:* historian of science who coined the term *paradigm*

1. Science emerged in Greece in the fourth century B.C. It spread to other nations over the next 300 years. As the Church gained in power, people turned away from science and toward philosophy and religion for explanations of the workings of the natural world. It was not until the 1300s that the rebirth of European science began. Four factors contributed to this rebirth: the Renaissance, the growth of knowledge concerning mining and metallurgy, the Age of Exploration, and the Protestant Reformation. The Renaissance was in part a by-product of trade with the East. The wealth produced by such trade provided merchants, bankers, and nobility with the leisure time to pursue art and learning. Advances in mining and metallurgy led to the printing press, which in turn made inexpensive books available and thus assisted in the spread of scientific knowledge. The Age of Exploration increased the demand for knowledge in astronomy and mathematics. And finally, the Protestant Reformation lessened public resistance to scientific inquiry by including science among the good works that could lead to salvation. By the 1700s, these various factors combined to produce a revolution in scientific thought that redefined the nature of the universe, the methods of scientific research, and the functions of science.

2. The four basic norms of science are universalism, organized skepticism, communalism, and disinterestedness. The norm of universalism holds that scientific research should be judged solely on the basis of quality, not on the characteristics of the scientist. The norm of organized skepticism holds that no scientific finding or theory is immune to questioning. The norm of communalism holds that all scientific knowledge should be made available to everyone in the scientific community. The norm of disinterestedness holds that scientists should seek truth, not personal gain.

3. **(a)** Scientific research suffers from four problems: fraud, the negative effects of competition, the Matthew effect, and conflicting views of reality. **(b)** Fraud and the negative effects of competition represent violations of the norm of disinterestedness. People seek personal gain over the pursuit of knowledge. The fear of being "beaten to the punch" on an important discovery also can cause scientists to refuse

to share unpublished information with their colleagues. This represents a violation of the norm of communalism. The Matthew effect—the tendency for scientific honors and recognition to go to scientists who have already achieved recognition and be withheld from scientists who have not as yet made their mark—represents a violation of the norms of organized skepticism and disinterestedness. And, finally, conflicts over competing paradigms represent a violation of the norm of organized skepticism.

SECTION 2 *(pages 386–395)*

SPORT AS A SOCIAL INSTITUTION

Section Overview

Sociologists use the term *sport* to refer to competitive games that are won or lost on the basis of physical skills and are played according to specific rules. Throughout history, people have played games. Sport as a social institution, however, is a relatively recent development. Modern sport is distinguished by seven characteristics: secularization, equality, specialization, rationalization, bureaucratization, quantification, and the quest for records.

Sociologists differ on how they view the effect of sport on society. Sociologists who adopt a functionalist perspective view sport as serving at least two important functions for society: social integration and the reinforcement of important social norms and values. Sociologists who adopt a conflict perspective, on the other hand, view sport as a mechanism to promote social inequality.

Social scientists have devoted considerable attention to the analysis of American sport. Two issues that have been of particular interest to sociologists are the continuing problem of racial discrimination in organized sports and the social and social-psychological factors associated with women's professional and amateur athletics.

Previewing Key Terms

Section 2 contains the following key terms: **sport, secularization, rationalization, stacking**. Copy the following "vocabulary pretest" on the chalkboard:

1. The process by which every feature of human behavior becomes subject to calculation, measurement, and control is called _____.
2. Movement away from the realm of the sacred to the realm of the profane is called _____.
3. _____ refers to competitive games that are won or lost on the basis of physical skills and are played according to specific rules.
4. _____ is the tendency to assign people to central or noncentral athletic positions on the basis of race or ethnicity.

Now have the class discuss possible answers for each question listed. With which terms is the class already familiar? Which terms are new? If students cannot answer one or more of the questions, have a volunteer find the correct terms in Section 2. End by telling students that all of these terms pertain to the social institution of sport.

Introducing the Section

Ask the students if any of them are surprised to find that sociologists consider sport to be a social institution. If any students answer affirmatively, ask them why they are surprised. Next tell the class that sport, like the other social institutions, is based on a system of statuses, roles, norms, and values, and can be analyzed in much the same way as the more familiar social institutions. Then assign the reading of Section 2.

Suggested Teaching Strategies

1. **Understanding Ideas (I)** List on the chalkboard the seven characteristics that define sport as a social institution. Then ask students to provide examples of how sports in the United States reflect these characteristics.
2. **Solving Problems (I)** Tell students that the problem of steroid abuse has become a major concern throughout the nation. Then show the class the film *Steroids: Shortcut to Make-Believe Muscles* (rental information can be found in the introductory section of this *Teacher's Manual*). Have the students discuss the views of those people portrayed in the film and then suggest ways to discourage young people from using steroids. Consider having volunteers use the suggestions to write an editorial for submission to the school newspaper.
3. **Gathering Information (I, II)** Have students read the Case Study on textbook page 390. Then have interested students compile lists of the types of and number of hours of sports coverage available in your area during any given week. Discuss the extent of coverage in class and whether such coverage is positive or negative for society.

Suggested Enrichment Activities

1. **Exploring Cross-Cultural Perspectives (I)** Have students complete the appropriate Cross-Cultural Perspectives Worksheet, found in the *Teacher's Resource Binder*.
2. **Debating Ideas (II, III)** Organize interested students into two groups and have the groups debate the following statement: "All professional athletes should be subject to drug testing on a regular basis."

Suggested Assignments

1. **Stating a Point of View (I)** As homework, have students write a critique of the functionalist and conflict perspectives on sport, and state which of the two perspectives they believe best explains the effects of sport on society.
2. **Making Inferences (I)** Have students complete the appropriate Critical Skills Mastery Worksheet, found in the *Teacher's Resource Binder*.
3. **Making Oral Presentations (III)** Have interested students research and prepare oral presentations on one of the following topics: the role of sports in nations other than the United States, racial discrimination in sports, or the state of women's athletics.

Closing the Section

Close the section by having students complete the appropriate Understanding Sociological Ideas Worksheet, found in the *Teacher's Resource Binder*.

Assessing the Section

Have students complete the Section 2 Review.

Answers to Section 2 Review *(page 395)*

Define *sport:* competitive games that are won or lost on the basis of physical skills and are played according to specific rules; ***stacking:*** tendency to assign people to central or noncentral athletic positions on the basis of race or ethnicity

1. The characteristics that distinguish sport as a social institution are secularization, equality, specialization, rationalization, bureaucratization, quantification, and the quest for records. Secularization is the movement away from the realm of the sacred to the realm of the profane. Equality means that sports competition is open to everyone and that the same rules apply to all contestants. Specialization refers to the fact that most serious athletes concentrate on one sport, as do most persons employed in athletics. Rationalization refers to the processes by which every feature of human behavior becomes subject to calculation, measurement, and control. In relation to sport, this means that every major sport is played according to established rules that are periodically revised. Bureaucratization goes hand-in-hand with rationalization. If a sport is to be played according to specific rules, there must be a formal organization charged with the task of developing and enforcing rules, settling disputes, and organizing competitions. Quantification refers to the evaluation of performance in terms of time or numerical scores so that athletes can be compared. Finally, the quest for records refers to the emphasis on winning and the setting of new performance records. Quantification and the quest for records are an outgrowth of the emphasis on achievement that is a central feature of industrial society.
2. Functionalists argue that sport performs at least two important functions for society. First, by providing a common interest for people with different racial, ethnic, and economic characteristics, sport serves to unite members of society. Second, sport teaches people to value hard work, team spirit, and obedience to authority. Conflict theorists, on the other hand, focus on the negative aspects of sport. According to many conflict theorists, sport helps to maintain social inequality by drawing people's attention away from personal and social problems. In addition, contact sports legitimate violence, thereby making it more acceptable in other areas of life. And finally, because sport reinforces the idea that achievement comes to those who work hard, it provides an excuse for the unequal distribution of wealth.

3. One of the major issues of interest to sociologists of sport is racial discrimination in organized sports. Studies on racial discrimination in sports tend to focus on one of two areas: the practice of stacking and pay differences between white and African American players. Stacking refers to the tendency to assign people to central or noncentral athletic positions on the basis of race or ethnicity. Social scientists have found that African American players tend to occupy noncentral positions in college and professional team sports, while white players occupy central positions. Social scientists also have found evidence of racial discrimination in pay differences between white and African American professional athletes. A second issue of interest to sociologists of sport is women's athletics. Research has found that women in professional sports have lower earnings potential than their male counterparts. Women's prize money in professional tennis, for instance, lags behind men's prize money by about 30 percent. The situation is no better in college athletics. Funding for women's college athletics generally is much lower than the funding provided for men's athletics. Many sociologists also are interested in the degree to which female participation in organized sports is considered socially acceptable. Research has indicated that traditional gender-role stereotypes still influence which sports are considered appropriate for women.

Answers to Developing Sociological Imagination *(pages 396–397)*

1. (a) The main idea of the passage is that human beings are inherently aggressive. **(b)** The author concludes that humans, like all animals, are genetically predisposed to carve out and defend their territory.

2. A single-cause fallacy found in this passage is that aggression is caused by genetics. Other factors from the social environment affect an individual's use of violence.

3. A correlation-as-cause fallacy is found in the statement that Americans have fences in their yards. Just because people have fences in their yards and are sometimes aggressive does not mean that people are genetically predisposed to carve out and defend their territory.

4. An insufficient-evidence fallacy is contained in the argument that finding the bones of our ancestors among the ashes of prehistoric fires is evidence that humans used fire as a weapon. Finding bones in the ashes of prehistoric fires is not enough evidence to support the idea that fire was used as a weapon. Additional evidence would be needed to determine how the bones got into the fire and whether the humans were dead or alive at the time.

5. A majority-view fallacy is contained in the statement that everyone knows that humans are inherently aggressive. The author has not supported the statement with testable facts.

Closing the Chapter

Have students complete the Chapter 15 Review Worksheet, found in the *Teacher's Resource Binder.*

Assessing the Chapter

Have students complete the Chapter 15 Review, found on page 398 of the *Pupil's Edition.*

Give students the Chapter 15 Form A Test and, if desired, the Chapter 15 Reteaching Worksheet and Form B Test, found in the *Teacher's Resource Binder.*

Answers to Chapter 15 Review *(page 398)*

Reviewing Sociological Terms

1. stacking
2. Science
3. paradigm
4. sociology of science
5. Sport

Thinking Critically about Sociology

1. The Enlightenment, which promoted reason over religious dogma, relied on the scientific method and scientific knowledge to achieve the goal of democratic government. One of the consequences of the Enlightenment—and of the French Revolution, which it helped spark—was a state-supported educational system. This system helped to spread scientific knowledge and provided new positions in research and teaching. The Industrial Revolution also emphasized progress through science. In addition to pure research, scientists increasingly saw as their task the creation of new technologies that could improve the human condition.

2. Science during the time of ancient Greeks and Romans was linked to the study of philosophy and religion. Great thinkers explored the fields of mathematics, astronomy, the biological sciences, physics, and medicine. In Egypt, great libraries and centers of learning were established, providing employment for scholars and scientists.

3. (a) The seven characteristics of sport outlined by Allen Guttman are secularization, equality, specialization, rationalization, bureaucratization, quantification, and the quest for records. Secularization refers to the movement away from the realm of the sacred to the realm of the profane. Equality means that sports competition is open to everyone and that the same rules apply to all contestants. Specialization refers to the fact that most serious athletes concentrate on one sport, as do most persons employed in athletics. Rationalization refers to the processes by which every feature of human behavior becomes subject to calculation, measurement, and control. In relation to sport, this means that every major sport is played according to established rules that are periodically revised. Bureaucratization goes hand-in-hand with rationalization. If a sport is to be played according to specific rules, there must be a formal organization whose task it is to develop and enforce rules, settle disputes, and organize competitions. Quantification refers to the evaluation of athletic performance in terms of time or numerical scores so that athletes can be compared. Finally, the quest for records refers to the emphasis on winning and the setting of new performance records. Quantification and the quest for records are an outgrowth of the emphasis on achievement that is a central feature of modern industrial society. **(b)** The central themes of the Enlightenment and the Industrial Revolution—democracy, achievement, competition, efficiency, and the desire for measurable progress—can be found in modern sports. Thus the rise of sport as a social institution closely follows the rise of modern industrial society. Among the core features of the social structure produced by the Industrial Revolution were a high degree of secularization, an emphasis on equality of opportunity and the distribution of rewards based on merit, a division of labor based on specialization, extreme rationalization and bureaucratization, and an emphasis on achievement as measured by quantifiable progress. All of these features are present in modern sport.

4. Social scientists have found that African American players tend to occupy noncentral positions in college and professional team sports, while white players occupy central positions. Social scientists also have found evidence of racial discrimination in pay differences between white and African American professional athletes. Furthermore, research has indicated that women in professional sports have lower earnings potential than their male counterparts. And the situation for women is no better in college athletics. The funding provided for women's college athletics generally is much lower than the funding provided for men's athletics.

5. The Renaissance was a by-product of trade with the East. The wealth produced by such trade provided bankers, merchants, and the nobility with the leisure time to pursue art and learning. Advances in mining and metallurgy led to the printing press, which in turn made inexpensive books available and thus assisted in the spread of scientific knowledge. The Age of Exploration increased the demand for knowledge in astronomy and mathematics. And finally, the Protestant Reformation lessened public resistance to scientific inquiry by including science among the good works that could lead to salvation.

6. Functionalists argue that sport performs at least two functions for society. First, sport tends to unite members of society by providing a common interest for people of different racial, ethnic, and economic characteristics. Second, sport teaches people to value hard work, team spirit, and obedience to authority. Conflict theorists, on the other hand, focus on the negative aspects of sport. According to many conflict theorists, sport helps maintain social inequality by drawing people's attention away from personal and social problems. In addition, contact sports legitimate violence, thereby making it more acceptable in other areas of life. And finally, because sport reinforces the idea that achievement comes to those who work hard, it provides an excuse for the unequal distribution of wealth. Answers regarding personal views on these perspectives will vary, but students should use sound reasoning in their responses.

7. **(a)** Conflicting views of reality may lead to the development of new paradigms. Paradigms determine what topics are appropriate for scientific inquiry, what methods can be used to collect and analyze data, and what interpretations of data are considered legitimate. During transitions between paradigms, conflicts often arise between supporters of the old and new paradigms. The perceptions of the general public or of the government also can affect science by limiting the areas of scientific inquiry that are considered appropriate. **(b)** The Matthew effect refers to the tendency for scientific honors and recognition to go to those scientists who have already achieved recognition. Such honors and recognition tend to be withheld from those who have not yet been recognized. The Matthew effect can have positive and negative consequences for science. On the negative side, the Matthew effect can hamper the careers of young scientists. However, science as a whole may benefit from the Matthew effect insofar as the findings of respected scientists are more readily incorporated into the existing body of knowledge.

8. Information for the chart should be drawn from textbook pages 379–381 and 384–385.

Exercising Sociological Skills

1. Steps that might be taken to improve scientific literacy in the United States include developing a "hands-on" approach to education and pursuing new scientific education standards in the schools.
2. Answers will vary, but students should base their essays on the information contained on textbook page 390.
3. Answers will vary, but students should follow the guidelines presented in the Developing Sociological Imagination feature on textbook pages 396–397.

Extending Sociological Imagination

1. Answers will vary.
2. Answers will vary.

Answers to Interpreting Primary Sources *(page 399)*

1. The physical effects of steroid abuse include severe acne, early balding, yellowing of the skin and eyes, and shrinking of the sex organs. In females, the breasts shrink, the sex organ swells, and hair is lost from the head but grows on the face and body. Young people also risk stunting their growth.
2. The psychological effects of steroid abuse include irritability, anger, and rage.

Closing the Unit

Have students complete the Unit 4 Review Worksheet, found in the *Teacher's Resource Binder.*

Assessing the Unit

Have students complete the Unit 4 Review, found on page 401 of the *Pupil's Edition.*

Give students the Unit 4 Form A Test and, if desired, the Unit 4 Reteaching Worksheet and Form B Test, found in the *Teacher's Resource Binder.*

Reviewing Sociological Ideas

1. **(a)** A social institution is the system of statuses, roles, norms, and values that is organized to satisfy one or more of the basic needs of society. **(b)** The family is a group of people who are related by marriage, blood, or adoption and who live together and share economic resources. The economic institution is the system of roles and norms that governs the production, distribution, and consumption of goods and services. The political institution is the system of roles and norms that governs the distribution and exercise of power in society. Education is the system of roles and norms that ensures the transmission of knowledge, values, and patterns of behavior from one generation to the next. Religion is the system of roles and norms organized around the sacred realm that binds people together in social groups. Science is the pursuit of knowledge through systematic methods. Sport is competitive games that are won or lost on the basis of physical skills and are played according to specific rules.

2. **(a)** The primary sector deals with the extraction of raw materials from the environment. The secondary sector deals with the manufacture of goods from raw materials. The tertiary sector is involved in the provision of services. **(b)** Labor in preindustrial societies is heavily concentrated in the primary sector. In industrial societies, the emphasis shifts to the secondary sector. In postindustrial societies, the tertiary sector becomes the most important area of the economy.

3. **(a)** In an authoritarian government, power rests firmly with the state. Members of such societies have little or no say in the political decision-making process. **(b)** There are several different forms of authoritarian governments. Absolute monarchies are societies in which a ruler who has inherited his or her position has absolute power. Dictatorships are governments in which one individual has complete power. Juntas are systems in which power has been seized from the previous government by force. Totalitarian societies are those in which leaders allow no limits on their authority. The lives of the members of such societies are rigidly controlled.

4. **(a)** A nuclear family is one or both parents and their children. **(b)** A family of orientation is the nuclear family into which a person is born. **(c)** A family of procreation is the family an individual forms through marriage, consisting of the individual, his or her spouse, and their children. **(d)** An extended family is three or more generations of a family sharing the same residence. **(e)** Kinship is a network of people who are related by marriage, birth, or adoption.

5. **(a)** Religion has three important functions. First, religion strengthens the bonds between societal members, thus increasing social cohesion. Participating in religious rituals and sharing religious beliefs create a sense of belonging among individuals. A second major function of religion is to encourage conformity to social norms. Norms surrounding important social issues often not only are formalized in law but also are supported by religious doctrine. Religion also provides formalized ways for individuals to relieve their guilt for disobeying norms and laws. Finally, religion provides emotional support for people during difficult times and provides answers to questions of life and death that cannot be answered by science or common sense. Such answers lend strength and calm as people approach the unknown. **(b)** The three basic elements of religion are rituals, belief systems, and organizational structures. Rituals are established patterns of behavior through which believers experience the sacred. Rituals unite believers, reinforce faith, and often mark major life events such as birth, marriage, or death. Belief systems are composed of sets of beliefs used to provide guidelines for behavior. There are three major belief systems. Animism is a belief system in which spirits are active in influencing human life. Theism is the belief in a god or gods. Ethicalism is a belief system in which moral principles have a sacred quality. There are four types of organizational structures: ecclesia, denominations, sects, and cults. An ecclesia is a type of religious organization to which people belong simply because of their birth. Denominations are formal, bureaucratic organizations, involving trained officials, to which a substantial proportion of the population belong. Sects are relatively small organizations that have split off from a denomination because of differences in doctrine. Cults are religious groups that are founded on the revelations of a person believed to have special knowledge.

6. **(a)** Power is the ability to control the behavior of other people, with or without their consent. **(b)** When power is exercised with the consent of the people being governed, it is considered legitimate. Power is considered illegitimate, on the other hand, when it is exercised against the will or without the approval of those being controlled. **(c)** The three forms of legitimate power outlined by Weber are traditional authority, charismatic authority, and rational-legal authority. Traditional authority is power that is legitimated by long-standing custom. Charismatic authority is power that is legitimated by the personal characteristics of the individual exercising the power. Rational-legal authority is power that is legitimated by formal rules and regulations.

7. **(a)** Homogamy is marriage between individuals with similar social characteristics. **(b)** Heterogamy is marriage between individuals who have different social characteristics.

8. **(a)** A democracy is a type of government in which power is exercised through the people. **(b)** The following conditions are needed for a democracy to thrive: industrialization and literate, urban populations that expect to have a voice in the political process; access to information; limits on government powers; and shared values.

9. The seven characteristics that distinguish sport as a social institution are secularization, equality, specialization, rationalization, bureaucratization, quantification, and the quest for records. Secularization is the movement away from the realm of the sacred to the realm of the profane. Equality means that sports

competition is open to everyone and that the same rules apply to all contestants. Specialization refers to the fact that most serious athletes concentrate on one sport, as do most persons employed in athletics. Rationalization refers to the processes by which every feature of human behavior becomes subject to calculation, measurement, and control. In relation to sport, this means that every major sport is played according to established rules that are periodically revised. Bureaucratization goes hand-in-hand with rationalization. If a sport is to be played according to specific rules, there must be a formal organization whose task it is to develop and enforce rules, settle disputes, and organize competitions. Quantification refers to the evaluation of performance in terms of time or numerical scores so that athletes can be compared. Finally, the quest for records refers to the emphasis on winning and the setting of new performance records.

Synthesizing Sociological Ideas

1. **(a)** Science emerged in Greece in the fourth century B.C. It spread to other nations over the next 300 years. As the Church gained in power, people turned away from science and toward philosophy and religion for explanations of the workings of the natural world. It was not until the 1300s that the rebirth of European science began. Four factors contributed to this rebirth: the Renaissance, the growth of knowledge concerning mining and metallurgy, the Age of Exploration, and the Protestant Reformation. The Renaissance was in part a by-product of trade with the East. The wealth produced by such trade provided merchants, bankers, and nobility with the leisure time to pursue art and learning. Advances in mining and metallurgy led to the printing press, which in turn made inexpensive books available and thus assisted in the spread of scientific knowledge. The Age of Exploration increased the demand for knowledge in astronomy and mathematics. And finally, the Protestant Reformation lessened public resistance to scientific inquiry by including science among the good works that could lead to salvation. By the 1700s, these various factors combined to produce a revolution in scientific thought that redefined the nature of the universe, the methods of scientific research, and the functions of science. **(b)** The four basic norms of science are universalism, organized skepticism, communalism, and disinterestedness. The norm of universalism holds that scientific research should be judged solely on the basis of quality, not on the characteristics of the scientist. The norm of organized skepticism holds that no scientific finding or theory is immune to questioning. The norm of communalism holds that all scientific knowledge should be made available to everyone in the scientific community. The norm of disinterestedness holds that scientists should seek truth, not personal gain. In reality, though, scientific research suffers from four problems: fraud, the negative effects of competition, the Matthew effect, and conflicting views of reality. Fraud and the negative effects of competition represent violations of the norm of disinterestedness. People seek personal gain over the pursuit of knowledge. The fear of being "beaten to the punch" on an important discovery also can cause scientists to refuse to share unpublished information with their colleagues. This represents a violation of the norm of communalism. The Matthew effect—the tendency for scientific honors and recognition to go to scientists who have already achieved recognition and be withheld from scientists who have not as yet made their mark—represents a violation of the norms of organized skepticism and disinterestedness. In addition, pressures from the public and from the government can affect the norms of science. Two norms—the norm of disinterestedness and the norm of organized skepticism—are particularly vulnerable to public and government pressures.

2. **(a)** Societies vary in terms of the number of marriage partners an individual can have. Societies that practice monogamy allow people to have only one marriage partner. Societies that practice polygamy allow people to have multiple marriage partners. Polygyny—the marriage of one man to multiple wives—and polyandry—the marriage of one women to multiple husbands—are types of polygamy. **(b)** Family patterns also vary in terms of residential rules. Some societies practice patrilocality and require newly married couples to live with or near the husband's family. Societies that practice matrilocality require newlyweds to live with or near the wife's family. In other societies, the newlyweds can choose to live near either the husband's or the wife's family, a system called bilocality. Finally, some societies, especially industrialized societies, practice neolocality and allow newlyweds to live apart from both sets of parents. **(c)** Societies also differ in terms of the way family descent is traced. Those that trace kinship through the father's family are patrilineal. Those that trace kinship through the mother's family, on the other hand, are matrilineal. Those that trace kinship through both the mother's and the father's families are bilateral. **(d)** There are three possible patterns of authority in families. In patriarchal systems, fathers hold most of the power. In matriarchal systems, mothers hold most of the power. In egalitarian systems, authority is shared by both mother and father.

3. The family has four central functions. It regulates sexual activity, enforcing an incest taboo that forbids sexual relations between certain relatives. Families also reproduce societal members, replacing those who die or move away. Within this function, they set up rules concerning childbearing and parenting obligations. Families also socialize children, teaching them the values and norms of society. Finally, families act as the basic economic units of societies. Basic needs are met through the division of labor among family members.

4. **(a)** Sociologists who follow the functionalist perspective view education as a force for the stability and smooth operation of society. Education does this by producing citizens who share a common set of values. **(b)** Sociologists who follow the conflict perspective, on the other hand, view education as a way of creating and maintaining unequal access to

positions of power in society. Education does this by producing citizens who will accept the basic inequalities of society and who will not question the existing order.

5. There are several common characteristics among marriages that are happy. These characteristics are having parents who are successfully married; having known each other for at least two years prior to marriage; marrying at an older age; holding traditional values; having a conflict-free engagement; being of the same race and religion; having a college education; and having parental approval of the marriage. Two additional factors affect marital satisfaction: gender and the presence of children. In general, men are more satisfied with marriage than are women. And, couples with no dependent children are more satisfied than parents.

6. In a pure capitalist system, the economy is regulated by self-interest and market competition. Self-interest leads consumers to try to purchase the goods and services they desire at the lowest prices possible. Producers, on the other hand, are guided by self-interest to undertake only those business ventures that have the potential to make a profit. In a pure socialist system, the economy is controlled by social need, rather than by self-interest, and by centralized government planning, rather than by market forces. What to produce is determined by the needs of society. How to produce is determined by central planners. For whom to produce is determined by need rather than by the ability to pay.

7. The structured overview should be patterned after the one presented on textbook page 41.

8. **(a)** The American free enterprise system has been affected by the rise of corporate capitalism, the globalization of the economy, the expanding role of government, and the changing nature of work. **(b)** The rise of corporate capitalism has changed the relationship between business ownership and control. Early capitalists managed the day-to-day affairs of the businesses they owned, Today, few corporate stockholders participate in daily business operations. Also, most American corporate stocks are owned by other corporations. The globalization of the economy has made nations economically interdependent. As a result, the economic policies of one nation often affect the policies of other nations. Population growth and the rise of corporate capitalism have led the government to take on more responsibility for the economy. The government has taken action to regulate economic activity, to protect consumers, to provide public goods, and to promote economic well-being. Automation and increased efficiency have reduced the number of workers needed to meet the demand in manufacturing. The demand for workers has increased in the service sector. This has led the government and business leaders to call for a strengthened commitment to quality education.

9. Social scientists have found that African American athletes tend to occupy noncentral positions in college and professional team sports, while white athletes occupy central positions. Social scientists also have found evidence of racial discrimination in salary differences between white and African American professional athletes. Moreover, research has indicated that women in professional sports have lower earnings potential than their male counterparts. A similar situation is present in college athletics. The funding provided for women's college athletics generally is much lower than the funding provided for men's college athletics.

Applying Sociological Imagination

1. Several trends in family life have been noted in recent years. First, people now are delaying marriage and marrying at older ages. Accompanying the delay in marriage is a delay in childbearing. Women now are waiting longer to have their first child. Additionally, the number of childless couples has been on the rise. A third trend is the increase in female labor force participation and in the number of dual-earner families. A fourth major trend involves an increase in the number of single-parent families. Finally, remarriages and stepfamilies have been on the rise over the years.

2. Answers will vary.

3. Answers will vary.

UNIT 5 *(pages 402–483)*

THE CHANGING SOCIAL WORLD

CHAPTER 16
COLLECTIVE BEHAVIOR AND
SOCIAL MOVEMENTS

CHAPTER 17
POPULATION AND URBANIZATION

CHAPTER 18
SOCIAL CHANGE AND MODERNIZATION

Unit Overview

All of history is the story of change. In the modern world, however, the pace of change has accelerated. Each week brings new material goods, new styles of dress, new ways of doing things, and new ideas to challenge existing knowledge and beliefs. Thus it is not surprising that the analysis of the causes and consequences of social change is a major theme in sociology. Unit 5 examines three areas of interest to sociologists studying the changing social world: collective behavior and social movements, population change and urbanization, and social change and modernization.

Unit Goals

At the end of the unit, students should be able to

1. Define collective behavior, and identify the six preconditions that guide the outcome of collective behavior.
2. Explain how collectivities differ from other types of social groups, and recognize the stages in the lifecycle of social movements.
3. Describe types of collectivities and types of social movements.
4. Compare the theories developed to explain collective behavior, and compare those developed to explain social movements.
5. Describe the characteristics of population change and the process of urbanization.
6. Compare the theories developed to describe population change, and compare those developed to explain city life.
7. Discuss the principal theories of social change and modernization.
8. Recognize some of the positive and negative social and environmental consequences of the modernization process.

Unit Skills

Three skills are developed in Unit 5.

★ WRITING ABOUT SOCIOLOGY: *Investigating Oral History* (Chapter 16; PE pages 424–425; TM page 112)
★ INTERPRETING THE VISUAL RECORD: *Analyzing Sociological-Data Maps* (Chapter 17; PE pages 454–455; TM page 119)
★ WRITING ABOUT SOCIOLOGY: *Composing a Comparative Essay* (Chapter 18; PE pages 478–479; TM page 123)

Suggestions for teaching the skills appear on the TM pages mentioned above. The suggestions are clearly identified by the ★ symbol. Each skill is reinforced in the Chapter Review under Exercising Sociological Skills. Answers to the questions in the textbook's skill features appear in the Answers to Developing Sociological Imagination sections of this *Teacher's Manual*.

Introducing the Unit

Write on the chalkboard the following quotation from the work of social scientist Daniel Chirot:

No social change occurs outside the world context; and though the strengths and weaknesses of individual states and societies are largely determined by internal causes, it is the way these characteristics of societies interact with the world systems that determines the direction, intensity, and speed of further internal change.

Ask students to describe what they think Chirot is saying about the nature of social change in the modern world. Then discuss the implications of this type of social change for (a) the world in general and (b) the United States in particular. Have students note current historical developments to support their arguments. Close the discussion by noting that Unit 5 will explore the nature of the changing social world in the late twentieth century.

References for Teachers

Aaseng, Nathan. *Overpopulation: Crisis or Challenge?* New York: Franklin Watts, 1991. Provides a historical overview of population growth and explores the problems associated with overpopulation.

Boorstin, Daniel J. *The Image: A Guide to Pseudo-Events in America*. New York: Vintage Books, 1992. Examines the ways in which the media manipulate information and events to sway public opinion.

Brown, Lester. *State of the World 1992: A Worldwatch Institute Report on Progress Toward a Sustainable Future*. New York: W.W. Norton, 1992. Annually updated report that focuses on a variety of issues relating to our changing social world.

Goldfarb, Theodore D., ed. *Taking Sides: Clashing Views on Controversial Environmental Issues*. Guilford, CT: Dushkin Press, 1991. Presents 18 point-counterpoint essays on a variety of environmental issues.

Hammond, Allen, ed. *The 1993 Information Please Environmental Almanac*. Boston, MA: Houghton

Mifflin, 1993. Almanac containing statistical information and stimulating essays on the state of the environment throughout the world.

Menard, Scott W., and Moen, Elizabeth. *Perspectives on Population: An Introduction to Concepts and Issues.* New York: Oxford University Press, 1987. Collection of scholarly essays on basic demographic principles and concepts.

Pratkanis, Anthony, and Aronson, Elliot. *The Age of Propaganda: The Everyday Use and Abuse of Persuasion.* New York: W.H. Freeman, 1991. Social-psychological approach to the analysis of propaganda techniques.

Schwab, William R. *The Sociology of Cities,* 2nd ed. Englewood Cliffs, NJ: Prentice-Hall, 1992. Overview of theory and research on urban sociology.

Senechal, Roberta. *The Sociogenesis of a Race Riot: Springfield, Illinois, in 1908.* Champaign, IL: University of Illinois Press, 1990. Case study analysis of collective behavior.

Volti, Rudi. *Society and Technological Change,* 2nd ed. New York: St. Martin's Press, 1992. Examines the influence of technology on social change.

Readings for Student Enrichment

Brunvand, Jan Harold. *The Baby Train and Other Urban Legends.* New York: W.W. Norton, 1993. Collection of urban legends from around the world; enables students to explore collective communication.

The Emerald Realm: Earth's Precious Rain Forests. Washington, DC: National Geographic Society, 1990. Scholarly examination of the world's tropical rain forests; enables students to explore what experts are doing to preserve and protect the vanishing rain forests.

Frank, Pat. *Alas, Babylon.* New York: Bantam Books, 1976. Small group of men and women band together to rebuild their world after a global disaster; enables students to explore the effects of drastic social change on human interaction.

Gay, Kathlyn. *Caution! This May Be an Advertisement: A Teen Guide to Advertising.* New York: Franklin Watts, 1992. Describes the techniques used by advertisers to persuade consumers to buy their products; helps students to recognize propaganda techniques and to become wise consumers.

MacEachern, Diane. *Save Our Planet: 750 Everyday Ways You Can Help Clean Up the Earth.* New York: Dell, 1990. Provides simple and effective ways to combat such problems as acid rain, the greenhouse effect, and water shortages; enables students to think critically about environmental problems and to work toward solutions.

Orwell, George. *1984.* New York: New American Library, 1983. Pessimistic prediction of the future of society; enables students to examine how society can use mass media to control the population.

Salak, John. *The Los Angeles Riots—America's Cities in Crisis: Headliners.* Brookfield, CT: Millbrook, 1993. Examines the 1992 Los Angeles riots in the context of America's turbulent past; provides students with insights into collective behavior.

Sinclair, Upton. *The Jungle.* New York: New American Library, 1906. Examination of the deplorable working and living conditions facing immigrants employed in the Chicago stockyards at the turn of the century; allows students to examine some of the consequences of rapid urbanization and industrialization.

Spencer, William. *The Challenge of World Hunger.* Hillside, NJ: Enslow Press, 1991. Examines the social, economic, environmental, and political causes of world hunger; enables students to understand the factors that make world hunger a persistent and challenging problem.

Weisel, Elie. *Night.* New York: Bantam Books, 1982. Novel about a young boy's imprisonment in a Nazi concentration camp; enables students to explore collective behavior from the standpoint of the Nazis and their victims.

Multimedia Materials

The selected materials listed below may be useful during the study of Unit 5. The following abbreviations are used in the list:

c = color	lvd = laser videodisc
b&w = black & white	sim = simulation
f = film	sw = software
fs = filmstrip	g = game
vhs = videocassette	

Chapter 16

The Civil Rights Movement (vhs; 15 min.) GA. Uses historical footage to document the history of the civil rights movement.

The Growth of the Labor Movement (fs on vhs; 37 min.) GA. Presents the historical development and the current status of the American labor movement.

Martin the Emancipator (vhs; 21 min.) EBEC. Examines the life of Dr. Martin Luther King, Jr., and how he inspired different factions of the civil rights movement to work together for social change.

The Propaganda Kit (g; entire class; 1 or more class periods) SSSS. Game kit designed to teach students how to recognize and think criticially about various propaganda techniques.

Psycho-Sell: Advertising and Persuasion (vhs, c; 25 min.) SSSS. Examines the methods used by advertisers to manipulate public opinion and persuade the public to buy their products.

The Rise of Labor (vhs; 30 min.) EBEC. Surveys the history of the American labor movement.

Search for the Master Terrorist: The Hunt for the Jackal (vhs, c; 90 min.) FHS. Documents the seven-year search for the world's most wanted man, terrorist Ilyich Ramirez Sanchez, known as "Carlos the Jackal."

30-Second Seduction (vhs; 25 min.) FIV. Advertisers and a sociologist explain how television commercials are designed to manipulate human emotions.

Unraveling Hitler's Conspiracy (vhs, c; 28 min.) FHS. Reveals how Heinrich Himmler, head of the German Gestapo, manipulated information about the past to legitimize the genocidal policies of Hitler and his Nazi regime.

Vietnam: A Television History, 11—Homefront U.S.A. (vhs, c; 60 min.) FIV. Documents the domestic upheaval caused by the Vietnam War.

The Witches of Salem: The Horror and the Hope (lvd; 34 min.) CMFV. Dramatization of the Salem witch trials of 1692, ignited by the hysterical accusations of a few young girls.

Zero Hour (vhs; 21 min.) EBEC. Ray Bradbury story about a new game sweeping the country and the dire implications of its appeal.

Chapter 17

The Development of Transportation (vhs; 10 min.) EBEC. Explores the relationship between the growth of the United States and the expansion of its transportation systems.

A Feast Amid Famine: The World Food Paradox (vhs; 60 min.) GA. Examines the worldwide problem of hunger and how such hunger often is made worse by economic systems that reward waste rather than efficiency.

The Industrial Revolution: Beginnings in the United States (vhs, c, b&w; 23 min.) EBEC. Traces the growth of the Industrial Revolution in the United States.

Jing, A Chinese Girl (vhs; 18 min.) AM. Chronicles two days in the life of Jing, a Chinese girl, to examine issues such as the role of children in a one-child-family society and how modern influences are affecting urban Chinese life.

The People Bomb (vhs, c; 106 min.) ZM. CNN correspondents report from Africa, Asia, and Latin America on how population growth is affecting the environment, global resources, and the social structure.

A Population Story: Collision with the Future? (vhs; 24 min.) EBEC. Animated sequences and live footage combine to tell the story of a future world where overpopulation has reached a critical level.

The Rise of the American City (vhs; 32 min.) EBEC. Discusses how the rise of cities has transformed the American nation and how these cities are now dealing with a host of social problems.

Simcity: School Edition (sim, sw) SSSS. Simulation that gives students hands-on experience in urban planning and urban development.

Street Children of Africa (vhs, c; 52 min.) FHS. Discusses the children of Africa who are homeless and who have no means of support other than what they can scrounge for themselves.

The Urban Dilemma (vhs, c; 28 min.) SSSS. Focuses on the explosive growth and resulting problems experienced by cities in less developed countries, and proposes solutions to the needs of these megacities.

U.S. Cities: Growth and Development (vhs; 19 min.) EBEC. Examines the origins and growth patterns of the great American cities.

World Population: A Graphic Simulation of the History of Human Population Growth (vhs, c; 6 min.) SSSS. Startling visual representation of the growth of the human population from 1 A.D. to the present.

Chapter 18

The Big Spill (vhs; 58 min.) CFV. *Nova* documentary that examines how and why the ecological disaster produced by the *Exxon Valdez* occurred, and what the ecological future of Prince William Sound might be.

Cope: A Simulation of Adapting to Change and Anticipating the Future (sim; entire class; 3 weeks) SSSS. Simulation in which students live in the era of 2000–2040 and must cope with a computer that has taken over all facets of human activity.

Deforestation: Exploring Issues (vhs, c; 13 min.) SSSS. Two high school students examine varied points of view concerning the issue of deforestation.

The Environment: Decisions, Decisions (sim, sw; 24 student booklets) SSSS. Simulation in which students consider crucial environmental questions from the perspective of a town mayor.

The Garbage Explosion (vhs; 15 min.) EBEC. Discusses the fact that America's cities are running out of landfill space and shows alternative ways to manage waste.

A Hole in the Sky: A Special Report on the Global Ozone Crisis (vhs, c; 35 min.) SSSS. Bernard Shaw narrates this overview of the international ozone crisis, including its causes, its effects on human beings, and its prospective solutions.

The International Monetary Fund at Work (vhs; 22 min.) EBEC. Explores how the International Monetary Fund encourages international cooperation to help underdeveloped countries around the world.

Modern Times (b&w; 87 min.) ZM. Satire of modern industrial society produced, written, and directed by Charlie Chaplin in 1936.

Nuclear Winter (vhs, c; 21 min.) FHS. Describes the nuclear winter in the northern and southern hemispheres that would be the inevitable result of a nuclear war.

Politics, People, and Pollution (vhs; 60 min.) PBS. Bill Moyers talks to environmentalists and industry representatives about corporate America's willingness to protect the public's health and safety.

Rachel Carson's Silent Spring (vhs; 60 min.) PBS. Details the struggle of biologist Rachel Carson to bring to public awareness the destructive potential of the unregulated usage of herbicides and pesticides in farming.

The Robotic Revolution (f, vhs, c; 24 min.) EBEC. Explores what robots can and cannot do and examines the social implications of robots in the workplace.

Survival of Spaceship Earth (vhs; 63 min.) CSS. Examines how the recent explosion in population is affecting our ability to cope with heretofore unforeseen environmental problems.

Technology's Price (vhs, c; 25 min.) EBEC. Explores the environmental and human costs of our dependence on technology.

Who'll Save Abacaxi? A Third-World Government Simulation (sim, sw) FM. Simulation in which students role-play the newly elected president and staff of the developing country of Abacaxi, making decisions that will have both internal and global implications.

Women of Kerala (vhs; 27 min.) FIV. Examines how the women of Kerala in India have been successful in reducing the birthrate and raising the standard of living in their area.

World Hunger: Current Issues Series (vhs, c; 30 min.) SSSS. Larry Hollar, spokesperson for Bread for the World, examines a variety of issues that focus on world hunger.

CHAPTER 16 *(pages 404–427)*

COLLECTIVE BEHAVIOR AND SOCIAL MOVEMENTS

SECTION 1
COLLECTIVE BEHAVIOR

SECTION 2
SOCIAL MOVEMENTS

Chapter Overview

In general, social behavior is patterned and predictable. People expect others to act in accord with established norms and in most instances they do. In fact, without this predictability and cooperative spirit, social interaction would be impossible.

Sometimes, however, situations occur in which the norms of behavior are unclear. Often in these situations, it appears as though people are making up new norms as they go along. Sociologists refer to this action as collective behavior. Chapter 16 examines the characteristics of collective behavior, types of collectivities, and the sociological theories that have been developed to explain collective behavior.

Chapter Objectives

At the conclusion of the chapter, students will be able to

1. Identify the preconditions that guide the outcome of collective behavior, and explain how these preconditions build on one another.
2. Recognize the characteristics of collectivities, and explain how various types of collectivities differ.
3. Discuss the theories that have been developed to explain collective behavior.
4. Distinguish between the various types of social movements, and trace the stages in the life-cycle of social movements.
5. Discuss the theories that have been developed to explain social movements.

Introducing the Chapter

Ask students to respond to the following scenario: "You are sitting in a movie theater watching a film, and the film breaks. How does the audience respond?" Most likely, the students will say that the audience starts stamping its feet, clapping, or booing. Then ask: "Why does the audience respond in this way, since these actions do nothing to fix the film?" Guide students to the realization that these actions are a spontaneous response to a situation in which there are no clear standards for behavior. Usually what happens in a situation such as the scenario in the movie theater is that one person starts the

action and then everyone else joins in. New norms for behavior thus are initiated, and most people feel obligated to conform to the group's norms. Tell students that this is a form of collective behavior, the relatively spontaneous social behavior that occurs when people try to develop common solutions to unclear situations. Then distinguish between collective behavior and social movements, and discuss the importance of each during periods of rapid social change. Close the discussion by noting that Chapter 16 will examine the types of collectivities and social movements found in modern society and the theories used to explain such behavior.

Chapter 16 Suggested Lesson Plans

Day 1	**Suggested Procedures:** Introducing the Unit; Introducing the Chapter; Section 1 Previewing Key Terms; Introducing the Section **Materials:** PE: pp. 402–416; TM: pp. 108–112
Day 2	**Suggested Procedures:** Section 1 Strategies and Assignments **Materials:** PE: pp. 406–416; TM: pp. 112–113; TRB: Assorted Worksheets
Day 3	**Suggested Procedures:** Section 2 Previewing Key Terms; Introducing the Section; Strategies and Assignments **Materials:** PE: pp. 417–425; TM: pp. 113–115; TRB: Assorted Worksheets
Day 4	**Suggested Procedures:** Closing the Chapter; Assessing the Chapter **Materials:** PE: pp. 426–427; TM: pp. 115–116; TRB: Review Worksheet, Tests, Reteaching Worksheet

SECTION 1 *(pages 406–416)*

COLLECTIVE BEHAVIOR

Section Overview

People in a society generally follow established norms. Thus behavior tends to be patterned and predictable. Sometimes, however, situations arise in which social norms are unclear or absent. The responses that people have to such situations fall under the umbrella of collective behavior. According to sociologist Neil Smelser, there are six preconditions that guide the outcome of collective behavior: structural conduciveness, structural strain, growth and spread of a generalized belief, precipitating factors, mobilization for action, and social control.

Collective behavior takes place within collectivities. Three factors distinguish collectivities from social groups: limited interaction, unclear norms, and limited unity. There are many types of collectivities, the most common of which are crowds, mobs and riots, panics, mass hysteria, fashions and fads, rumors and urban legends, and public opinion.

A number of theories have been developed to explain collective behavior. Most contemporary sociologists favor the emergent-norm theory of collective behavior. According to the emergent-norm theory, new norms emerge in situations in which conventional norms are absent or lacking.

Previewing Key Terms

Section 1 contains the following key terms: **collective behavior, collectivity, crowd, mob, riot, panic, mass hysteria, fashions, fad, rumor, urban legends, public, public opinion, propaganda, contagion theory, emergent-norm theory**. Ask students to create a Word Search puzzle using each of these terms. Then have students exchange papers and complete the puzzles. Students then may place the puzzles in their study notebooks for later review.

Introducing the Section

When class begins, go to the back of the classroom, sit in a chair, and begin to read a book. Ignore the actions and the vocalizations of your students. Do this for about five minutes or until the class becomes truly annoyed. Then explain to the students that they have just encountered a situation in which no clear norms of behavior exist, and ask them to describe how the class responded. Tell the students that most behavior in society tends to be predictable and patterned, and it is this predictability that makes social interaction possible. Yet sometimes situations occur in which social norms are unclear or absent. The responses that people have to such situations falls under the area of study known as collective behavior, the focus of Section 1.

Suggested Teaching Strategies

1. **Clarifying Ideas (I)** After reviewing the six preconditions of collective behavior outlined by Smelser, have students apply the preconditions to the analysis of actual examples of collective behavior. If desired, have interested students research additional examples and report their findings to the class.
2. **Learning from Films (I)** Show the film *The Witches of Salem: The Horror and the Hope* (rental information can be found in the introductory section of this *Teacher's Manual*). Then ask the students to debate whether a mass hysteria such as that portrayed in the film could happen today.
3. **Recognizing Propaganda (I)** Have students give real-life examples of each of the six propaganda techniques described in the section. Then ask: "Why is it crucial in a democracy such as the United States that citizens be alert to the techniques used by propagandists?" Help students to understand the ease with which persuasive orators such as Hitler can sway public opinion to grievous ends.

4. **Seeing Relationships (II)** Organize the class into groups and have each group complete the research assignment outlined in the Applying Sociology feature on textbook pages 414–415. Tally the data in class and discuss the findings.
5. **Working in Groups (II, III)** After discussing the definition of each type of collectivity in class, organize the class into small groups and assign each group one type of collectivity (such as fads). Have each group research current and historical examples of their collectivity and share their examples with the class.

Suggested Enrichment Activities

1. **Reading for Detail (I)** Have students complete the appropriate Developing Research Skills Worksheet, found in the *Teacher's Resource Binder.*
2. **Identifying Ideas (III)** Have interested students collect examples of urban legends from family members, neighbors, and friends. Ask the students to share the urban legends with the class and have the class try to determine the moral lesson contained in each legend.

Suggested Assignments

1. **Organizing Ideas (I)** As homework, have students complete the appropriate Graphic Organizer Worksheet, found in the *Teacher's Resource Binder.*
2. **Drawing Conclusions (I)** Have students read the Interpreting Primary Sources feature on textbook page 427 and answer the accompanying questions. Discuss the answers in class.
3. **★Writing about Sociology: Investigating Oral History (I)** Instruct students to read the Developing Sociological Imagination feature on textbook pages 424–425 and then complete the assignment under Practicing the Skill.
4. **Using Sociological Imagination (I, II)** Have students, either individually or in groups, create a piece of art that illustrates a fad or craze currently in vogue with teenagers. Art may take the form of a song, a poem, a painting, a collage, a dance, and so on. Have students display their pieces of art in the classroom or perform them for the class. Discuss the appeal of fads and why they are short-lived.

Closing the Section

Close the section by having students write an essay describing a personal experience with collective behavior (such as being in a crowd or hearing a rumor). Ask students to analyze the collective behavior from a sociological perspective and then give their personal reactions to the collective behavior. Have volunteers read their essays to the class for class discussion.

Assessing the Section

Have students complete the Section 1 Review.

Answers to Applying Sociology (pages 414–415)

Answers will vary, but students should discern the varying techniques used by advertisers to sway public opinion toward their products.

Answers to Section 1 Review *(page 416)*

Define *collective behavior:* relatively spontaneous social behavior that occurs when people try to develop common solutions to unclear situations; *collectivity:* collection of people who have limited interaction with each other and who do not share clearly defined, conventional norms

1. According to sociologist Neil Smelser, there are six preconditions for collective behavior: structural conduciveness, structural strain, growth and spread of a generalized belief, precipitating factors, mobilization for action, and social control. Structural conduciveness refers to the fact that the surrounding social structure must include elements that will enable a certain type of collective behavior to occur. The second precondition, structural strain, refers to the fact that there must be a social condition that puts a strain on people and encourages them to seek some collective means to relieve the strain. Growth and spread of a generalized belief begins when a belief about the severity of a structural strain begins to spread throughout the society. The fourth precondition, precipitating factors, begins when some kind of triggering mechanism sets off the collective behavior by reinforcing the belief about the severity of the strain. By the fifth stage, mobilization for action, people begin to act in an attempt to remedy the situation. This action increases the strain. Finally, if there are inadequate social controls to prevent or minimize individual actions, full-fledged collective behavior occurs.
2. Collectivities differ from social groups in three ways. First, members of social groups generally interact with each other directly, often for long periods of time. Interaction among members of collectivities, however, is limited and sometimes nonexistent. Second, the norms that guide behavior in social groups are clearly defined and widely understood. In collectivities, however, norms for behavior either are unclear or they are unconventional. Finally, the people who form social groups generally are united by an awareness that they are members of these groups. Members of collectivities, on the other hand, seldom share a sense of group unity.
3. Students' outlines should include information on the types of collectivities found on textbook pages 408–413.
4. Contagion theory, proposed by Gustav Le Bon, holds that the hypnotic power of the crowd encourages people to give up their individuality to the stronger pull of the group. Individuals become anonymous, with no will power or sense of responsibility. The crowd in effect becomes a single organism operating under a collective mind. Conventional social norms lose their meaning, and, as emotion sweeps through the crowd, behavior becomes unrestrained. According to emergent-norm theory, the people in a crowd often are faced with a situation in which the traditional norms of behavior do not apply. Gradually through interaction, however, new norms emerge when one or more leaders initiate new behaviors. These new norms provide a common motivation for group action where none existed before.

SECTION 2 *(pages 417–423)*

SOCIAL MOVEMENTS

Section Overview

Social movements are forms of collective behavior that are intended either to promote or prevent social change. Social movements may develop around any social issue. Four general types of social movements have been identified by sociologists: resistance movements, reform movements, utopian movements, and revolutionary movements. Although social movements differ in their goals, all successful social movements appear to go through the same four stages: agitation, legitimation, bureaucratization, and institutionalization.

Contemporary sociologists look to the social environment for explanations of social movements. Deprivation theory holds that social movements arise when large numbers of people feel economically or socially deprived. Resource-mobilization theorists, however, believe that deprivation alone is insufficient to explain social movements. According to these theorists, social movements will not arise unless people can mobilize the necessary resources.

Previewing Key Terms

Section 2 contains the following key terms: **social movement, resistance movements, reform movements, utopian movements, revolutionary movements, terrorism, deprivation theory, absolute deprivation, relative deprivation, resource mobilization, resource-mobilization theory**. Ask students to write a definition for each of these terms, based on what they think it means. Then have students look up each of these terms in the Glossary and revise their definitions based on what they have learned.

Introducing the Section

Show to the class the film *The Civil Rights Movement* (rental information can be found in the introductory section of this *Teacher's Manual*), which documents the history of the civil rights movement in the United States. After discussing the film with the class, tell students that the purpose of the civil rights movement was to promote social change. Some social movements, however, work toward preventing social change. Ask students if they can think of any examples of social movements, current or historical, that worked toward that end. Next tell students that, while the goals of various social movements may differ, all successful social movements appear to go through a set series of stages. Then assign the reading of Section 2.

Suggested Teaching Strategies

1. **Contrasting Ideas (I)** After reading Section 2, have students define the term *social movement* and then distinguish in writing between the following types of social movements: resistance movements, reform

movements, utopian movements, and revolutionary movements.

2. **Expressing Viewpoints (I)** Have students read the Case Study on textbook page 419 and then discuss the following questions in class: (a) How should the United States respond to acts of terrorism? (b) Does the media give too much attention to terrorists? (c) What can be done to discourage acts of terrorism in the United States?

3. **Working in Groups (II, III)** Organize the class into four small groups and assign each group one of the four types of social movements discussed in the section. Tell the members of each group that they are to imagine themselves the leaders of a fictional social movement of the type assigned. Have the groups choose a focus for their social movement (approved by the teacher) and prepare a strong argument explaining why other people should join their movement. Then have the groups present their arguments to the class for class discussion.

Suggested Enrichment Activities

1. **Exploring Cross-Cultural Perspectives (I)** Have students complete the appropriate Cross-Cultural Perspectives Worksheet, found in the *Teacher's Resource Binder.*

2. **Making Oral Presentations (III)** Have interested students research and prepare oral presentations on specific social movements. The social movements can be either historical or contemporary. After students have made their oral presentations to the class, have the class discuss why the movements either succeeded or failed.

Suggested Assignments

1. **Analyzing Ideas (I)** As homework, have students analyze the two theories of social movements and write an essay identifying which of the two they think best explains the existence of social movements and why. Have volunteers read their essays aloud to the class for class discussion.

2. **Summarizing Information (I)** Have students complete the appropriate Critical Skills Mastery Worksheet, found in the *Teacher's Resource Binder.*

3. **Making a Time Line (III)** Have interested students conduct library research to learn about the accomplishments of a successful social movement, such as the civil rights movement, the American labor union movement, or the women's movement. Instruct students to organize the information in the form of a time line. Have students display their time lines in class and give brief overviews of the movements' goals and successes.

Closing the Section

Close the section by having students complete the appropriate Understanding Sociological Ideas Worksheet, found in the *Teacher's Resource Binder.*

Assessing the Section

Have students complete the Section 2 Review.

Answers to Section 2 Review *(page 423)*

Define *social movement:* long-term conscious effort to promote or prevent social change; ***absolute deprivation:*** situation in which people lack one or more social rewards; ***relative deprivation:*** situation in which people have a lesser portion of social rewards compared to other people or groups; ***resource mobilization:*** organization and effective use of resources

1. The main goal of resistance movements is to return to traditional ways of acting and thinking. The members of resistance groups typically are suspicious of and hostile toward social change. Reform movements generally focus on a single issue and make effective use of political lobbyists, the media, and the courts in seeking reform. The members of utopian movements generally are dissatisfied with society, so they seek to create their own ideal society. The main goal of revolutionary movements is a total and radical change in the existing social structure. Typically, revolutionary movements involve violent or illegal actions and sometimes can result in dramatic and widespread social change.

2. All successful social movements go through four stages. The first stage of a social movement, agitation, occurs with the perception that a problem exists. In this stage, a small group of people attempt to stir up public awareness of the issue, often with the intent of gaining widespread support for a social movement. In the second stage, legitimation, the social movement becomes more respectable as it gains acceptance among the population. The leaders of the movement become accepted as legitimate spokespersons for a reasonable cause. The third stage, bureaucratization, begins as the movement becomes more formally organized. As the movement becomes increasingly bureaucratized, the original goals may be swept aside because more time is needed to handle daily administrative tasks. The final stage, institutionalization, is marked by the establishment of the movement as an accepted part of society. The original excitement generated by the movement is gone and the movement may resist proposals for further social change.

3. Deprivation theory explains the emergence of social movements as the result of feelings of economic or social deprivation on the part of large numbers of people. These feelings of deprivation cause people to feel dissatisfied with the way things are and to organize themselves into a social movement to demand change. Resource-mobilization theory argues that feelings of deprivation alone are not sufficient to trigger social movements. According to this theory, only groups of people who can effectively organize and use resources, such as a body of supporters, money, and access to the media, will be able to bring about change.

Answers to Developing Sociological Imagination *(pages 424–425)*

Answers will vary, but students might suggest that Terkel asked some of the following questions: "What kind of work did your father do?" "What was it like being a coal miner in the early part of this century?" "Why did coal miners want to unionize?" "What happened to your husband when he and the other miners tried to unionize?"

Closing the Chapter

Have students complete the Chapter 16 Review Worksheet, found in the *Teacher's Resource Binder.*

Assessing the Chapter

Have students complete the Chapter 16 Review, found on page 426 of the *Pupil's Edition.*

Give students the Chapter 16 Form A Test and, if desired, the Chapter 16 Reteaching Worksheet and Form B Test, found in the *Teacher's Resource Binder.*

Answers to Chapter 16 Review *(page 426)*

Reviewing Sociological Terms

1. Panic
2. public
3. social movement
4. propaganda
5. Terrorism
6. resource mobilization

Thinking Critically about Sociology

1. Relative deprivation is a situation in which people have a lesser portion of social rewards compared to other people or groups. Absolute deprivation, on the other hand, is a situation in which people lack one or more social rewards.
2. **(a)** The six basic preconditions for collective behavior are structural conduciveness, structural strain, growth and spread of a generalized belief, precipitating factors, mobilization for action, and social control. Structural conduciveness refers to the fact that the surrounding social structure must include elements that will enable a certain type of collective behavior to occur. The second precondition, structural strain, refers to the fact that there must be a social condition that puts a strain on people and encourages them to seek some collective means to relieve the strain. Growth and spread of a generalized belief begins when a belief about the severity of a structural strain begins to spread throughout the society. The fourth precondition, precipitating factors, begins when some kind of triggering mechanism sets off the collective behavior by reinforcing the belief about the severity of the strain. By the fifth stage, mobilization for action, people begin to act in an attempt to remedy the situation. This action increases the strain. Finally, if there are inadequate social controls to prevent or minimize individual actions, full-fledged collective behavior occurs. **(b)** Answers will vary, but students should present scenarios in which are all six preconditions are present.
3. **(a)** The resource-mobilization theory holds that social movements can come about only if the people involved can effectively generate and use fundamental resources such as a group of supporters with time to devote to the effort, financial backing, and access to the media. **(b)** Resource-mobilization theory has been criticized for minimizing the importance of deprivation and dissatisfaction.
4. **(a)** A group is a temporary collection of people who are in close enough proximity to interact. **(b)** Answers will vary. Students' charts should include the information on crowds presented on textbook pages 408–409.
5. **(a)** According to deprivation theory, social movements arise when large numbers of people feel economically or socially deprived of what they think is necessary for their well-being. **(b)** Deprivation theory is similar to Marx's theory of revolution. Marx believed that capitalist economies deprive and frustrate workers by keeping their access to wages and power at minimal levels. According to Marx, once workers realize that employers are mistreating them, the workers will band together and overthrow the system.
6. Answers will vary, but students should use the four stages of social movements identified in the chapter to trace the progress of the social movements they have chosen.
7. Collective behavior is the relatively spontaneous social behavior that occurs when people try to develop common solutions to unclear situations. Collective behavior is a difficult topic to study. One reason for the difficulty is the fact that the range of material covered under the umbrella of collective behavior is quite large. Collective behavior also is difficult to study because it is relatively short-lived, spontaneous, and emotional. This sometimes makes it difficult to understand how the behavior arises and to measure the reactions of people to the situations that spark the behavior. Adding to the problem is the fact that collective behavior usually involves large numbers of people who do not know each other. Because episodes of collective behavior are not enduring aspects of society, it is difficult to subject them to systematic, scientific study.
8. A collectivity is a collection of people who have limited interaction with each other and who do not share clearly defined, conventional norms. The three major characteristics of a collectivity are limited or nonexistent interaction among members, unclear or unconventional norms, and a limited sense of unity among members.
9. Answers will vary, but students should locate two occurrences for each of the four phenomena listed.

Exercising Sociological Skills

1. Answers will vary, but students should follow the steps outlined in the feature on textbook pages 414–415.
2. There are two major reasons why terrorists use violence rather than peaceful means to achieve their goals. First, terrorists are fanatics who believe that nothing, including human life, is more important than their cause. They therefore justify any act that will further their goals. Second, terrorists are people who lack the patience and power to bring about change through peaceful means. They therefore seek to equalize the balance of power through the spread of fear and destruction.

3. Answers will vary, but students should follow the steps outlined in the feature on textbook pages 424–425 when analyzing their chosen oral histories.

Extending Sociological Imagination

1. Answers will vary.
2. Answers will vary.

Answers to Interpreting Primary Sources *(page 427)*

1. Listeners believed that the fictional Mars invasion was real because they trusted radio and did not pay close attention to the radio program's opening signature. Listeners also were conditioned by earlier news reports of widespread political turmoil.

2. The broadcast caused a mass hysteria. People panicked, believing their chances of escape from the Martians were nonexistent. The fear fueled miscommunication about the event and people began to ignore conventional norms. The fear generated by the panic, and its subsequent results, underscore how the public can react in situations when conventional norms no longer apply. Such reactions make the public particularly vulnerable to fanatics and terrorists.

CHAPTER 17 *(pages 428–457)*

POPULATION AND URBANIZATION

SECTION 1
POPULATION CHANGE

SECTION 2
URBAN LIFE

Chapter Overview

Until relatively recently in human history, the world was populated by small bands of people who lived and roamed in primary groups. Today, there are more than 5 billion people living in the world, and even more growth in expected in the near future. The growth of the population in recent years has had a tremendous impact on many aspects of our changing social world.

Nowhere is the impact of population growth felt more clearly than in the cities. The movement of large numbers of people from the countryside to the cities is a relatively recent phenomenon. The effect on social life, however, has been tremendous. It is estimated that by the year 2000, nearly half of the world's population will be concentrated in urban areas.

These two major forces—population growth and urbanization—have changed the face of the world. Thus it is not surprising that sociologists have devoted considerable time to studying the ways in which population

and urbanization have affected the social world and the nature of human interaction. The effects of population growth and urbanization are the focus of Chapter 17.

Chapter Objectives

At the conclusion of the chapter, students will be able to

1. Identify the factors that affect the size and structure of populations, and explain how sociologists measure these factors.
2. Compare the theories that have been developed to explain population change.
3. Describe the programs that have been instituted to control population growth.
4. Discuss the evolution of cities, and explain why urbanization is such a recent phenomenon.
5. Compare the theories that have been proposed to explain the structure of cities.
6. Discuss the theories that have been put forth to explain city life.

Introducing the Chapter

The population of the world is increasing. Many social scientists fear that the consequences could be catastrophic, not only for the less developed nations that are experiencing rapid population growth, but also for the more developed nations of the world. Prior to assigning the reading of Chapter 17, ask each student to make a list of the possible social and environmental consequences of an ever-increasing world population. Use the lists as the basis of a class discussion on the social significance of population growth.

Chapter 17 Suggested Lesson Plans

Day 1	**Suggested Procedures:** Introducing the Chapter; Section 1 Previewing Key Terms; Introducing the Section **Materials:** PE: pp. 428–444; TM: pp. 116–117
Day 2	**Suggested Procedures:** Section 1 Strategies and Assignments **Materials:** PE: pp. 430–444; TM: pp. 117–118; TRB: Transparencies 14–16, Assorted Worksheets
Day 3	**Suggested Procedures:** Section 2 Previewing Key Terms; Introducing the Section; Strategies and Assignments **Materials:** PE: pp. 445–455; TM: pp. 119–120; TRB: Transparency 17, Assorted Worksheets
Day 4	**Suggested Procedures:** Closing the Chapter; Assessing the Chapter **Materials:** PE: pp. 456–457; TM: pp. 120–122; TRB: Review Worksheet, Tests, Reteaching Worksheet

SECTION 1 *(pages 430–444)*

POPULATION CHANGE

Section Overview

Changes in population size result from three demographic processes: the birth rate, the death rate, and the migration rate. In addition to population size, demographers are interested in the composition, or structure, of a population.

Several theories have been proposed to explain population growth. Thomas Malthus, for example, believed that the inability of people to control the birth rate would result in worldwide starvation because the food supply would not be able to keep up with population growth. Demographic transition theory, on the other hand, argues that population growth goes through a series of stages, each tied to a society's level of technology.

Nations concerned about rapid population growth have adopted strategies to control this growth. Some nations have encouraged the use of family planning. Other nations have sought to control population size through economic improvements.

Previewing Key Terms

Section 1 contains the following key terms: **population, demography, birth rate, fertility, fecundity, mortality, death rate, infant mortality rate, more developed nations, less developed nations, life expectancy, life span, migration, migration rate, growth rate, doubling time, population pyramid, Malthusian theory, demographic transition theory, zero population growth, family planning, antinatalism**. Have students choose 15 of the key terms and prepare 15 riddles, using the chosen terms as answers. For example: "I am the birth rate minus the death rate. What am I?" *(growth rate)* Tell students to write their riddles on one side of the paper and the answers on the other side. Completed sets of riddles can be exchanged among students and answered. Then have students put their papers in their study notebooks for later review.

Introducing the Section

Ask students to turn to the Section 1 Review on textbook page 444. Then write the following sentence on the chalkboard: "Based on the review questions, I expect to learn at least 10 things from this section:"

1. _____
2. _____
3. _____
etc.

Ask students to copy the sentence and to fill in the blanks. When the activity has been completed, ask volunteers to discuss their answers with the class. Instruct students to keep their list of items in their study notebooks for later use.

Suggested Teaching Strategies

1. **Learning from Charts (I)** Many of the sociological concepts in Section 1 can best be illustrated through the use of charts and graphs. Complement your discussion of the section material by placing, at the appropriate times, Transparencies 14–16 on an overhead projector and asking the questions contained in the accompanying teacher's notes. Transparencies and accompanying teacher's notes are found in the *Teacher's Resource Binder*.
2. **Contrasting Ideas (I)** Have students write a short essay contrasting Malthusian theory with demographic transition theory.
3. **Learning from Films (I)** Show to the class the film *The People Bomb* (rental information can be found in the introductory section of this *Teacher's Manual*), which focuses on population growth in Africa, Asia, and Latin America. Following the film, discuss with the class how population growth in these areas is affecting the environment, global resources, and the social structure.
4. **Debating Ideas (II, III)** Organize interested students into two groups and have the groups debate the following statement: "Antinatalism policies violate basic human rights."

Suggested Enrichment Activities

1. **Locating Information (I)** Have students complete the appropriate Critical Skills Mastery Worksheet, found in the *Teacher's Resource Binder*.
2. **Constructing Population Pyramids (III)** Have interested students prepare population pyramids for several nations from each of the geographic regions listed in the chart on textbook page 435. Compare the pyramids in class and discuss the social significance of the variations.

Suggested Assignments

1. **Organizing Ideas (I)** As homework, have students complete the appropriate Graphic Organizer Worksheet, found in the *Teacher's Resource Binder*.
2. **Using Sociological Imagination (I)** Have students write an imaginative short story about a society in which overpopulation has reached a critical level. Ask volunteers to read their stories aloud to the class for class discussion.
3. **Linking the Past to the Present (II, III)** Have interested students use library sources to locate historical quotations that focus on the push factors and pull factors encouraging immigrants to come to the United States. Conduct a class discussion in which students evaluate how valid these quotations are for immigrants coming to the United States today.

Closing the Section

Close the section by having students retrieve the lists of items they prepared during the Introducing the Section activity. Ask volunteers to read items from their lists aloud and have the class discuss how their expectations for learning the section material have been fulfilled. Offer any necessary clarifications at this time.

Assessing the Section

Have students complete the Section 1 Review.

Answers to Applying Sociology (pages 440–441)

1. **(a)** In 1980, Austria, Germany, and Sweden had more than 15 percent of their populations in the age 65 and over group. **(b)** In 1980, Australia, Canada, Iceland, Japan, New Zealand, and Turkey had less than 10 percent of their populations in the age 65 and over group.
2. **(a)** The nations of France, Germany, Greece, Italy, Japan, Luxembourg, Sweden, and Switzerland are projected to have more than 15 percent of their populations in the age 65 and over category by the year 2000. **(b)** Only Turkey is expected to have less than 10 percent of its population in the age 65 and older group by the year 2000.
3. **(a)** All of the nations in the table except Australia, Ireland, Turkey, the United Kingdom, and the United States are projected to have more than 20 percent of their populations in the age 65 and over group by the year 2050. **(b)** Turkey is the only nation expected to have less than 15 percent of its population in the age 65 and over group by the year 2050.
4. **(a)** Australia, 9.8 percent; Austria, 6.2 percent; Belgium, 6.4 percent; Canada, 11.8 percent; Denmark, 8.8 percent; Finland, 10.7 percent; France, 8.3 percent; Germany, 9.0 percent; Greece, 8.0 percent; Iceland, 11.2 percent; Ireland, 8.2 percent; Italy, 9.1 percent; Japan, 13.2 percent; Luxembourg, 6.8 percent; Netherlands, 11.1 percent; New Zealand, 11.6 percent; Norway, 7.1 percent; Portugal, 10.4 percent; Spain, 12.0 percent; Sweden, 5.1 percent; Switzerland, 12.5 percent; Turkey, 6.8 percent; United Kingdom, 3.8 percent; United States, 8.0 percent. **(b)** Canada, Finland, Iceland, Japan, Netherlands, New Zealand, Portugal, Spain, and Switzerland are projected to have greater than a 10 percent increase in their aged populations between the years 1980 and 2050.
5. The proportion of the work force aged 15–44 will increase until 2020, then it will decrease slightly through 2050. The proportion of the work force aged 45 and over will decrease until 2020, then it will increase slightly.
6. **(a)** Social spending will increase in the areas of health and pensions between 1980 and 2040. **(b)** The greatest increase in social spending will be in pensions.
7. As populations age, they must spend more money on health and retirement benefits.

Answers to Section 1 Review (page 444)

Define *demography:* scientific study of human populations; ***fecundity;*** biological potential for reproduction; ***infant mortality rate:*** annual number of deaths among infants under one year of age per 1,000 live births in a population; ***more developed nations;*** nations that have high levels of per capita income, industrialization, and modernization; ***less developed nations;*** nations that have low levels of per capita income, industrialization, and modernization; ***zero population growth:*** point at which nearly equal birth rates and death rates produce a growth rate of zero

1. **(a)** Three factors affect the growth or decline of a population: the birth rate, the death rate, and the migration rate. The birth rate is the annual number of live births per 1,000 members of a population. The death rate is the annual number of deaths per 1,000 members of a population. The migration rate is the annual difference between in-migration and out-migration. **(b)** The growth rate of a population is related to its doubling time, the number of years necessary for a population to double in size, given its current rate of growth. For example, a growth rate of 1 percent will cause a population to double in size in about 70 years. A growth rate of 3.2 percent will cause a population to double in size in about 22 years.
2. Because population pyramids show the age and sex composition of a population, they indicate the population's potential for growth. For example, a population with a large proportion of children has a high potential for growth because these children will grow up to have children themselves. A population with a small proportion of children has a limited potential for growth because there are not as many people who later will have children.
3. Malthus predicted that population growth eventually would outpace the earth's ability to produce food because population progresses geometrically, while the food supply increases only arithmetically. From this, Malthus predicted that worldwide starvation would result. Demographic transition theory, on the other hand, holds that population patterns are tied to a society's level of technological development. According to this theory, a society's population moves through three stages. In Stage 1, typical of preindustrial societies, both the birth rate and the death rate are high, leading to slow population growth. As societies enter the industrial phase, Stage 2, improved medical techniques, sanitation, and increased food production work to reduce the death rate. The birth rate, however, remains high. These factors lead to rapid population growth. Stage 3 societies have a fully developed industrial economy. The birth rate falls and the death rate remains low. The low birth rate and the low death rate produce fairly stable populations in which population growth occurs very slowly.
4. **(a)** There are two primary strategies used to control population growth. The first strategy is to lower the birth rate through family planning programs or antinatalism programs. Family planning allows the couple to decide how many children to have. Antinatalism, on the other hand, involves official policies designed to discourage births. A second strategy involves increasing living standards, especially income and education, to decrease the birth rate. **(b)** Family planning strategies are problematic because when couples are allowed to decide how many children to have, they often have more than the population can bear. Antinatalism policies tend to be more forceful than family planning programs but generally are successful. Economic programs designed to increase the standard of living in nations have only done so for a small proportion of the population. As a result, the majority of the population remains in poverty and the birth rates remain high.

SECTION 2 *(pages 445–453)*

URBAN LIFE

Section Overview

Urbanization is a relatively recent phenomenon and appears to be tied to two important developments: the Agricultural Revolution and the Industrial Revolution. The evolution of cities advanced very rapidly with the development of industrialization.

Urban ecology examines the relationship between people and the urban environment. Three major models of urban structure have been proposed: the concentric zone model, the sector model, and the multiple-nuclei model.

The nature of urban life has long interested sociologists. Urban anomie theory views the city as an unfriendly, anonymous place. Compositional theory argues that people are protected from the anonymous nature of city life by their primary group associations. Subcultural theory, on the other hand, views the city as a place that encourages rather than discourages the development of primary group relationships.

Previewing Key Terms

Section 2 contains the following key terms: **urbanization, city, overurbanization, urban ecology, suburb, metropolitan statistical area (MSA), megalopolis, urban renewal, regentrification, concentric zone model, sector model, multiple-nuclei model, urban anomie theory, compositional theory, subcultural theory**. Have students look up each term in the Glossary, and then use eight of the terms to write a paragraph about urban life. Although the eight terms should be used in the paragraph, students should indicate these terms only with numbered blanks. The correct answer for each number may be put on the back of the paper. When students have finished their paragraphs, have them exchange papers and fill in the blanks with the correct terms.

Introducing the Section

Show to the class the film *The Rise of the American City* (rental information can be found in the introductory section of this *Teacher's Manual*). This film focuses on how the rise of cities has transformed the American nation and how cities now are dealing with a host of social problems. After discussing the film, tell students that urbanization is a relatively recent phenomenon in world history, but that now urbanization is fast becoming commonplace the world over. Then assign the reading of Section 2.

Suggested Teaching Strategies

1. **Outlining Information (I)** After discussing the evolution of the city, have students write an outline of this information to place in their study notebooks.
2. **Learning from Graphs (I)** Place Transparency 17, which focuses on models of city structure, on an overhead projector and ask the questions contained in the accompanying teacher's notes. Transparencies and accompanying teacher's notes are found in the *Teacher's Resource Binder*.
3. **Practicing Interviewing Skills (I)** Invite a member of a historical society in your community to speak to the class about how your community has changed over the past 50 years. Have students compile a list of questions beforehand to ask the speaker. Following the presentation, discuss the consequences of these changes for your community.
4. **Solving Problems (I, II)** Organize the class into small groups and have the members of each group discuss the social problems that might be common to your community. Ask each group to compile a list of five things that could be done to combat one of these social problems. Have representatives from each group present the lists to the class and have the class discuss the feasibility of the suggestions.
5. **Conducting a Debate (II, III)** Have students read the Case Study on textbook page 448. Then organize the class into three groups: one group to argue in favor of regentrification, one group to argue against regentrification, and a larger group to act as an audience. Have the debate teams conduct additional research on the issues surrounding regentrification before engaging in the debate.

Suggested Enrichment Activities

1. **Exploring Cross-Cultural Perspectives (I)** Have students complete the appropriate Cross-Cultural Perspectives Worksheet, found in the *Teacher's Resource Binder*.
2. **Dramatizing Sociology (II, III)** Have groups of interested students write and perform short skits about urban life from the perspective of one of the three theories of city life discussed in the section. For example, students may choose to write a skit from the urban anomie perspective that focuses on the impersonal nature of city life. Have the class critique the skits for sociological accuracy.

Suggested Assignments

1. **Conducting a Poll (I)** As homework, have students ask five people (friends, neighbors, family members, other students) the following questions: "What is the best thing about city life?" "What is the worst thing about city life?" Instruct students to take notes on the reasons why the interviewees have answered a certain way. Then, in class, tally the responses and use the results as the basis of a class discussion on theories of city life.
2. **Summarizing Information (I)** Have students complete the appropriate Developing Research Skills Worksheet, found in the *Teacher's Resource Binder*.
3. **★Interpreting the Visual Record: Analyzing Sociological-Data Maps (I)** Instruct students to read the Developing Sociological Imagination feature on textbook pages 454–455 and then complete the assignment under Practicing the Skill.
4. **Exploring Multicultural Perspectives (III)** Have interested students conduct library research to locate

poems about life in the city written by members of various American cultural groups. Have students read the poems aloud to the class and have the class discuss the social and cultural factors that might account for the varied perspectives on city life contained in the poems.

Closing the Section

Close the section by having students complete the appropriate Understanding Sociological Ideas Worksheet, found in the *Teacher's Resource Binder*.

Assessing the Section

Have students complete the Section 2 Review.

Answers to Section 2 Review *(page 453)*

Define urbanization: concentration of the population in cities; **overurbanization:** situation in which more people live in the city than the city can support in terms of jobs and facilities

1. The first cities appeared about 6,000 years ago, but even as late as 1850, only about 2 percent of the world's population lived in cities. The rise of cities was tied to the Agricultural Revolution and the Industrial Revolution. The Agricultural Revolution increased the efficiency of food production and created a surplus of food for the first time. This freed workers from farming and allowed them to pursue other types of work. Some went to central areas where they could most easily engage in specialized types of work, encouraging the development of cities. The Industrial Revolution replaced traditional human and animal sources of power with new sources such as coal, water, and steam. The Industrial Revolution also replaced hand tools with machines and led to the development and growth of factories. Cities also became able to support increasing numbers of people. Preindustrial cities were small. Living conditions were characterized by a lack of sanitation, ineffective medical technologies, crowding, and lack of sewage facilities. Epidemics were common. Life was organized around kinship and extended families. Governments were organized as monarchies or oligarchies. Citizens were segregated into classes or castes, with the poor living on the city's outskirts and the rich living in the center. Compared to preindustrial cities, industrial cities were larger and had a greater diversity of people. Commerce became the focal point of cities. The rise of industrial cities brought social problems such as crime, overcrowding, and pollution, but they also brought high literacy rates, economic opportunities, and health care.
2. The three models of urban ecology are the concentric zone model, the sector model, and the multiple-nuclei model. Burgess developed the concentric zone model to describe the structure of urban areas. In this model, the city spreads outward from the center, resulting in a series of circles within circles. Each of these circles, or zones, differs in terms of the way in which the land is used. The sector model, developed by Hoyt, also holds that cities grow outward from the

center. However, according to this model, growth occurs in wedges from the center outward. Transportation patterns affect land use. Harris and Ullman developed the multiple-nuclei model, which proposes that cities have a number of specialized centers that influence the land use around them. This model acknowledges the influence of automobiles and highways on the development of cities.
3. The three theories of urban life are urban anomie theory, developed by Louis Wirth, compositional theory, developed by Herbert J. Gans, and subcultural theory, developed by Claude Fischer. According to urban anomie theory, life in cities is marked by interactions that involve only impersonal secondary groups. The formation of close primary group relations is discouraged by the size, density, and diversity of urban life. The lack of primary group relations creates anomie, or normlessness, which leads to mental illness, crime, and delinquency. Compositional theory focuses on the way the city's makeup in terms of age, race, ethnicity, income, and occupation influences the life of its residents. The wide diversity of people leads to a variety of life-styles. Groups formed around these characteristics provide city dwellers with a sense of solidarity and community. Subcultural theory also emphasizes the formation of primary group relationships. People in cities have a much greater chance of finding others who have similar interests than do people in rural areas.

Answers to Developing Sociological Imagination *(pages 454–455)*

1. **(a)** The title of the map is "Age of Housing." **(b)** The map shows the geographic distribution of houses by age in an urban area.
2. The colors on the map indicate commercial districts, industrial areas, parks, and rivers and lakes.
3. The age ranges of the houses are indicated by different patterns.
4. **(a)** The oldest and next-to-the-oldest houses are in the center of the urban area, around the central lake, and in the north central area. **(b)** The newest and next-to-the-newest houses are in the outer parts of the urban areas.
5. The town grew westward first and then eastward.
6. The newer houses in the southwest and northwest and in the east are owned by upper-class and middle-class families. The new houses in the central western area are in middle-class neighborhoods.

Closing the Chapter

Have students complete the Chapter 17 Review Worksheet, found in the *Teacher's Resource Binder*.

Assessing the Chapter

Have students complete the Chapter 17 Review, found on page 456 of the *Pupil's Edition*.

Give students the Chapter 17 Form A Test and, if desired, the Chapter 17 Reteaching Worksheet and Form B Test, found in the *Teacher's Resource Binder*.

Answers to Chapter 17 Review *(page 456)*

Reviewing Sociological Terms

1. Mortality
2. population
3. family planning
4. Overurbanization
5. urban ecology
6. migration
7. Zero population growth

Thinking Critically about Sociology

1. Urban anomie theory holds that life in cities is marked by interactions that involve only impersonal secondary groups. The formation of close primary group relations is discouraged by the size, density, and diversity of urban life. The lack of primary group relationships in cities creates anomie, or normlessness, which can lead to problems such as mental illness, crime, and delinquency. The compositional theory of city life focuses on the way that the city's makeup in terms of age, race, ethnicity, income, and occupation influences the life of the residents. The wide diversity of people leads to a variety of lifestyles. Groups that form around these social characteristics provide city residents with a sense of solidarity and community. The subcultural theory of city life also emphasizes the formation of primary group relationships. According to subcultural theory, people who live in cities have a much greater chance of finding other people who have similar interests than do people who live in rural areas.

2. **(a)** The birth rate is the annual number of births per 1,000 members of a population. The death rate is the annual number of deaths per 1,000 members of a population. Demographers often refer to the birth rate as a crude rate because it is based on the total population, which includes males, children, and women who are past the age of childbearing. The crude birth rate also does not take into account the fact that, within a single society, various ethnic, racial, and religious groups may have different birth rates. The death rate is considered a crude rate because it does not take into account the varying death rates found among subgroups in the population. The death rate also is crude because it is misleading to compare the rates of different nations. **(b)** The growth rate of a population is equal to the birth rate minus the death rate.

3. **(a)** Preindustrial cities were small. Living conditions were shaped by a lack of sanitation, ineffective medical technologies, and crowding. Epidemics were common. Life in these cities was organized around kinship and extended families. Governments were organized as monarchies or oligarchies. Citizens were segregated into castes or classes, with the poor living on the outskirts of the city and the rich living in the center of the city. **(b)** Compared to preindustrial cities, industrial cities were larger and had a greater diversity of people. Commerce became the focal point of cities. The rise of industrial cities brought social problems such as crime, overcrowding, and pollution, but they also brought high literacy rates, economic opportunities, and improved health care.

(c) Urbanization in less developed nations has been less orderly and more rapid than it was in the more developed nations. As a result, cities in some less developed nations are experiencing overurbanization. In such cities, there are inadequate housing, food, sewage disposal, and medical services. The crowded and unsanitary living conditions common to overurbanized cities cause high rates of illness and death.

4. **(a)** Migration is the movement of people from one specified area to another. The migration rate is the annual difference between in-migration and out-migration. **(b)** Migration occurs as a result of push factors and pull factors. A push factor is something that encourages people to move out of a certain area, such as religious or political persecution. A pull factor is something that encourages people to move into a certain area, such as religious freedom or job opportunities.

5. **(a)** Malthus predicted that population growth eventually would outpace the earth's ability to produce food because population progresses geometrically, while the food supply increases only arithmetically. From this, Malthus predicted that worldwide starvation would result. Demographic transition theory, on the other hand, holds that population patterns are tied to a society's level of technological development. According to this theory, a society's population moves through three stages. In Stage 1, typical of preindustrial societies, both the birth rate and the death rate are high, leading to slow population growth. As societies enter the industrial phase, Stage 2, improved medical techniques, sanitation, and increased food production work to reduce the death rate. The birth rate, however, remains high. These factors lead to rapid population growth. Stage 3 societies have a fully developed industrial economy. The birth rate falls and the death rate remains low. The low birth rate and the low death rate produce fairly stable populations in which population growth occurs very slowly. **(b)** Malthus failed to anticipate that advances in agricultural technology would allow farmers to produce vastly increased yields on their available land. He also foresaw neither the development of effective birth control methods nor their widespread acceptance and use. Critics of demographic transition theory believe it is unlikely that all nations will follow the stages of technological development found in Europe and North America over the past few decades.

6. According to the population pyramid on textbook page 436, the age group 35–39 is the youngest group in which the percentage of women is higher than the percentage of men.

7. The three models of urban ecology are the concentric zone model, the sector model, and the multiple-nuclei model. Burgess developed the concentric zone model to describe the structure of urban areas. In this model, the city spreads outward from the center, resulting in a series of circles within circles. Each of these circles, or zones, differs in terms of the way in which the land is used. The sector model, developed by Hoyt, also holds that cities grow outward from the center. However, according to this model, growth occurs in wedges from the center outward.

Transportation patterns affect the way the land is used. Harris and Ullman developed the multiple-nuclei model, which proposes that cities have a number of specialized centers that influence the land use around them. This model acknowledges the influence of automobiles and highways on the development of cities.

8. Answers will vary, but students should provide two examples of nations that are using family planning strategies, two that are using antinatalism strategies, and two that are using economic improvement strategies.

Exercising Sociological Skills

1. According to the table on textbook page 440, Turkey will have the smallest percentage of elderly in the year 2000.
2. Regentrification is the upgrading of specific neighborhoods in an attempt to encourage the middle and upper classes to relocate to the cities. Critics of regentrification charge that this process further reduces the availability of housing for the poor.
3. Answers will vary, but students should analyze the map using the skills presented in the Developing Sociological Imagination feature on textbook pages 454–455.

Extending Sociological Imagination

1. Answers will vary.
2. Answers will vary.

Answers to Interpreting Primary Sources *(page 457)*

1. In Cairo, children often dig through ox dung looking for kernels of undigested corn. Young, homeless thieves in Port Moresby often do not know their last names or the names of the villages where they were born. In Mexico City, air pollution has reached critical levels. Tokyo is being overwhelmed by the amount of garbage produced by its citizens.
2. It is important that we solve the problems of the megacities because the future of the world is entwined with the fate of the world's largest cities.

CHAPTER 18 *(pages 458–481)*

SOCIAL CHANGE AND MODERNIZATION

SECTION 1
EXPLAINING SOCIAL CHANGE

SECTION 2
MODERNIZATION

Chapter Overview

Sociology grew out of the social turmoil of the seventeenth and eighteenth centuries. Thus it is not surprising that sociologists have devoted considerable attention to the study of social change. Sociologists define social change as alterations in various aspects of a society over time. Chapter 18 first examines the theories that sociologists have developed to explain how and why societies change, and then examines the causes and consequences of modernization for social life and for the natural environment.

Chapter Objectives

At the conclusion of the chapter, students will be able to

1. Identify and describe the various theories that have been developed to explain the process of social change.
2. Explain how modernization theory and world-system theory differ in their views on modernization in less developed nations.
3. Discuss some of the positive and negative consequences of modernization for social life and for the natural environment.

Introducing the Chapter

Review with students the discussion of social change found in Section 3 of Chapter 3. Then show one of the following films: *The International Monetary Fund at Work*—which explores how the International Monetary Fund helps underdeveloped countries around the world— or *Women of Kerala*—which examines how the women of Kerala in India have been raising the standard of living in their area. Following the film, ask students to discuss which of the sources of social change described in Chapter 3 are evident in the society or societies depicted in the film. Close the discussion by noting that Chapter 18 will examine the causes and consequences of social change and modernization.

Chapter 18 Suggested Lesson Plans

Day 1	**Suggested Procedures:** Introducing the Chapter; Section 1 Previewing Key Terms; Introducing the Section **Materials:** PE: pp. 458–465; TM: pp. 122–123
Day 2	**Suggested Procedures:** Section 1 Strategies and Assignments **Materials:** PE: pp. 460–465; TM: pp. 123–124; TRB: Assorted Worksheets
Day 3	**Suggested Procedures:** Section 2 Previewing Key Terms; Introducing the Section; Strategies and Assignments **Materials:** PE: pp. 466–479; TM: pp. 124–126; TRB: Transparency 18, Assorted Worksheets

Day 4	**Suggested Procedures:** Closing the Chapter; Assessing the Chapter **Materials:** PE: pp. 480–481; TM: pp. 126–127; TRB: Review Worksheet, Tests, Reteaching Worksheet
Day 5	**Suggested Procedures:** Closing the Unit; Assessing the Unit **Materials:** PE: pp. 482–483; TM: pp. 127–129; TRB: Review Worksheet, Tests, Reteaching Worksheet

SECTION 1 *(pages 460–465)*

EXPLAINING SOCIAL CHANGE

Section Overview

Sociologists define social change as alterations in various aspects of society over time. Sociological theories of social change can be grouped into four broad categories: cyclical theory, evolutionary theory, equilibrium theory, and conflict theory.

Cyclical theories of social change view change from a historical perspective. Societies are seen as moving back and forth between stages of development. Evolutionary theories, on the other hand, view change as a process that moves in one direction. Although early evolutionary theories have been discredited, modern evolutionary theories enjoy continued support.

According to equilibrium theory, change results from a society's attempts to maintain stability. When stability is disrupted by change in one part of the system, all parts of the system must change slightly to restore equilibrium. Conflict theory, on the other hand, sees change as resulting from conflicts between social groups with opposing interests. Conflict theory is rooted in the class-based theories of Karl Marx.

Previewing Key Terms

Section 1 contains the following key terms: **cyclical theory of social change, ideational culture, sensate culture, idealistic culture, principle of immanent change, evolutionary theory of social change, equilibrium theory of social change, conflict theory of social change**. Have students prepare a matching test using these terms and their definitions, found in the Glossary. Answers should appear on the back of the paper. Then have students exchange papers and complete the tests. Students then may place the papers in their study notebooks for later review.

Introducing the Section

Tell students that they are going to practice their outlining skills in this section. First, ask a volunteer to copy the headings and subheadings in Section 1 on the chalkboard. Then have the class provide the important details that should appear under each item in the outline. Have students copy the final outline into their notebooks for later review.

Suggested Teaching Strategies

1. **Comparing Ideas (I)** After discussing the characteristics of the four categories of theories concerning social change, have students compare the theories in terms of source of change and direction of change. Discuss the comparisons in class.
2. **Clarifying Ideas (I)** Have students define in writing each of the following concepts: ideational culture, sensate culture, idealistic culture, and principle of immanent change. Then have groups of interested students find historical and current examples of each of the three types of culture and share their examples with the class.
3. **Analyzing Ideas (I)** Have students examine the photographs on textbook page 465 and read the accompanying caption. Then ask students to consider the following question: "Why does violence sometimes accompany social change?" Have students try to come up with additional contemporary examples of nations experiencing violent social change.
4. **Making Oral Presentations (III)** Have interested students research and prepare oral presentations on the social changes now taking place in Eastern Europe and the former Soviet Union. Then have the class discuss how the various theoretical perspectives would explain these changes.

Suggested Enrichment Activities

1. **Making Generalizations (I)** Have students complete the appropriate Developing Research Skills Worksheet, found in the *Teacher's Resource Binder*.
2. **Researching Biographies (III)** Have interested students research the life and works of the theorists mentioned in Section 1. Ask students to share their findings with the class.

Suggested Assignments

1. **Organizing Ideas (I)** As homework, have students complete the appropriate Graphic Organizer Worksheet, found in the *Teacher's Resource Binder*.
2. **★Writing about Sociology: Composing a Comparative Essay (I)** Instruct students to read the Developing Sociological Imagination feature on textbook pages 478–479 and then complete the assignment under Practicing the Skill.

Closing the Section

Close the section by having students write position papers stating which of the four broad theoretical perspectives on social change they believe offers the best explanation of social change. Caution students to provide sound reasons for their positions. Have volunteers read their papers to the class for class discussion.

Assessing the Section

Have students complete the Section 1 Review.

Identify *Oswald Spengler:* German historian who proposed a cyclical theory of social change. According to Spengler, societies do not continuously progress toward higher levels of complexity or achievement. Rather, each society develops to a certain level and then declines to the point of death; *Pitirim Sorokin:* Russian American sociologist who developed a cyclical theory of social change. According to Sorokin, all societies fluctuate between two extreme forms of culture. External factors—such as war or contact with other societies—can hasten a shift from one form of culture to another; *Gerhard Lenski:* sociologist who proposed an evolutionary theory of social change. According to Lenski, social evolution takes place because of changes in a society's economic base and its level of technology; *Talcott Parsons:* functionalist sociologist who developed the equilibrium theory of social change. According to Parsons, change in one part of the social system produces social change because the other parts of the system adjust to the degree necessary to bring the system back into balance. Order is restored, but the new system is slightly different from the old system; *Ralf Dahrendorf:* theorist who proposed a conflict theory of social change. According to Dahrendorf, various kinds of conflict between different groups in the population can lead to social change

1. **(a)** The cyclical theory of social change views change from a historical perspective. Societies are seen as rising and then falling or as continuously moving back and forth between stages of development. **(b)** According to Spengler's view of social change, societies do not continuously progress toward higher levels of complexity or achievement. Rather, each society develops to a certain level and then declines to the point of death. Sorokin, on the other hand, viewed social change as the fluctuation of societies between two extreme forms of culture—ideational culture and sensate culture. In an ideational culture, truth and knowledge are sought through faith and religion. In a sensate culture, on the other hand, knowledge is sought through science. Sorokin also identified the type of culture present during the shift from one extreme to the other as the idealistic culture, a culture that contains both ideational and sensate characteristics. Sorokin believed that the tendency toward change is natural and present at the birth of a society.

2. Early evolutionary theories held that all societies progress through the same distinct stages of social development. According to this view, each stage of development was believed to bring with it improved social conditions and increased societal complexity. Modern evolutionary theories, on the other hand, do not claim that all societies pass through a single set of distinct stages on the way toward an ideal society. Rather, modern evolutionary theories hold that societies only have a tendency to become more complex over time. They also do not assume that change always produces progress or that progress means the same thing in all societies. Another difference between early and modern evolutionary theory is that modern theories attempt to explain why societies change, whereas early theories did not.

3. **(a)** The equilibrium theory of social change holds that change in one part of the social system produces change in all other parts of the system. This occurs because social systems are like living organisms, which attempt to maintain stability. According to this view, change in one part of the social system produces social change because the other parts of the system adjust to the degree necessary to bring the system back into balance. Order is restored, but the new system is slightly different from the old system. **(b)** According to Parsons, evolution takes place through a two-step process of differentiation and integration. As societies become more complex, their social institutions become more numerous and more distinct. The new institutions must work effectively with other parts of the society if the system is to be stable. New norms and values are created to resolve the conflict between old and new elements of the society. Thus, equilibrium is maintained even when societies are undergoing periods of change.

4. Karl Marx believed that class conflict is the central force for social change. Ralf Dahrendorf, on the other hand, believes that various kinds of conflict between different groups in the population can lead to social change. In addition, Marx believed that violence is a necessary part of social change. Dahrendorf, on the other hand, believes that various interest groups in society may bring about social change through compromise and adaptation.

SECTION 2 *(pages 466–477)*

MODERNIZATION

Section Overview

Many sociologists who are interested in social change focus on the process of modernization in less developed nations. Modernization is the process by which a society's institutions become increasingly complex as the society moves toward industrialization. The two major theories used to explain this process are modernization theory and world-system theory.

Modernization theory holds that the more developed nations of the world were the first to modernize because they were the first to industrialize. Once the less developed nations of the world begin to industrialize, they too will undergo modernization.

World-system theory offers a different explanation for why societies modernize at varying rates. According to world-system theory, the spread of capitalism has resulted in an international division of labor between more developed and less developed nations. According to this view, the more developed nations control the factors of production, while the less developed nations serve as sources of cheap labor and raw materials. As a result, the economies of the less developed nations face severe handicaps.

Other sociologists who are interested in social change focus on how modernization affects the social and natural environments. Among the positive effects of modernization is an increase in the standard of living. Negative effects include a loss of traditional values, feelings of social isolation, an increase in the number of moral and ethical issues facing members of society, and serious environmental problems.

Previewing Key Terms

Section 2 contains the following key terms: **modernization, modernization theory, world-system theory, core societies, peripheral societies, ecology**. Copy the following "vocabulary pretest" on the chalkboard:

1. The term _____ _____ describes those more developed nations that are at the center of the world economy and upon which less developed societies are economically dependent.
2. _____ _____ _____ holds the view that the spread of capitalism has produced an international division of labor between more developed nations and less developed nations.
3. _____ is the process by which a society's social institutions become increasingly complex as the society moves toward industrialization.
4. The term _____ refers to the science that studies the relationship between living organisms and their environment.
5. _____ _____ argues that the more developed nations of the world were the first to modernize because they were the first to industrialize.
6. Less developed nations that are economically dependent on more developed nations are called _____ _____.

Now have the class suggest possible answers for each question listed. With which terms are students already familiar? Which terms are new? If students cannot provide one or more of these terms, have volunteers find the correct terms in Section 2. Close the activity by telling the class that all of these terms relate to the process of modernization in some way.

Introducing the Section

Tell students to imagine that it is 200 years ago and that they are looking out the window of a one-room schoolhouse. Ask: "What does your environment look like?" "What does the land look like?" "What animals live in the area?" Have a volunteer write student suggestions on the chalkboard. Now have students look out the window of your classroom and describe the environment as it appears today. How does this environment compare to the environment of the same place 200 years ago? When students have completed their comparisons, ask: "What effects have human beings had on this area?" "Are the effects positive or negative?" Then tell students that the effects they are discussing are all outcomes of the process of modernization. Help students to see that modernization has brought positive effects such as an increased standard of living and higher literacy rates. But it has also brought negative effects such as pollution and a loss of traditional values. Close by telling students that Section 2 will introduce them to the sociological perspective on modernization.

Suggested Teaching Strategies

1. **Learning from Maps (I)** Place Transparency 18, which focuses on the status of human welfare, on an overhead projector and ask the questions contained in the accompanying teacher's notes. Transparencies and accompanying teacher's notes are found in the *Teacher's Resource Binder*.
2. **Conducting a Debate (I, II)** Modernization theory and world-system theory have very different views of modernization and the role of more developed nations in the process. Because modernization theorists believe that modernization is tied to political and social reform, they hold that more developed nations serve as positive models for the less developed nations of the world. World-system theorists, on the other hand, view more developed nations as the exploitive partner in an international division of labor. After discussing in class the characteristics of each theory, organize the class into three groups: one group to argue in support of modernization theory, one group to argue in support of world-system theory, and a larger group to act as an audience.
3. **Solving Problems (II, III)** Ask interested students to research the latest facts on pollution and the environment. Then have these students form a panel to discuss ways of solving the problems of water, air, and ground pollution. In a follow-up activity, members of the class can suggest ways of dealing with these problems in your own community.
4. **Extending Ideas (III)** Modernization is often a difficult and painful process. Have interested students conduct research on the struggles for economic and social reform in nations such as the People's Republic of China and the former Soviet Union and report their findings to the class.

Suggested Enrichment Activities

1. **Exploring Cross-Cultural Perspectives (I)** Have students complete the appropriate Cross-Cultural Perspectives Worksheet, found in the *Teacher's Resource Binder*.
2. **Making Oral Presentations (III)** Have all students read the Case Study feature on textbook page 467, the Applying Sociology feature on textbook pages 474–475, and the Interpreting Primary Sources feature on textbook page 481. Then have interested students prepare and present oral presentations on various environmental and social consequences of modernization.

Suggested Assignments

1. **Drawing Conclusions (I)** As homework, have students complete the appropriate Critical Skills Mastery Worksheet, found in the *Teacher's Resource Binder*.
2. ★**Writing about Sociology: Composing a Comparative Essay (I)** Instruct students to read the Developing Sociological Imagination feature on textbook pages 478–479 and then complete the assignment under Practicing the Skill.
3. **Using Sociological Imagination (I, II)** Have students write imaginative short stories depicting what

life in the United States will be like in the year 2050 if pollution is not brought under control today. Ask volunteers to share their short stories with the class for class discussion.

Closing the Section

Close the section by having students complete the appropriate Understanding Sociological Ideas Worksheet, found in the *Teacher's Resource Binder.*

Assessing the Section

Have students complete the Section 2 Review.

Answers to Applying Sociology *(pages 474–475)*

Answers will vary, but students should use sound reasoning in their responses to the three questions.

Answers to Section 2 Review *(page 477)*

Define *modernization:* process by which a society's social institutions become increasingly complex as the society moves toward industrialization; ***core societies:*** term used in world-system theory to describe those nations that are at the center of the world economy and upon which less developed nations are economically dependent; ***peripheral societies:*** term used in world-system theory to describe those less developed nations that are economically dependent on the core, or more developed, societies; ***ecology:*** science that studies the relationship between living organisms and their environment

1. **(a)** According to modernization theory, once less developed nations begin to industrialize, they will undergo a modernization process similar to that of more developed nations. As a result, less developed nations eventually will resemble more developed nations in terms of social structure, norms, and values. World-system theory, on the other hand, holds that most less developed nations will remain at a low level of modernization because the more developed nations control the factors of production. As a result of this control, less developed nations lack economic diversity, depend on exports and foreign assistance, and are economically stratified. These factors work to block modernization in less developed nations. **(b)** Critics of modernization theory argue that it has failed to take into account the fact that less developed nations face very different social conditions than those faced by the more developed nations during their modernization. Critics of world-system theory point out that the theory is unable to explain why some nations that were not under colonial rule have low levels of economic growth and development. The theory also is unable to explain why some less developed nations are following a modernization path similar to the one followed by the more developed nations of the West.
2. Modernization can have both positive and negative consequences. On the positive side, modernization brings higher life expectancies, lower birth rates, higher rates of literacy, the freedom to compete, and more personal comforts. On the negative side, modernization can decrease the role of religion and the family in society, while increasing the role of the government. Modernization also can weaken social ties and lead to feelings of social isolation. In addition, modernization can result in role conflict and confusion and pollution of the environment.

Answers to Developing Sociological Imagination *(pages 478–479)*

1. The information terms are "social change," "early evolutionary theorists," and "modern evolutionary theorists." The performance term is "contrast."
2. Students should develop charts with the specified headings.
3. Answers will vary.

Closing the Chapter

Have students complete the Chapter 18 Review Worksheet, found in the *Teacher's Resource Binder.*

Assessing the Chapter

Have students complete the Chapter 18 Review, found on page 480 of the *Pupil's Edition.*

Give students the Chapter 18 Form A Test and, if desired, the Chapter 18 Reteaching Worksheet and Form B Test, found in the *Teacher's Resource Binder.*

Answers to Chapter 18 Review *(page 480)*

Reviewing Sociological Terms

1. Ecology
2. modernization
3. idealistic culture
4. Social change

Thinking Critically about Sociology

1. The relationship between core societies and peripheral societies is like an international division of labor because the more developed nations (core societies) control the factors of production, while the less developed nations (peripheral societies) serve as sources of cheap labor and raw materials.
2. **(a)** The cyclical theory of social change views change from a historical perspective, whereby societies are seen as rising and then falling or as continuously moving back and forth between stages of development. **(b)** Cyclical theories of social change are popular during periods of social upheaval because social events and conditions usually are considered to be beyond the control of human actions.
3. Ralf Dahrendorf proposed a conflict theory of social change. Dahrendorf believes that various kinds of conflict between different groups in the population can lead to social change. Dahrendorf's view of conflict differs from the view of Karl Marx in that Marx considered class conflict to be the central force for social change. Dahrendorf also believes that interest groups in society may bring about social change through compromise and adaptation. Marx, on the other hand, believed that violence is a necessary part of social change.

4. Modern evolutionary theories have attempted to avoid the criticisms leveled against the early evolutionary theories. Modern evolutionary theories do not claim, as the early theories did, that all societies pass through a single set of distinct stages on the way toward an ideal society. Rather, modern evolutionary theories hold that societies have only a tendency to become more complex over time. They also do not assume that change always produces progress or that progress means the same thing in all societies. Another difference between early and modern evolutionary theory is that modern theories attempt to explain why societies change, whereas early theories did not.

5. (a) According to modernization theory, the more developed nations of the world were the first to modernize because they were the first to industrialize. Once less developed nations begin to industrialize, they too will undergo modernization. As a result, less developed nations eventually will resemble the more developed nations in their social structure, norms, and values. **(b)** According to world-system theory, most less developed nations will remain at a low level of modernization because the more developed nations of the world control the factors of production. As a result, less developed nations lack economic diversity, depend on exports and foreign assistance, and are economically stratified. These factors work to block modernization in the less developed nations. **(c)** Answers will vary.

6. Students' answers should resemble the format given on textbook page 41.

7. (a) According to Sorokin, all societies fluctuate between ideational cultures and sensate cultures. **(b)** Ideational cultures seek truth and knowledge through faith and religion and are "otherworldly." Sensate cultures, on the other hand, seek knowledge through science and are practical and materialistic. **(c)** According to Sorokin, the tendency for societies to shift back and forth between cultures is a natural tendency, one present at the birth of a society. However, external factors such as war and contact with other societies can hasten a society's shift from one form of culture to another.

Exercising Sociological Skills

1. Answers will vary, but students should write stories similar to the one written by Rachel Carson.

2. The tropical rain forests are being destroyed because of clearing for cattle ranching and logging, efforts to ease population pressures, and slash-and-burn agriculture. The destruction of the tropical rain forests has many negative consequences for the environment. First, the land cleared by the deforestation loses its nutrients in a few years and becomes useless in farming unless chemical nutrients are used. Second, the use of slash-and-burn agriculture releases tons of carbon into the air each year. This contributes to acid rain. Third, the deforestation is leading to the extinction of countless species of plants and animals.

3. Answers will vary, but students should use the skills presented on textbook pages 478–479 to write an essay concerning the information presented on textbook pages 463–464.

Extending Sociological Imagination

1. Answers will vary.
2. Answers will vary.
3. Answers will vary.

Answers to Interpreting Primary Sources *(page 481)*

1. There are several reasons why communist rule led to environmental problems in the former Soviet Union. First, the Soviet Union for many years maintained a "growth-at-any-cost" mentality. Second, much of the secret military activity of the communist government was carried on without environmental controls. Third, industry was under no constraints to consider environmental repercussions. And finally, the people of the Soviet Union were given no information about environmental problems or ecological disasters.

2. It will be difficult for the former Soviet Union to solve its environmental problems because it faces both economic pressures and environmental pressures and has too few resources to solve either problem at this time.

Closing the Unit

Have students complete the Unit 5 Review Worksheet, found in the *Teacher's Resource Binder*.

Assessing the Unit

Have students complete the Unit 5 Review, found on page 483 of the *Pupil's Edition*.

Give students the Unit 5 Form A Test and, if desired, the Unit 5 Reteaching Worksheet and Form B Test, found in the *Teacher's Resource Binder*.

Answers to Unit 5 Review *(page 483)*

Reviewing Sociological Ideas

1. (a) A social movement is a long-term conscious effort to promote or prevent social change. **(b)** All successful social movements go through a series of four stages: agitation, legitimation, bureaucratization, and institutionalization. The first stage, agitation, occurs with the perception that a problem exists. In this stage, a small group of people attempt to stir up public awareness of the issue, often with the intent of gaining widespread support for a social movement. In the second stage, legitimation, the social movement becomes more respectable as it gains acceptance among the population. The leaders of the movement become accepted as legitimate spokespersons for a reasonable cause. The third stage, bureaucratization, begins as the movement becomes more formally organized. As the movement becomes increasingly bureaucratized, the original goals may be swept aside because more time is needed to handle daily administrative tasks. The final stage, institutionalization, is marked by the establishment of the movement as an accepted part of society. The original excitement generated by the movement is gone and the movement may resist proposals for further social change.

2. (a) Population is the number of people living in an area at a particular time. **(b)** Three factors affect the size and structure of a population: the birth rate, the death rate, and the migration rate. **(c)** The birth rate is calculated by dividing the number of live births in a particular year by the total population of the society for that year. This figure then is multiplied by 1,000. The death rate is calculated by dividing the number of deaths in a particular year by the total population of the society for that year. This figure then is multiplied by 1,000. The migration rate is based on the annual difference between in-migration and out-migration. This is calculated by determining the annual number of persons who move into a specified area per 1,000 members of a population minus the annual number of persons who move out of a specified area per 1,000 members of a population.

3. (a) Collective behavior is the relatively spontaneous social behavior that occurs when people try to develop common solutions to unclear situations. **(b)** There are six basic preconditions for collective behavior: structural conduciveness, structural strain, growth and spread of a generalized belief, precipitating factors, mobilization for action, and social control. These six preconditions guide the outcome of collective behavior.

4. (a) There are two primary strategies used to control population growth. The first strategy is to lower the birth rate through family planning or antinatalism. Family planning allows the couple to decide how many children to have. Antinatalism, on the other hand, involves official policies designed to discourage births. A second strategy involves increasing living standards, especially income and education, to decrease the birth rate. **(b)** Family planning strategies are problematic because when couples are allowed to decide how many children to have, they often have more than the population can bear. Antinatalism policies tend to be more forceful than family planning but generally are successful. Economic programs designed to increase the standard of living in nations have only done so for a small proportion of the population. As a result, the majority of the population remains in poverty and the birth rates remain high.

5. (a) Urban ecology is an approach that examines the relationship between people and the urban environment. **(b)** The three models of urban ecology are the concentric zone model, the sector model, and the multiple-nuclei model. Burgess developed the concentric zone model to describe the structure of urban areas. In this model, the city spreads outward from the center, resulting in a series of circles within circles. Each of these circles, or zones, differs in terms of the way in which the land is used. The sector model, developed by Hoyt, also holds that cities grow outward from the center. However, according to this model, growth occurs in wedges from the center outward. Transportation patterns affect land use. Harris and Ullman developed the multiple-nuclei model, which proposes that cities have a number of specialized centers that influence the land use around them. This model acknowledges the influence of automobiles and highways on the development of cities.

6. (a) Modernization is the process by which a society's social institutions become increasingly complex as the society moves toward industrialization. **(b)** Modernization can have both positive and negative consequences. On the positive side, modernization brings higher life expectancies, lower birth rates, higher rates of literacy, a decrease in economic and social inequality, and more personal comforts. On the negative side, modernization can decrease the role of religion and the family in society, while increasing the role of the government. Modernization also can weaken social ties and lead to feelings of social isolation. In addition, modernization can result in role conflict and confusion and pollution of the environment.

7. (a) A collectivity is a collection of people who have limited interaction with each other and who do not share clearly defined, conventional norms. **(b)** Collectivities differ from social groups in three ways. First, members of social groups generally interact with each other directly, often for long periods of time. Interaction among members of collectivities, however, is limited and sometimes nonexistent. Second, the norms that guide behavior in social groups are clearly defined and widely understood. In collectivities, however, norms for behavior either are unclear or they are unconventional. Finally, the people who form social groups generally are united by an awareness that they are members of these groups. Members of collectivities, on the other hand, seldom share a sense of group unity.

Synthesizing Sociological Ideas

1. Contagion theory, proposed by Gustav Le Bon, holds that the hypnotic power of the crowd encourages people to give up their individuality to the stronger pull of the group. Individuals become anonymous, with no will power or sense of responsibility. The crowd in effect becomes a single organism operating under a collective mind. Conventional social norms lose their meaning, and, as emotion sweeps through the crowd, behavior becomes unrestrained. According to emergent-norm theory, the people in a crowd often are faced with a situation in which the traditional norms of behavior do not apply. Gradually through interaction, however, new norms emerge when one or more leaders initiate new behaviors. These new norms provide a common motivation for group action where none existed before.

2. (a) The first cities appeared about 6,000 years ago, but even as late as 1850, only about 2 percent of the world's population lived in cities. The rise of cities was tied to the Agricultural Revolution and the Industrial Revolution. The Agricultural Revolution increased the efficiency of food production and created a surplus of food for the first time. This freed workers from farming and allowed them to pursue other types of work. Some went to central areas where they could most easily engage in specialized types of work, encouraging the development of cities. The Industrial Revolution replaced traditional human and animal sources of power with new sources such as coal, water, and steam. The Industrial Revolution also replaced hand tools with machines and led to the development and growth of factories. Cities also became able to support increasing numbers of people. Preindustrial cities were small. Living conditions were characterized by a lack of sanitation, ineffective medical technologies, crowding, and lack of sewage facilities. Epidemics were common. Life was organized around kinship and extended families. Governments were organized as monarchies or oligarchies. Citizens were segregated into classes or castes, with the poor living on the city's outskirts and the rich living in the center. Compared to preindustrial cities, industrial cities were larger and had a greater diversity of people. Commerce became the focal point of cities. The rise of industrial cities brought social problems such as crime, overcrowding, and pollution, but they also brought high literacy rates, economic opportunities, and health care. **(b)** Urbanization is a recent phenomenon because the Agricultural Revolution and the Industrial Revolution, the two major developments responsible for urbanization, occurred centuries apart. The Industrial Revolution occurred only a short time ago.

3. Students' summaries should be based on information contained on textbook pages 408–413.

4. **(a)** Social change refers to alterations in various aspects of a society over time. **(b)** The cyclical theory of social change is a historical view of social change in which societies are seen as rising and then falling or as continuously moving back and forth between stages of development. The evolutionary theory of social change views change as a process that moves in one direction—toward increasing complexity. The equilibrium theory of social change likens society to a living organism. Change in one part of the social system produces change in all other parts, as the system attempts to regain balance, or equilibrium. The conflict theory of social change views social change as the result of conflicts between groups with opposing interests.

5. **(a)** According to urban anomie theory, life in cities is marked by interactions that involve only impersonal secondary groups. The formation of close primary group relations is discouraged by the size, density, and diversity of urban life. The lack of primary group relations creates anomie, or normlessness, which leads to mental illness, crime, and delinquency. Compositional theory focuses on the way the city's makeup in terms of age, race, ethnicity, income, and occupation influences the life of its residents. The wide diversity of people leads to a variety of life-styles. Groups formed around these characteristics provide city dwellers with a sense of solidarity and community. Subcultural theory also emphasizes the formation of primary group relationships. People in cities have a much greater chance of finding others who have similar interests than do people in rural areas. **(b)** Urban anomie

theory views the city as an unfriendly, anonymous place for people to live. Compositional theory argues that people are protected from the anonymous nature of city life by their primary group associations. Subcultural theory, on the other hand, views the city as a place that encourages rather than discourages the development of primary group relationships.

6. **(a)** According to Malthusian theory, the food supply increases only arithmetically, while the population increases geometrically. From this, Malthus predicted that overpopulation would result in worldwide starvation. Malthus believed that the only possible ways to stop the coming disaster were through birth control, sexual self-control, and delayed marriage. He believed that disease and famine were the most likely ways in which nature would attempt to control the enormous population growth. **(b)** According to demographic transition theory, population changes are tied to a society's level of technological development. According to this theory, a society's population moves through three stages. In Stage 1, typical of preindustrial societies, both the birth rate and the death rate are high, leading to slow population growth. As societies enter the industrial phase, Stage 2, improved medical techniques, sanitation, and increased food production work to reduce the death rate. The birth rate, however, remains high. These factors lead to rapid population growth. Stage 3 societies have a fully developed industrial economy. The birth rate falls and the death rate remains low. The low birth rate and the low death rate produce fairly stable populations in which population growth occurs very slowly.

7. Students' charts should be based on information contained on textbook pages 417–418.

8. **(a)** Deprivation theory explains the emergence of social movements as the result of feelings of economic or social deprivation on the part of large numbers of people. These feelings of deprivation cause people to feel dissatisfied with the way things are and to organize themselves into a social movement to demand change. Resource-mobilization theory argues that feelings of deprivation alone are not sufficient to trigger social movements. According to this theory, only groups of people who can effectively organize and use resources, such as a body of supporters, money, and access to the media, will be able to bring about change. **(b)** Answers will vary.

Applying Sociological Imagination

1. Answers will vary.
2. Answers will vary.
3. Students' charts should contain information presented on textbook pages 408–409.
4. Answers will vary.